D0428771

INTRODUCTION TO FOREST RESOURCE MANAGEMENT c.1

WILLIAM A. LEUSCHNER

School of Forestry and Wildlife Resources
Virginia Polytechnic Institute and State University

JOHN WILEY & SONS
New York   Chichester   Brisbane   Toronto   Singapore

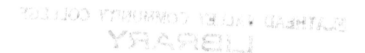

Library of Congress Cataloging in Publication Data

Leuschner, William A.

  Introduction to forest resource management.

  Includes index.
  1. Forest management. I. Title.
SD373.L45 1984   634.9′28   83-21602
ISBN 0-471-08668-1

Printed in the United States of America

10 9 8 7 6 5 4 3 2 1

PREFACE

THIS BOOK IS designed to help the decision maker evaluate his alternatives and their constraints and then reach his objectives. Certain techniques are particularly applicable to forest management decisions and provide the manager with guidelines.

This text has three major parts. The first deals with appraising alternatives and techniques for calculating decision guidelines. Many forest management decisions are investment decisions in which forests and funds are committed for long time periods. Therefore, the time value of money and investment decision models are discussed. There are also chapters on choosing the interest rate and on adjusting analyses for inflation, taxation, and risk.

The text's second part focuses on cutting the forest because cutting is one of the main alternatives for obtaining forest management objectives. The traditional methods for regulating even- and uneven-aged forests are presented, as are rotation determination and allowable cut calculations. The traditional models are important both because they are still used on smaller forests and because they provide the foundation for understanding more sophisticated techniques.

Part III contains the more advanced management techniques and may be thought of as having three sections of its own. First, two chapters appear on mathematical programming and its use for harvest scheduling. Second, multiple-use management practices and principles are discussed. Finally, forest management planning systems are addressed and suggestions for writing a forest management plan are offered.

The book is written for classroom use by upper-division undergraduates. It is intended as a teaching text, rather than a reference book, and contains those items believed to be the minimum needed by baccalaureate foresters to function in management positions. Such a foundation is required for a forester to function effectively as a professional or to understand more sophisticated techniques. My intention is to err on the side of simplicity in explanations, hoping that the basic concepts will thereby be understood. This text is written for students who have had algebra and trigonometry, but not calculus or matrix algebra, and who have studied introductory economics, but not forest economics.

WILLIAM A. LEUSCHNER

CONTENTS

INTRODUCTION TO FOREST RESOURCE MANAGEMENT

1

FOREST MANAGEMENT, IN the broadest sense, integrates all of the biological, social, economic, and other factors that affect management decisions about the forest. Everything affects everything else in this view of forest management and, therefore, one must know everything about everything to make informed decisions. This may be ultimately true, but only in varying degrees. The partial effects of some factors will be greater than the partial effects of other factors, and the effects of some factors will be so small that they can be ignored completely. This broad view of forest management has not been adopted in this book because the required knowledge is impossible to attain and because forest management decisions are not currently being made this way.

A second view, which is a bit lower hierarchically, is that forest management encompasses all those decisions needed to operate a forest on a continuing basis. This view focuses more directly on those areas of knowledge used on the forest for its management. This means personnel management is part of forest management because people are used, mechanical engineering is part of forest management because machinery is used, and so on. Sometimes social interactions at the first or second level beyond the forest are also included.

This view has merit but does not recognize that this knowledge is needed any time resources are combined for production. The knowledge is needed for all management decisions from government through manufacturing. It defines a broader field of management that is sometimes taught in schools with a general rather than professional orientation.

This second view is not adopted in this book either. First, most forest organizations hire experts in the needed fields, such as personnel managers or engineers. Second, many of the general subjects are better taught by schools that specialize in them, such as schools of business, public administration, or engineering. Foresters attending schools at large universities usually can obtain desired training by attending classes in these schools.

What then is forest management? Historically, forest management has dealt primarily with silviculture and the biological management of the forests. Many earlier forest management texts contained primarily the silvicultural aspects of forest management. This definition derived from the profession's biological foundation.

At various times, forest management has also been defined as including watershed management, mensuration, and other aspects of forestry. These were, and are, integral parts of forest management. However, as the profession has grown, these have developed into separate fields. The situation is somewhat analogous to the medical profession in which the general practitioner has been augmented by experts in obstetrics, pediatrics, or internal medicine. These necessary aspects of forest management are now being taught by experts in those fields and at a greater depth than would be possible in a single forest management course. Therefore, this view of forest management is not used because of its breadth.

Forest management does have a definition in its current usage. In some circles, such as the USDA Forest Service, the broader biological definition is still retained and so usage can be ambiguous. In other circles, forest management refers to *the study and application of analytical techniques to aid in choosing those management alternatives that contribute most to organizational objectives*. This is the definition of forest management used in this book. However, forestry remains dynamic and the student should not be surprised at continuing changes in usage over time.

FOREST MANAGEMENT OBJECTIVES

There are several points that should be recognized about the objectives mentioned in the definition. The first is that "objectives" implies that there is a desired point that the forest organization wishes to reach. The desired point is almost always the goods or services that the forest produces. These goods and services can be material things, such as timber, fuelwood, or fodder, but they can also be nonmaterial things, such as scenic beauty or the vicarious use of a unique natural area. However, it is this desired end point, this objective, that makes the forest worth managing. The forest would be unmanaged if its products were useless to society.

Second, objectives may or may not be identified. Objective identification can be very difficult, and the objectives can change with each user group. Mills want timber, hunters want game, and backpackers want undisturbed wilderness. Thus, objectives can change depending on which user group or mix of user groups the owner wishes to accomodate or which becomes dominant over time. This also means that objectives can change once they have been identified and so must be identified again. Change can be good in that it makes the forest responsive to societal needs. It can be bad if it occurs too frequently and destroys the continuity of management. This is particularly true in forest and resource management where the production process is slow and long time periods are needed to modify it.

Third, objective identification may result from careful thought with much planning and public consultation, or it can be the result of an emotional or intuitive reaction. Many public and private organizations spend a great deal of time and money to develop management plans and objectives. The extent of some of this planning can be seen in Chapter 16 on harvest scheduling. In other cases, objectives can result from intuitive feelings.

Fourth, objectives are usually determined by the forest landowner. Often, a central tendency of objectives can be identified by an owner group. The national forests are owned by the public at large and are managed for a wide variety of goods and services. Some public groups want timber, some campgrounds, and some wilderness. The USDA Forest Service, which manages the national forests, tries to meet these objectives through multiple-use management. The USDI Bureau of Land Management and state, county, and municipal agencies are the other major public land managers.

Nonindustrial private landowners, which include farmers, are the largest single landowner group. They also have a large variety of diverse management objectives. Farmers may want a minimum revenue flow to pay taxes while building growing stock as a form of savings. Absentee owners, living in the city, may want the land primarily as a real estate investment and care little about forestry. Second home owners may be concerned with maintaining an esthetically pleasing environment around that home. The diversity of objectives makes the management activities of this group difficult to predict.

Industrial owner objectives may be the easiest to predict. They own forests to provide raw materials for their manufacturing plants at reasonable costs. Thus, timber production is a primary objective. However, other objectives, such as recreation and hunting, have received increasing recognition over the last several decades.

Another point is that the management objectives are the owner's objectives. One can speak of "correct" objectives in the sense that a higher objective has already been identified and a criterion for judging correctness, such as efficiency, has been adopted. The beginning forester is seldom involved in these deliberations; thus, this book adopts the position that the correct objective is the landowner's objective as a useful, operational first approximation.

Finally, it should be recognized that there is seldom a single management objective, even though this and many other presentations speak in these terms to facilitate learning and analysis. Owners usually have multiple objectives and they often conflict with each other. Then, the owner must give up some or all of one objective to obtain the other. For example, maximizing the forest's present net worth and maintaining a continuous wood flow may conflict. The owner can smooth out wood flow by cutting some stands before or after the age at which their present net worth is maximum. But doing this causes the total present net worth to be less than the absolute maximum. Some objectives may be mutually exclusive, for example, producing timber and maintaining wilderness on the same acre.

Actual management objectives, whether stated or unstated, are a mixture of several management objectives. There is no one correct mixture. This depends on the owner's objectives and the relative importance placed on them. Assigning relative importance is one reason for valuation, which is discussed in the next section. The forest manager helps the landowner evaluate his objectives. He provides the owner with information to help him decide on the objectives he wants and their relative importance. The forest manager does not decide on the objectives unless, of course, he is an owner–manager.

FOREST MANAGEMENT ALTERNATIVES AND ANALYSES

The alternatives mentioned in the definition of forest management may be viewed as the many actions that a forest owner may take to achieve his objectives. These are the actions that can be taken in the field that will cause production of one or another, or some mix, of forest products. The actions an owner takes can include cutting, reforestation, and construction.

Cutting the forest, or not cutting it, is one of the primary tools for accomplishing management objectives. Cutting is used to manipulate the forest to obtain the desired forest products at the desired point in time. The different kinds of cuts, such as clearcutting or shelterwood cutting, have different effects on the residual stand and hence on the products. Thus, both the timing and type of cut are management alternatives that must be decided on.

Reforestation practices are a second major set of alternatives that must be chosen to obtain management objectives. Choices must be made between natural and artificial reforestation, the kind of site preparation if any, and the species to be regenerated. Reforestation practices affect density and species and hence forest production possibilities.

Construction is a third major set of alternatives that must be chosen. There are many kinds of construction and each can affect the amount of an objective obtained. For example, road placement not only affects timber harvest but also affects access for recreation and hunting, aesthetic values, and soil stability. The location and layout of campgrounds affect not only the quality of recreation experience but also timber management. Similarly, placement of ponds affects both grazing and wildlife production.

Forest management alternatives may be viewed in another, more general way. The alternatives are defined by the physical production possibilities of the forest. The physical production possibilities are determined by the basic biology of the forest being managed. Thus, the alternatives flow from and are defined by the many topics you have studied. These include silviculture, protection, mensuration, and electives. This is why there are entire curricula designated "Forest Management" as well as individual courses that bear the same title.

"Analytical techniques" are also part of the forest management definition. This book contains many of these techniques for choosing between alternatives. Many are well known and not unique to forestry. Others are special cases of general techniques that have been developed to answer particular forestry problems. Some were developed especially for forestry. For example, discounting and present net worth are general techniques applied to forestry problems. Concepts such as land expectation value and the Faustman Formula are special cases of discounting developed for forestry problems. The harvest scheduling model ECHO (Walker, 1971) also may be considered a unique development for analyzing forestry problems.

These analytical techniques provide guidelines for choosing between the courses of action. The techniques can tell you what will happen if all the assumptions and projections used in the analysis are fulfilled. However, the real world is filled with risk, and the end result is not always what was predicted. Analytical results must be considered guidelines and not irrevocable answers, because projections of variables (such as yield) contain errors and are not always met and the analytical models are seldom perfect.

A DECISION-MAKING MODEL

We have been talking about forest management, objectives, and alternatives. These can all be brought together in a decision-making model. Figure 1.1 represents one of the more basic decision-making models. There are many variants, some more complicated, some less complicated. It is not the only model, but rather one that is useful to our purposes.

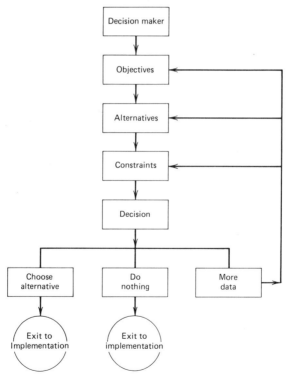

FIGURE 1.1 *A rudimentary decision-making model.*

The decision maker is at the top and is ultimately responsible for deciding which alternative is chosen. Whoever is in this position may have staff members present data and analyses or may perform these tasks unassisted.

Next come the goals or objectives. These terms are used synonymously in this book but some classification schemes use them to mean different things. Management objectives have been discussed at some length in the preceding pages, so little space is devoted to them here. Their inclusion implies that they have been identified and that conflicting objectives have been resolved. This is not always true, and the decision-making process often focuses on these problems and causes their resolution. Ideally, the decision maker has one or more objectives identified and they provide information for the next step, listing alternatives.

Alternatives are the different courses of action that managers may take to reach their objectives. There are often several different ways to reach these objectives. In the idealized system the decision makers list the alternative courses of action they must take to reach their objectives. Each alternative may partially or fully achieve the objective.

There are barriers or constraints to reaching objectives. They are what must be given up to reach the objective or what prevents one from reaching the objective. Both physical and economic constraints can be identified.

Physical constraints may exist in the forest production process that do not allow reaching some objectives or that may determine just how closely the objective can be reached. For example, site quality may determine how much timber can be grown and how responsive it is to cultural treatments. There can be many economic constraints also. The cost of cultural treatments or other alternatives is determined by the market prices of land, labor, equipment, and materials. There may also be a limited amount of funds available for forestry investment or perhaps alternative nonforestry investments with high returns against which one must compete. The forest manager therefore must choose those alternatives to reach the desired objective within these constraints.

Once the objective is identified, the alternatives for reaching the objective are listed along with the constraints on each alternative. Analyses can be made at this point and one of three decisions can be made: (1) choose an alternative, (2) do nothing, or (3) go back and obtain more data for further analyses.

Choosing an alternative from among those listed means that a course of action has been defined. The next step (after the EXIT) would be to implement the alternative. It may be decided to do nothing. This is a decision not to actively try to reach the objective but rather to let things continue as they are. Note this is a valid alternative but it should be pursued consciously, not taken by default.

Finally, more information can be sought. It can be sought at any of the preceding levels. Objectives can be reformulated in the light of analyses performed during the decision-making process; new alternatives can be sought or more data about existing alternatives obtained; and/or additional information about constraints and ways to circumvent them can be found. Seeking more data brings us back to the model at these levels until an exit point is reached—either a "no" or "alternative" decision.

FOREST
VALUATION

PART

INTRODUCTION TO FOREST VALUATION

2

PEOPLE MUST CONSTANTLY choose between alternative courses of action. Some choices may be mundane, such as deciding which of two movies to attend or deciding which shirt to wear. Other choices, such as those in our professional lives, can involve large dollar expenditures whose outcomes will affect many other people. For example, choosing the location of a new mill may not only affect the firm's profitability but also local employment.

Choosing between alternatives is greatly simplified if weights can be assigned to the alternatives. These weights may indicate the amount of usefulness or cost that the organization will accrue if the alternative is followed. The alternative that is most useful, or least costly, can then be followed. Of course, each unit of the weight must have the same value and, ideally, measure in terms relevant to the organization.

Valuation is placing a value on something. Forest valuation is the placing of a value on forest production. This may include valuing the resources consumed in that production. These values can guide forest management decisions if we assume that the organizational objective is to maximize production value and if production is widely defined.

Maximization of production value, or value net of costs, is a good first approximation of a general management objective. Managing a forest almost always requires the use of scarce resources, and it is unlikely that society or an individual would allocate the resources without something in return. The "something in return" is forest production. Further, it is also likely that people would like to get the most in return for their resources. For example, for the same expenditure, 45 cords of wood is preferred to 30 cords or $1000 worth of forest products is preferred to $500 worth.

Defining forest production provides no conceptual problem. The familiar wood, water, range, wildlife, and recreation are included. Esthetic values and vicarious use by urban dwellers might also be added to the list. This first list can then be further divided. For example, recreation can be divided into campground and wilderness recreation, and wilderness recreation can be divided still further into wilderness hiking and wilderness rafting.

These are the forest products to be valued. Some are easier to value than others but, generally, the more specific the product definition the easier it is to value. The quantities produced must be measured before valuation. Some products' quantities are easier to measure than others, such as cubic feet of timber as opposed to vicarious use of a forest. Some products are bought and sold in a market, such as timber and grazing rights, and are easier to value than those that are not, such as esthetic values or a wilderness experience. The latter are called "nonmarket" products because they are not regularly exchanged in a readily recognized market. Nonmarket valuation is not addressed to any major extent in this book.

But what unit of measurement should be used to value forest products? The unit most commonly used is the monetary unit of the nation in which the forest is located. Thus, the U.S. dollar will be used most often throughout this book.

Do not interpret the preceding statement as advocating that "everything should have a dollar value." Rather, a least common denominator is being sought that can weigh the importance of resources and the products made from them. This common denominator can then be used for valuation and to guide forest management decisions.

The unit of measurement that is the least common denominator for the greatest number of resources and products is usually the monetary unit of the nation, particularly if a well-developed market economy exists. Further, and particularly with free-floating currency, the monetary unit of one nation can be expressed in terms of another; hence, international comparisons are possible.

Nonmarket products are difficult or impossible to value in dollars. Therefore, the weighting scheme is imperfect and gives only partial answers. This is another reason why valuation models provide only guidelines. Social scientists are constantly trying to put dollar values on nonmarket products. Implicitly, it is judged easier to apply a dollar value than to find a new common denominator.

In summary, the dollar is used for valuation because it is the most ubiquitous measure and the best available, not because it is perfect and without fault.

WHAT IS VALUE?

The proper theoretical determination of value often confuses students. The basic reason a good or service has value is because it does something that is desired by an individual or society. It provides a certain amount of utility. This utility may be from using the good or service for personal consumption, for example, from eating a steak or going on a camping trip. The utility may also be from earning money with which to purchase goods and services that in turn have utility.

The "demand value" of a good or service is what people would be willing to give up to obtain it. Demand value is based on the utility that the good or service will produce for the individual. It reflects the usefulness of the item to the person, in relation to that person's own tastes and preferences and the alternative items available.

The relationship between the number of units of any specific good or service that would be purchased and the price that an individual or group of individuals would pay for that number of units is called a demand schedule or demand curve. The demand schedule is a list of the quantity of the good or service that would be sold at a specific price. The demand curve is a curve of the demand schedule with dollars (or price) on the y axis and quantity demanded at that price on the x axis. The demand curve shows the quantity that will be purchased at the indicated price. The higher the price, the less will be purchased.

The demand curve or demand value reflects the usefulness of the good or service to the individual or society in dollar terms. It reflects the value of the consumption or use to those who use it.

The "supply value" of a good or service is what people who produce it require in order to sell it to someone else. It is the minimum price for which they would sell an item.

Supply value is based on the production costs for the person making the good or service. The producer must believe that a product can be sold at a price at least equal to the production costs; otherwise, there is no point in producing it. The costs of producing an additional unit of an item form the marginal cost curve. This is the supply curve in the short run once the fixed production costs are met. The supply curve shows the quantities that a producer would be willing to produce at different prices. Usually, the higher the price, the more an item will be produced.

Determination of value depends on both the demand and supply values. The demand value alone does not establish value because people may not be willing to pay enough to meet the costs of production. A supplier cannot produce the item because no one is willing to pay production costs. Society will be implicitly indicating that the resources needed to supply the item are better used elsewhere. It may, for example, not be worth reducing the production of game to increase the production of timber. Demand exists but the item's usefulness is simply too small relative to its cost.

Similarly, supply value alone does not establish value because the costs of production may far exceed what people are willing to pay for the item. An item cannot be worth its supply value unless people buy it at that value. For example, some timber sales are advertised at a minimum bid price but no bids are received. The items' costs of production are simply too big relative to its usefulness.

The value of a good or service is established when the price people are willing to pay to obtain it is equal to the price people are willing to receive to produce it. This is the price at which the usefulness of the item is equal to the usefulness of resources taken from other uses to produce it. It is the intersection of the supply and demand curves or the simultaneous solution of the supply and demand functions. This is the market price that is generally accepted, with some limitations, as the best measure of dollar value. Market price will be used throughout this book to estimate the dollar value of a good or service, wherever possible.

The market value of an item is the best value indicator currently available, but it is not perfect. There are many imperfections, one of which is the existence of nonmarket values. These nonmarket values can be products not bought and sold in readily identifiable or observable markets or they can be externalities in production or consumption. The lack of a market means that prices are not observable and, hence, are difficult or impossible to estimate. The existence of externalities means that the market prices that are observable do not reflect the true social benefits or costs.

Another limitation is that the market price of an asset is often unknown until one tries to sell it or buy it. Two assets in forestry are seldom the same. Each acre of land may be more or less different than the other, so the comparison of observed prices to the investor's asset is imperfect. Furthermore, the observed market price may be in a different geographic area or may have occurred at a different point in time when the supply and demand for the asset were different. Therefore, the price in the investor's market today will not always be the same. This is less of a problem with some forest products such as timber, where the product is more homogeneous or where, in some cases, grades are established to increase homogeneity.

Market value is still the best indicator of value despite its limitations. One major reason is that it is the best estimate of the money that would have to be used to purchase an asset and that would therefore be unavailable to use elsewhere. Or, on the other side of the market, it indicates the money that could be obtained by selling an asset and therefore would be available to use elsewhere. Prices also can provide a good estimate of products' and resources' social value if the markets are reasonably free. These prices are useful in developing guidelines for public sector decision making.

As a practical matter, many organizations routinely use prices as a value measure, and the analyst will probably have to follow his or her organization's procedures and use them. One should recognize that many of the measures commonly used in forestry are imperfect and contain error, for example, diameter at breast height (dbh), volume tables, and wildlife censusing techniques. Once again, the main point is that market prices are the best value estimates generally available and so they are used.

OTHER VALUATION METHODS

Two other valuation methods are often proposed; hence, it is important they be discussed and their limitations noted.

Depreciated Cost or Net Book Value

The value of an asset or piece of property is calculated by subtracting the depreciation on the property from its purchase price. For example, assume a crawler tractor was purchased for $100,000, had an estimated life of 20,000 hours, and an estimated scrap value of $25,000. The tractor's value at the end of 10,000 hours use based on straight line depreciation is

$$\frac{(\$100,000 - \$25,000)}{20,000 \text{ hrs}} = \$3.75/\text{hr depreciation}$$

$\$3.75/\text{hr} \times 10,000 \text{ hr use} = \$37,500$ total depreciation

Value $= \$100,000 - \$37,500 = \$62,500$

There are several limitations to this valuation method. First, the scrap value may be wrong. The projection of the cash that will be paid for the machine when it is sold for scrap may either be higher or lower than that actually received; thus, the value could be over- or understated. This happens when the market for the asset changes during its lifetime. A good example is the rising market for housing. Most of us have parents or friends who have sold their homes, after living in them for many years, for tens of thousands of dollars more than they paid for them.

Second, the depreciation rate could be in error if the estimation of lifetime is incorrect. The depreciation rate is supposed to measure how fast the machine is consumed in production. This is difficult to estimate accurately. Another reason the rate may be incorrect is that many firms use accelerated depreciation rates for federal income tax purposes. These rates may depreciate the asset more rapidly than it is actually being consumed, thereby understating its value.

The depreciated cost procedure is sometimes used to estimate replacement or restoration costs. For example, many insurance companies use a depreciated cost value to settle claims on damaged or stolen household goods. Note that this procedure is used to estimate the replacement cost of the asset, that is, what it would cost on the market to replace the asset. Actual market values are not used because they are not conveniently available. For example, the market value of a 3-month-old wool suit lost by an airline is practically impossible to determine.

Depreciated cost is sometimes useful in estimating current market value, but market value is the value being estimated. Depreciated cost is simply the surrogate for market value, which for some reason is indeterminable.

Income Value

Some authors have suggested that an asset's value is based on the income it produces and they refer to this as the income value. For example, suppose you owned 30 acres of land on a 30-year rotation that produced one cord of pulpwood per acre per year; that the stumpage price was $10 per cord; and that you had the alternative of investing your funds at 8 percent interest. The income value of the asset is

$$\frac{30 \text{ acres} \times 1.0 \text{ cord/acre/year} \times \$10.00/\text{cord}}{0.08} = \$3,750.00 \qquad (2.1)$$

The annual income from the asset is the numerator of equation 2.1 or \$300 per year. This is *not* the income value because it is produced *each* year. Therefore, it should be replaced with an asset that produces at least \$300 per year income. You could invest your money, if you had it, in your next best alternative at 8 percent per year, so the question becomes "How much money must I invest at 8 percent per annum to obtain \$300 a year income?" or

$$0.08 \, X = \$300.00 \qquad (2.2)$$

$$X = \frac{\$300.00}{0.08} = \$3,750$$

The income value is \$3750. It is the dollar amount that must be invested in the next best alternative to produce the same income as the asset being valued.

A limitation of this procedure is that while it may tell you the asset's value to you personally it does not tell you the buying or selling price. You do not know how much you would have to pay to buy it or what you would receive if you sold it.

For example, the most you would be willing to pay for the asset if you were buying it is \$3700. But perhaps the owner is a better forest manager and could grow 1.25 cords per acre per year. Then he would only be willing to sell for \$4687.50. Or, suppose you owned the asset and that all the potential buyers had alternative investments that returned 10 percent as opposed to your 8 percent. Then the most they would be willing to pay is \$3000, whereas you desire \$3750.

Calculating income value is useful because it indicates the minimum selling price or the buying price for the asset. However, you might still take a different price because the calculations may not include all relevant factors. You might take a little less if you were selling because you wanted the money to take a long-promised vacation trip around the world. Or, you might pay a little more because you want the land for hunting in addition to growing pulpwood.

CAPITAL, INVESTMENT, AND INTEREST

Economists have traditionally divided the "factors of production" into three categories; land, labor, and capital. Land meant not only the earth itself but also the natural resource contained within it, such as metallic ores. Labor meant the hours of human time needed to produce a good or service and capital meant the fabricated assets needed for production.

The term fabricated is loosely interpreted in forestry investments. There are some obvious forms of capital that are fabricated such as the tools and machinery used for regeneration. Other less obvious forms of forest capital include the roads and dams constructed for management purposes and the growing stock on the forest itself.

The term investment can have different definitions for different people. To the accountant it can mean purchases of assets lasting longer than one year. The Internal Revenue Service may use this same definition but add a minimum dollar amount onto the purchase.

To the economist, investment is current consumption, which is foregone in order to build capital. The consumption foregone can be measured by the amount of money not used for consumption but used instead to purchase capital goods. Thus, capital investment, or investment, is the money used to purchase capital. Money is not capital unless it is needed in the production process, for example, the working capital needed by corporations.

Interest is the return to the owner of capital. It is the return that the owner of the man-made assets receives for investing his money in those assets. Interest can also be viewed as the cost of the capital for the person who is using it.

For example, in the preceding income value example the landowner invested funds in the productive capital of 30 acres of land. The $300 per year return from the sale of pulpwood was his return to capital or the interest on his investment. Interest is usually expressed as a percent per unit of time. The percent interest in this example would be 8 percent a year if the market value of the investment was $3750, namely, ($300/$3750) × 100 = 8 percent.

Taking the other view, suppose someone wanted to borrow the land, growing stock, and other capital assets to grow the trees. Many pulp and paper companies do just this in the southern United States when they take long-term leases on forest land. The landowner would insist on at least $300 per year income from the person borrowing the capital since this is the amount that would have been earned by the landowner had he or she kept it and grown the trees. The $300 is the interest the borrower must pay the owner for using the capital. If the assets were worth $3750 on the market, then the interest is 8 percent.

Interest has also been defined as the market price of money. Economists talk as if there were just one interest rate. However, there are many observable interest rates in the market. This is because there are many determinants of an interest rate other than just the supply and demand for money. These are discussed at greater length in the next chapter.

However, interest is a legitimate cost of business that must be considered even if it is not paid directly by the investor. There is almost always the alternative of selling capital assets at their market value and reinvesting the money from the sale in your next best alternative. These can include: alternative investments within a corporation, for example, building a new plant to make boxes out of the paper you manufacture instead of purchasing a tract of timber; savings accounts for individuals with no minimum deposit requirement, money withdrawable on demand, interest at over 5 percent, and the money insured by the federal government; or cash funds operated by stockbrokers requiring a $5000 minimum deposit with returns at the going interest rate, whatever that may be at the time.

An opportunity cost is the cost of an opportunity foregone. An opportunity cost is incurred if funds are invested at less than the maximum alternative. Suppose, in the preceding income value example, that the asset were sold for $3750 and this money were deposited in a bank account at 5 percent interest. The interest earned would then be $187.50 (0.05 × $3750) instead of $300 and the opportunity cost of this investment is $112.50 ($300 − $187.50).

THE ALTERNATIVE RATE OF RETURN

The alternative rate of return (ARR) is the interest rate that your best alternative investment can return. It is the return you would expect if you invested in the next best project other than the one you are currently considering.

Alternative rates of return must be determined on an individual basis because each organization or individual has different alternatives. Reasons for different alternatives include: not being able to raise the capital investment needed, not having the expertise to manage the alternative, or not having the marketing channels or integrated firm in which to place the investment.

The ARR is important because it establishes the opportunity cost of investing in a particular project. The prospective project must return at least the ARR to be worthwhile. Otherwise, you will lose the difference—the $112.50 in the opportunity cost example. The ARR is also called the guiding rate of interest (Duerr, 1960).

THE INTEREST RATE

3

CHAPTER 2 BRIEFLY discusses capital, investment, and interest. It introduces the idea that interest is a legitimate cost of business and should be considered in investment analyses. Interest is included in all the compound interest formulas as a variable (Chapter 4). It is one of the most important variables because it has a large effect on the analyses, particularly higher interest rates, and because different organizations or individuals can have different interest rates that are "right" for them.

This chapter begins with the Chapter 2 definition that interest is the market price of money and continues the theoretical discussion at greater depth. This is followed by a discussion of interest rate determination for the private and public sectors. This discussion explains how analysts can decide which interest rate to use in each formula.

COMPONENTS OF THE INTEREST RATE

Money may be considered a commodity, such as lumber, with both a supply and a demand. One theory states that money is demanded for transactions, precautionary purchases, and speculation. The money supply is controlled in part by the central bank of the nation, the Federal Reserve Bank in the United States, and partly by the amount of checks and credit that exists. The simultaneous solution of the supply and demand functions for money sets the interest rate. The interest rate is the price of money.

Economists speak of a single interest rate rather than several rates. This is similar to speaking of *the* price of food or *the* price of many commodities when everyone knows there are many prices even for the same good. For example, the price of a six-pack of your favorite beverage can vary from store to store on the same day, but a single beverage price is still meaningful, usually in terms of an implied average price.

However, there can be reasons for different beverage prices in different stores on the same day. There can be differences in the brand so that not all orange soda is "the same"; there can be differences in the containers in which the beverage is sold so that one is more or less convenient; and there can be differences in the size of the container in the six-pack so that more or less soda is obtained for the price. These are qualitative reasons for price differences and are discussed here with regard to interest rates.

It is perhaps best to start with the concept of the *pure interest rate*. The pure interest rate is the base price of money that is then modified for other qualitative components. It is a risk-free price that one would pay for funds.

Risk is the first major component that modifies the interest rate. It is the amount of certainty assigned to an alternative's outcome. An investment whose outcome, or return, is difficult to predict or is unknown is a risky investment. Some authors identify three categories: certainty, risk, and uncertainty.

Certainty exists if there is only one outcome for each alternative. Risk exists if a probability distribution can be assigned to a series of outcomes for each alternative. Uncertainty exists when no information exists about the probability distribution of the outcomes. These three definitions actually mark three areas along a continuum of knowledge about investment outcomes. Adjusting for these differences is discussed in Chapter 9.

All three categories are combined into a general category called risk when discussing the interest rate. The certainty category is the risk-free investment discussed above.

Generally, the greater an investment's risk, the higher the interest rate. This simply means that investors want to be paid more for placing their funds in an investment for which the likelihood of obtaining the predicted return is low or unknown.

Liquidity is a second interest rate component. Liquidity is the ease with which an investment can be ended. It is the investor's ability to "liquidate" an investment if such is the desired course. Liquidity is important for several reasons. First, a liquid investment allows termination of the investment if the predicted outcome seems incorrect. This, in effect, reduces the risk. Second, a liquid investment allows changing to an investment with a higher return if one should become available in the future. Thus, errors in estimating the ARR can be rectified.

The length of time money must be left in an investment is an expression of its liquidity. For example, bonds are sold with varying repayment periods; certificates of deposit are available in yearly increments for up to 8 years; and most savings accounts are now, at least in fact, payable on demand. Generally, the less liquid the investment, the larger the interest rate.

Time preference, a third component, is the degree to which an individual or organization desires current rather than future consumption. A boy who passes an ice cream store and decides he must have an ice cream cone now has a high time preference. He does not want to wait for the future. The person who does not mind postponing consumption until the future has a low time preference.

Individuals usually have shorter time preferences, organizations longer, and "society" the longest. An individual has the shortest life-span and must consume before death to derive any personal benefit. Some individuals have longer time preferences because they want to leave an estate to their heirs. Organizations, particularly business corporations, have a longer life, often exceeding that of their founders. Therefore, they tend to look more toward the future, although current sales and profits exert a very strong influence. Society's time preference is usually longest because it plans to exist in perpetuity. Society may feel a responsibility for "generations unborn" and thus be willing to give up current consumption for their benefits. Generally, the shorter the time preference, the higher the interest rate and the longer the time preference, the lower the interest rate.

Transaction costs are the resources consumed in making loans or exchanging money. Banks investigate the credit ratings of borrowers, attorneys write contracts, and someone must see that principal and interest are paid on time. These costs are added to the interest rate by the lender. Generally, the larger the loan, the smaller the interest rate because many transaction costs are fixed with respect to loan size.

The *inflation rate* expected also affects the interest rate. Prices, including the price of money, rise each year during inflationary times. The amount of price increase is difficult to predict, but an investor wants assurance that "full money value" will be obtained. Therefore, the investor will increase the asking price for the money *now*, to be sure it is worth relatively at least as much at the termination of the investment. Generally, the higher the expected inflation rate, the higher an interest rate the investor desires.

INTEREST RATES FOR THE PRIVATE SECTOR

Interest should be included in investment analyses because it is the market price of money and an individual or organization can be either a lender or a borrower of funds. Suppose you have money you can invest. Your choice may be either to invest it in capital, such as a sawmill, or to lend it in the money market. One can almost always lend money, even if it is only to the local bank in a 5 percent interest savings account. The interest rate obtained in the money market is your alternative rate of return. This rate of return must be equaled or exceeded by your sawmill or you will have incurred an opportunity cost for the difference in the returns. In this example the alternative rate of return of 5 percent bank interest is the interest rate to use in compounding and discounting calculations.

Strictly speaking, alternative investments should be comparable in all the components of the interest rate—risk, liquidity, inflation, and the others. In practice, alternatives are seldom comparable, and it is a matter of judgment how incomparable they are. This discussion continues, with comparability assumed not to be a problem. Adjustments for lack of comparability in certain components, such as risk and inflation, are discussed in later chapters.

Suppose you have several investment alternatives, such as a sawmill, a plywood mill, and a plant to manufacture corrugated boxes. You may then rank them by their rates of return and invest in those above the alternative rate of return, as long as funds last. This idea is expressed in Keynsian economics as the Marginal Efficiency of Capital (MEC). The MEC is a curve that represents the rates of return for investment possibilities in the economy plotted over the amount of funds required for those investments (Figure 3.1a).

The MEC curve for the economy, or a particular industry within the economy, is continuous because there are many investment possibilities. The curves for an individual or organization may be more like a histogram because there are only a few discrete investment alternatives (Figure 3.1b). The economy or industry would probably invest along the MEC curve until the rate of return on the investment equaled the alternative rate of return (ARR) and the amount invested equaled OA (Figure 3.1a).

The individual firm has discrete investment opportunities of OA, AB, and BC (Figure 3.1b). It would choose projects OA and AB though not BC because BC is below its ARR. But, the firm's choice is not quite this simple. For example, suppose a firm had investment funds limited to AB and could only invest in either OA or AB. We will not delve any deeper because at this point we are interested primarily in the principles.

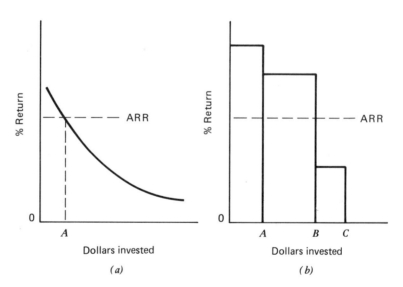

FIGURE 3.1   *Marginal efficiency of capital for (a) an industry or economy, and (b) an individual, organization, or firm.*

This is the basic idea of determining the interest rate from the lender's viewpoint. A person or organization with funds can either invest them internally or lend them in the market. The market interest rate is then the ARR, the interest rate to use for calculations. Funds should be invested internally for projects with returns greater than the market rate and loaned in the market after that. An opportunity cost would be incurred otherwise.

Now let us examine interest from the borrower's viewpoint. Suppose there are investment opportunities available but no funds to invest. You then must borrow funds in the market at the market interest rate. The market rate at which you can borrow becomes the alternative rate of return because the alternative is not borrowing and hence saving the interest charge. If we look at it another way, the borrower must at least earn the cost of the borrowed money, the interest, to make the investment worthwhile. This is often called the cost of capital.

The cost of capital is the interest rate that the borrower would pay for the funds to finance the project. This rate may be easily determined for an individual or small organization. For example, the owner of a small business can simply ask the local banker what the interest rate is for a 5-year loan. Or, the individual may be paying 19.56 percent interest on a credit card charge to replace funds used for an investment.

However, larger private organizations, such as large forest products companies, have many sources of funds. It is difficult to tell which source a dollar comes from because all dollars look alike and because one dollar bill is readily substitutable for another. Furthermore, financial experts believe a large corporation must keep the appropriate mix of debt and equity funds to have access to future capital funds markets. This means that over the years the average cost needed to maintain the proper mix is the minimum cost of capital and not the lower interest rate paid on debt or the higher rate paid on common stocks. Consequently, several techniques have been developed to estimate the cost of capital. Some of the more common ones are discussed here.

The *cost of capital* is yet another term that goes by a number of different names. It is variously called the cost of capital, the weighted average cost of capital, the composite cost of capital, and the overall cost of capital.* The objective is to find the cost of capital funds to use as the alternative rate of return, or cutoff rate, for analyzing investment alternatives. This rate, if properly set, should cause the price of stock in the firm to remain constant. A higher return would cause a price increase, a lower return a price decrease.

The basic procedure for calculating the cost of capital is to calculate the cost of each of the capital sources and then to combine them in a weighted average. The cost of capital is calculated after income taxes. Four sources of capital funds are generally available to publicly owned corporations; debt, preferred stock, common stock, and retained earnings. The last three sources constitute *equity*.

---

*This discussion closely follows Weston and Brigham's (1978) Chapter 19, where additional details may be found.

Some additional sources are variations of these, but we need not discuss them here. The cost of each of these sources of funds is calculated as follows:

The cost of new debt is

$$c_d = c'_d(1.0 - t) \tag{3.1}$$

where

c_d = the cost of new debt, after tax
c'_d = the cost of new debt, before tax
t = the marginal regular tax rate

The estimated cost is for new debt. Old debt, which was usually obtained at lower interest rates in these inflationary times, is not considered because those funds will not be available for investment.

The cost of preferred stock after tax is

$$c_p = \frac{d_p}{p_p} \tag{3.2}$$

where

c_p = the cost of new preferred stock, after tax
d_p = the dividends paid on the preferred stock
p_p = the price the firm would receive for the preferred stock at the dividend rate d_p

The price estimated, p_p, is the price the firm would receive for new preferred stock. This implies the price is the net of any issuance costs. The cost of new preferred stock is often estimated as the cost of old preferred stock.

The cost of retained earnings is the return that common stockholders require in order to invest or

$$c_r = \frac{d_c}{p_c} + g \tag{3.3}$$

where

c_r = the cost of retained earnings, after tax
d_c = the yearly expected dividend on common stock at the end of the year
p_c = the current price of common stock
g = the expected growth of the dividend in the coming year

Dividend and growth estimates (d_c and g) can be based on the past record of the firm, analyses made by securities analysts, or an analysis of the current stock market adjusted for the individual firm's risk. The past record is a bad estimate during unstable economic periods.

The cost of newly issued common stock is calculated by

$$c_c = \frac{d_c}{p_c(1.0 - f)} + g \tag{3.4}$$

where

    c_c — the cost of newly issued common stock
    f = the cost of issuing new stock per share as a proportion of its selling price

Equation 3.4 is exactly the same as Eq. 3.3 except that the cost of issuing the common stock is expressed directly in Eq. 3.4.

The cost of capital to use as the alternative rate of return, or the cutoff point, is the weighted average of these four sources, or

$$C = \sum w_i c_i \tag{3.5}$$

where

    C = the cost of capital
    w_i = the weight for the ith source of capital
    c_i = the cost of the ith source of capital

The cost of the ith source of capital is calculated as shown in Eqs. 3.1 to 3.4. The weights for the sources, w_i, should be those that will actually be in effect when the capital funds are obtained. These are often assumed to be the existing capital structure or the one that will exist if a new security issue is imminent.

Some authors recommend calculating the marginal cost of capital. This shows the changes in the cost of capital as the debt–equity ratio of the firm changes for different financing schemes. The ratio with the lowest cost of capital is chosen as the target; the firm's debt structure is managed to obtain that ratio. The cost of capital at that ratio is used as the ARR.

The basic idea in calculating the cost of capital is to estimate as accurately as possible the firm's future average capital costs. The average future cost is the return required to keep the stock of the firm at a constant price. This becomes the investment cutoff, or alternative rate of return. Only investments with returns greater than the cost are chosen; therefore, the value of the stock should rise. The costs must be calculated after tax and after any costs of issuing the securities have been deducted to truly reflect the cost of capital.

INTEREST RATES FOR
THE PUBLIC SECTOR

The appropriate conceptual model and estimating technique for the public sector interest rate have been and continue to be the subject of much discussion. One thing that all parties agree on is that the public sector should recognize the time value of money and use discounted investment analyses. The questions being discussed are (1) what is the "right" conceptual model and (2) how should the rate be estimated in practice once the right model is chosen.

Three frequently suggested conceptual models are the social rate of time preference, the cost of borrowing, and the opportunity cost of foregone private expenditures. The social rate of time preference is usually considered lower than the private rate for the reasons discussed above. Moreover, some economists believe that individuals have different values when acting collectively as a society than when acting as individuals. The interest rate reflecting their collective societal actions is the social rate of time preference. The cost of borrowing model parallels the cost of capital model presented above except that only government debt financing is considered. The opportunity cost model states that government spending reduces private spending and, therefore, the return on government spending must at least equal the foregone return in the private sector. The estimated interest rate must be weighted for the amount of consumption and investment expenditure foregone in the private sector.

The weight of opinion seems to favor the opportunity cost model, and it is suggested that this be estimated by the average current interest rate (not the coupon rate) on the long-term government bonds if a risk-free interest rate is desired. Several weighting schemes, which adjust for consumption and investment rates, can be applied to the private capital funds market if an interest rate including risk is desired.

The Joint Economic Committee found in 1968 that the risk-free interest rate was at least 5 percent and that the rates with risk were around 8 to 10 percent. In actual practice, the interest rate for most of the federal government has been set by the Office of Management and Budget (OMB).

The OMB is the "business manager" for the executive branch of our government. It monitors the managerial practices of the administrative agencies for the President, including the procedures used for investment analyses. Most natural resource agencies, including all those in the Departments of Agriculture and Interior, are executive branch agencies and therefore under OMB's guidance.

OMB requires that all agencies use a discounted analysis for "...program(s)...submitted...in support of legislative and budget programs." They further require that a 10 percent interest rate be used in the calculations (Office of Management and Budget, 1972). The analyses are to be performed in constant dollars, so that the effects of inflation are excluded. However, relative changes in the real price should be shown. The 10 percent interest rate is the noninflationary rate, before taxes. It is based on an estimate of rates of return on private investment and hence reflects a risk factor.

Projects of the Water Resources Council are specifically excepted from this interest rate. Their interest rate was set at $6\frac{7}{8}$ percent and is based on the cost of long-term federal borrowing (Water Resources Council, 1974).

THE TIME VALUE OF MONEY AND COMPOUND INTEREST

4

"TIME IS MONEY" is a meaningful phrase, particularly when one is growing trees or investing money, because both grow with time. A forest stand will grow with time and, with proper management, add increment each year for many years. Funds in a savings account will draw interest and funds invested in capital should also be earning their interest. An opportunity cost is incurred if they are not.

Invested funds earn interest and this interest can then be invested to earn its own interest. The $100 placed in a savings account may earn $5 interest this year. The $5 interest can be left in the bank account to earn $0.25 interest next year. This is the principle of compound interest. The interest rate is 5 percent a year in this example.

The amount of money originally invested is called the *principal amount*, and the amount of money to which it will grow when the interest is added is called the *future value*. The term *payment* indicates either a revenue (money received) or a cost (money paid). Formulas to calculate the future value of an investment once the interest rate is known are presented in this chapter.

A dollar invested today will be worth more in the future because it earns interest. It follows from this that a dollar received in the future is worth less than a dollar received today because it can not be invested and earn interest. The future payment is worth less because an opportunity cost of the interest payments foregone has been incurred. The value today of a future payment is called the *present value*. This chapter also presents formulas to calculate the present value of a future payment if the interest rate is known.

Calculating the future value of a payment or series of payments is called *compounding*. The payments are compounded forward to some future year *n*. Calculating the present value of a future payment is called *discounting*. Payments are discounted backward to the present. Compounding formulas are used to calculate the future value and discounting formulas are used to calculate the present value.

An example of future and present values may take these concepts clearer. Suppose $100 was invested at 8 percent interest per year. The future value of that investment in 1 year is $100 × 1.08, or $108. The present value of $100 received 1 year in the future is $100/1.08, or $92.59, because $92.59 invested today at 8 percent interest will grow to $100 in a year's time.

The terms future value and present value are expressed symbolically for convenience in using them in formulas. V_n is used to represent future value. V represents value and n represents the nth year in the future in which the value occurs. V_0 is used to represent present value. V is again value and 0 is time zero, today. Present value is a special case of V_n where $n = 0$.

The zero subscript defining "today" illustrates an important convention. The present is always considered time period zero. The subscript n implies that we can speak of a future value in any of the possible n future time periods. The time period (n) can be of any time length: days, weeks, months, or years. First, only years are considered until the principles of compounding are presented. Other time periods are then covered.

Interest always accrues at the end of the time period, say at the end of the year, unless there is instantaneous (sometimes called continuous) compounding. This leads to a second important convention. Payments, either costs or revenues, are always assumed to occur at the end of the time period in which they happen. A cost incurred in year "1" is incurred at the end of the first year. A revenue received in year "2" is received at the end of the second year. The most unambiguous way to correctly decide on the appropriate time period for a payment is to draw a *time line*. For example,

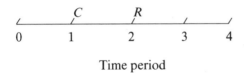

Time period

The cost occurring in year 1 is indicated by point C on the time line and the revenue by point R. The payment's timing is significant because it only bears interest after it is made. A cost cannot be charged interest until after it is paid and a revenue cannot earn interest until after it is received.

FORMULAS FOR SINGLE PAYMENTS

The simplest method of compounding or discounting is calculating future or present value of a single payment. We start with this method and then intuitively develop the other formulas.

The Future Value

Suppose the $100 used in the preceding example was allowed to remain invested for 3 years, and we wanted to calculate its future value at 8 percent interest. The value of V_n when $n = 3$, $V_0 = \$100$, and the interest rate, i, is 0.08 is desired. Using the notation previously discussed, we obtain

$$V_1 = \$100.00 \times 1.08 = \$108.00 \tag{4.1}$$

$$V_2 = \$108.00 \times 1.08 = \$116.64 \tag{4.2}$$

$$V_3 = \$116.64 \times 1.08 = \$125.97 \tag{4.3}$$

Equation 4.3 can be rewritten as

$$V_3 = V_2(1.0 + i) \tag{4.4}$$

and Eq. 4.2, which equals V_2, can be rewritten and substituted into Eq. 4.4 as

$$V_3 = V_1(1.0 + i)(1.0 + i) \tag{4.5}$$

Equation 4.1 can similarly be substituted into Eq. 4.5 as

$$V_3 = V_0(1.0 + i)(1.0 + i)(1.0 + i) \tag{4.6}$$

Finally, Eq. 4.6 can be rewritten and generalized as

$$V_3 = V_0(1.0 + i)^3$$
$$V_n = V_0(1.0 + i)^n \tag{4.7}$$

where

V_n = the future value of a single payment in year n
V_0 = the present value of a single payment
$\quad i$ = the interest rate
$\quad n$ = the year in which the payment occurs

Equation 4.7 is for calculating the future value (V_n) of a single payment (V_0) n years in the future when the interest rate is i. For example, calculate V_n when $V_0 = \$250$, $i = 8$ percent, and $n = 10$:

$$V_{10} = \$250.00(1.08)^{10}$$

$$V_{10} = \$250.00(2.1589)$$

$$V_{10} = \$539.73$$

The value $(1.0 + i)^n$ is the *multiplier* for the future value of a single payment. Tables of multipliers for this and all following formulas are readily available.* Table A.1 contains compounding multipliers for a single payment. The table shows the value of a dollar if it were compounded to the future for the indicated time period and interest rate. It is the amount to which one dollar would grow if it were put in the bank today for the indicated time and interest rate.

The Present Value

Calculating the present value of a single payment simply requires solving Eq. 4.7 for the present value and substituting the required variable values into the equation, as follows:

$$V_n = V_0(1.0 + i)^n$$

Divide both sides by $(1.0 + i)^n$, and move V_0 to the left-hand side to obtain

$$V_0 = \frac{V_n}{(1.0 + i)^n} \tag{4.8}$$

where all variables are as previously defined.

Equation 4.8 can be used to calculate the present value (V_0) of a future payment (V_n) that is made n years in the future when the interest rate is i. For example, calculate V_0 when $V_n = \$539.73$, $i = 8$ percent, and $n = 10$:

$$V_0 = \frac{\$539.73}{(1.08)^{10}} = \$100.00$$

The expression $1/(1.0 + i)^n$ solved for the indicated i and n is the multiplier for the present value of a single payment. It is the reciprocal of the corresponding future value multiplier in Table A.1. The present value multiplier may be interpreted as the value of a dollar if it were discounted to the present. It is the amount of money you would have to put in the bank today to receive a dollar in the future for the indicated time and interest rate.

The Interest Rate or Number of Years Invested

Equation 4.7 can also be solved for the interest rate earned by an investment or the number of years it will take to obtain a desired amount of money, as long as the other three variables are known. It is simply a matter of solving the equation for the desired variable.

---

*One of the more widely used tables in forestry is Lundgren, A. L. 1971. Tables of compound-discount interest rate multipliers for evaluating forestry investments. Research Paper NC-51 North Central Forest Experiment Station, USDA Forest Service, St. Paul, Minnesota.

Solving for the interest rate is done by starting with Eq. 4.7

$$V_n = V_0(1.0 + i)^n$$

dividing both sides by V_0,

$$\frac{V_n}{V_0} = (1.0 + i)^n$$

taking the nth root of both sides,

$$\sqrt[n]{\frac{V_n}{V_0}} = 1.0 + i$$

subtracting 1.0 from both sides and moving i to the left-hand side,

$$i = \sqrt[n]{\frac{V_n}{V_0}} - 1.0 \tag{4.9}$$

For example, suppose you invested $100 for 3 years and received $125 in return. What interest rate did you earn?

$$i = \sqrt[3]{\frac{\$125}{\$100}} - 1.0 = 1.077 - 1.0 = 0.077 = 7.7\%$$

Another method is to simply look up the value V_n/V_0 for the known number of years in Table A.1. For example, suppose a share of common stock was purchased in 1978 for $100 and sold in 1985 for $177. Assume further that no dividends were paid during the investment and no brokerage fees charged. What interest rate was earned? First, construct a time line to determine the number of years in the investment.

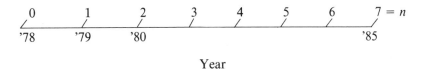

Year

Then calculate $V_n/V_0 = \$177/\$100 = 1.770$ and look across Table A.1 on the 7-year line until the compounding factor 1.770 is found under the 0.085 column. The interest rate earned is 8.5 percent.

Solving for the number of years is a bit more complicated. Start with Eq. 4.7 as before

$$V_n = V_0(1.0 + i)^n$$

and divide both sides by V_0

$$V_n/V_0 = (1.0 + i)^n$$

convert the equation to logarithms

$$\ln V_n/V_0 = n \ln (1.0 + i)$$

and divide both sides of the equation by $\ln (1.0 + i)$, and move n to the left-hand side so that

$$n = \frac{\ln V_n/V_0}{\ln (1.0 + i)} \tag{4.10}$$

For example, suppose you now had \$1500, you needed \$2000, and you could invest your funds at 7.5 percent interest. How many years would you have to invest your money before you had \$2000? Using Eq. 4.10, we obtain

$$n = \frac{\ln \$2000/\$1500}{\ln (1.075)} = \frac{0.28768}{0.07232} = 3.98 \text{ years} \tag{4.11}$$

Note that any base logarithms can be used for these calculations. Table A.1 could also be used again, this time going down the 7.5 percent column until the multiplier 1.3333 is found.

FORMULAS FOR SERIES OF PAYMENTS

Thus far only payments made at a *single* point in time have been discussed, for example, \$100 received in year 20. Suppose that a series of payments, all the same amount, were made at regular intervals for a specified number of time periods. These payments are called *terminating annual annuities*. Terminating means the series is finite, annuity means the payments are due at regular intervals, and annual means the payment is made each year or in the single unit of the time period. A \$100 payment each year for 20 years is a terminating annual annuity because the payment ends in 20 years, it is paid regularly every year, and it is paid each year rather than, say, every other year. The regular time intervals may be any time period such as a month, quarter, or year.

The present value and future value of terminating annual annuities are often calculated. The notation used in these calculations is similar to that used for a single payment. The subscript n is used to indicate the *number* of time periods in which the annuity occurs and the V is replaced with SA, which stands for "sum of the annuity." The amount of the annuity is indicated by the symbol a, which replaces the V_0 in Eq. 4.7.

Notation varies from author to author. This is often confusing. One of the best ways to avoid confusion is to understand what the formula does rather than simply learning to use it by rote.

The Future Value of a Terminating Annual Annuity

Suppose you are a landowner and a hunting club leases your land for $100 a year for the next 15 years. You want to know the value of the payments at the lease's expiration if you invest each payment at 8 percent as it is received. This is a future value of a terminating annual annuity problem. It is a future value because the value is desired as of the end of the lease. It is a terminating series because the lease ends in 15 years. It is an annuity because the payments occur at regular intervals, and it is an annual annuity because that interval is 1 year.

You already know how to solve this problem. It is a future value, so Eq. 4.7 applies. A time line shows how many years each payment in the series must be compounded.

Payment =		$100	$100	$100	$100		$100	$100
$n =$	0	1	2	3	4		14	15

If we take the timing convention into account, the first payment in the series occurs at the end of the first year, the second payment at the end of the second year, and so on, until the final payment occurs at the end of the 15th year.

The value at the end of the lease is desired; therefore, the value of the payments in year 15 is needed. The payment made in year 15 earns no interest because it occurs at the end of that year. Therefore, its value at year 15 is $100. The payment received in year 14 is available for 1 year and will be invested. Therefore, its value in year 15 is compounded forward for 1 year or, if we use Eq. 4.7,

$$V_{15} = \$100(1.0 + 0.8)^1 = \$108.00$$

The payment received in year 13 must be compounded forward 2 years and is worth $116.64 in year 15; the payment in year 12 is compounded 3 years, and so on, until the first payment, made in year 1, is compounded forward 14 years. The sum of each of these annual payments, compounded forward to year 15, is the future value of the lease.

These calculations are illustrated in Table 4.1. The first three columns show the year of payment, the number of years the payment must be compounded, and

TABLE 4.1 Calculating the Future Value of a Terminating Annual Annuity

Year of Payment	No. years compounded (n)	Amount of payment (a)	Future value multiplier $(1 + 0.08)^n$	Future value (V_n)
15	0	$100	1.0000	$100.00
14	1	100	1.0800	108.00
13	2	100	1.1664	116.64
12	3	100	1.2597	125.97
11	4	100	1.3605	136.05
10	5	100	1.4693	146.93
9	6	100	1.5869	158.69
8	7	100	1.7138	171.38
7	8	100	1.8509	185.09
6	9	100	1.9990	199.90
5	10	100	2.1589	215.89
4	11	100	2.3316	233.16
3	12	100	2.5182	251.82
2	13	100	2.7196	271.96
1	14	100	2.9372	293.72
Total			27.1520	$2,715.20

the amount of the payment. The fourth column contains the future value multiplier that is obtained either from Table A.1 or from the formula $(1.0 + i)^n$. The last column is the product of the third and fourth columns, the annuity multiplied by the future value multiplier. The future value of the lease is the sum of the fifth column or $2715.20.

A shortcut for calculating the future value of a terminating annual annuity is possible. In the example one number that is constant (the annuity) is multiplied by another number that is variable (the future value multiplier) and the results are summed. The variable values of the multiplier can be represented by the letters of the alphabet so that $A = 1.0$, $B = 1.08, \ldots 0 = 2.9372$. Then, the preceding calculations can be written

$$SA_{15} = (100 \times A) + (100 \times B) + \cdots + (100 \times 0)$$

which can be rewritten by the distributive law of multiplication as

$$SA_{15} = \$100.00(A + B + \cdots + 0)$$
$$SA_{15} = \$100.00(27.1520) = \$2,715.20$$

where 27.1520 is the sum of the future value multipliers—column 4 in Table 4.1.

The amount of the annuity is then simply multiplied by the multiplier to obtain the future value of the series.

The future value of a terminating annuity can be calculated directly by the formula

$$SA_n = a \frac{(1.0 + i)^n - 1.0}{i}$$ (4.12)

where

SA_n = the future value of a terminating annuity, or equivalently, the sum of the annuities at year n
a = amount of the annuity
n = the number of years the annuity is paid
i = the interest rate

The right-hand expression

$$\frac{(1.0 + i)^n - 1.0}{i}$$

is the future value multiplier. It may be calculated directly, it may be calculated by looking up the value of $(1.0 + i)^n$ in Table A.1 and substituting it in the expression, or it can often be found in a separate table. Table A.2 in this book contains the future value multipliers for terminating annual annuities.

The preceding problem may be solved using Eq. 4.12 as:

$$SA_{15} = \$100.00 \frac{(1.0 + 0.08)^{15} - 1.0}{0.08} = \$100.00 \times (27.1521) = \$2,715.21$$

The difference in the two answers is due to rounding. The multiplier 27.1521 can either be found in Table A.2 or be calculated.

The Present Value of a Terminating Annual Annuity

The present value of a terminating annual annuity parallels the future value except that annuity values are discounted instead of compounded. Suppose we had the same $100 a year, 15-year lease, only now the present value of the lease was desired. Start again by drawing a time line that will look exactly like the previous one.

Recalling the timing convention, we see that the first payment of $100 must be discounted back 1 year to year zero, the second payment must be discounted back 2 years, and so on, until the last payment is discounted back 15 years. You already know how to do this. The present value of the first payment, from year 1, can be calculated using Eq. 4.8 as

$$V_0 = \frac{\$100.00}{(1.0 + 0.08)^1} = \$92.59$$

This procedure can be follows for each of the 15 payments and summed to find the present value of the lease. These calculations are illustrated in Table 4.2 where the first three columns are the year of payment, the number of years the payment must be discounted, and the amount of the annuity. The fourth column is the present value multiplier, which can be calculated either from the formula $(1/1.0 + i)^n$ or as the reciprocal of the corresponding value from Table A.1. The fifth column is the product of the third and fourth columns in the table. The present value of the series is the sum of the fifth column or $855.94.

As before, a short-cut method is available. A constant is still being multiplied by a variable and the results are summed. Therefore, the present value of the terminating annuity can be written

$$V_0 = \$100.00(A + B + \ldots + 0)$$
$$V_0 = \$100.00(8.5595) = \$855.95$$

TABLE 4.2 Calculating the Present Value of a Terminating Annual Annuity

Year of payment	No. years discounted (n)	Amount of payment (a)	Present value multiplier $\left(\dfrac{1}{(1 + 0.08)^n}\right)$	Present value (V_0)
1	1	$100	0.9259	$92.59
2	2	100	0.8573	85.73
3	3	100	0.7938	79.38
4	4	100	0.7350	73.50
5	5	100	0.6806	68.06
6	6	100	0.6302	63.02
7	7	100	0.5835	58.35
8	8	100	0.5403	54.03
9	9	100	0.5002	50.02
10	10	100	0.4632	46.32
11	11	100	0.4289	42.89
12	12	100	0.3971	39.71
13	13	100	0.3677	36.77
14	14	100	0.3405	34.05
15	15	100	0.3152	31.52
Total			8.5595	$855.94

where 8.5595 is the sum of the present value multipliers in column four of Table 4.2. Once again, the payment is multiplied by the multiplier to obtain the desired value.

The present value of a terminating annual annuity can be calculated directly by the formula

$$SA_0 = a \frac{(1.0 + i)^n - 1.0}{i(1.0 + i)^n}$$ (4.13)

where

SA_0 = the present value of a terminating annuity, or equivalently, the sum of the annuities in year zero.

a = the amount of the annuity

n = the number of years the annuity is paid

i = the interest rate

The right-hand expression

$$\frac{(1.0 + i)^n - 1.0}{i(1.0 + i)^n}$$

is the present value multiplier. It may be calculated directly, it may be calculated by looking up the value for $(1.0 + i)^n$ in Table A.1 and substituting it into the expression, or it can often be found in a separate table. Table A.3 in this book contains the present value multipliers for terminating annual annuities.

The preceding problem may be solved using Eq. 4.13 as

$$SA_0 = \$100.00 \frac{(1.0 + 0.08)^{15} - 1.0}{0.08(1.0 + 0.08)^{15}} = \$100.00(8.5595) = \$855.95$$

The difference in the two answers is due to rounding. The multiplier 8.5595 can either be found in Table A.3 or be calculated.

The Present Value of a Perpetual Annual Annuity

Suppose the stream of payments did not terminate as in the preceding cases but went on forever. This is the implicit assumption made in many forest valuation problems when the analyst says the land will be forever forested.

We can begin to solve this problem by rewriting Eq. 4.13, the present value of a terminating annuity, with the terms spaced a bit further apart so that

$$SA_0 = a \frac{1}{i} \frac{(1.0 + i)^n - 1.0}{(1.0 + i)^n}$$

Now, when payments never terminate but continue in perpetuity, we are really saying that n becomes infinitely large. This makes the term $(1.0 + i)^n$ very large. For example,

$$n = 500, (1.0 + 0.08)^{500} = 5.15 \times 10^{16}$$

and

$$n = 1000, (1.0 + 0.08)^{1,000} = 2.65 \times 10^{33}$$

This means that when the term

$$\frac{(1.0 + i)^n - 1.0}{(1.0 + i)^n}$$

is calculated, the numerator will almost equal the denominator because 1.0 subtracted from such large numbers will hardly make them different. Therefore, the value of this fraction can be considered 1.0.

Equation 4.13 can then be written as

$$SA_0 = a \frac{1}{i} 1.0$$

$$SA_0 = \frac{a}{i} \qquad\qquad (4.14)$$

where

> SA_0 = the present value of a perpetual annuity
> a = the amount of the annuity
> i = the interest rate

The payment is simply divided by the interest rate to find the present value.

Suppose, for example, the hunting lease of $100 discussed earlier was perpetual. Then, the present value of these payments at 8 percent interest is

$$SA_0 = \frac{\$100.00}{0.08} = \$1,250.00$$

Similarly, the present value of $2 per acre year property taxes with an alternative rate of return of 12 percent is

$$SA_0 = \frac{\$2.00}{0.12} = \$16.67$$

This type of calculation is very useful during investment analyses.

The Present Value of a Perpetual Periodic Annuity

The present value of a perpetual periodic annuity refers to the case in which the payment series does not occur yearly, or every time period, but rather in multiplies of years or the time period. For example, a multiaged forest may be on a 5-year cutting cycle and it is estimated that 50,000 board feet will be harvested every 5 years. Another example occurs in even-aged management where the harvest cut is made at the end of the rotation, say every 25 years, and it is assumed that there will be perpetual rotations. The identifying characteristic of this case is that the same sized payment occurs in constant multiples of the time period in perpetuity.

You can very closely approximate the present value calculation using techniques you already know. Simply calculate the present values of the payments using Eq. 4.8 until the present value becomes very small, say only a few pennies, and then sum the present values.

Suppose, as a simplified example, a forest has a 25-year pulpwood rotation, that there magically is no expense during the rotation, that your income is $500 an acre, and that your alternative rate of return is 8 percent. You desire to know the minimum sale price you should receive for the land.

The calculations are illustrated in Table 4.3. The first and second columns contain the year in which the payment is made and the amount of the payment. Note that there is a constant number of years between each payment and that the first payment occurs the same number of years into the future. The third column is the present value multiplier and the fourth column is the product of the second and third columns. The sum of the fourth column is $85.49 and is the amount of money you would have to invest today at 8 percent interest to have $500 in 25 years and every 25 years thereafter.

As before, a short-cut method is available. A constant is still being multiplied by a variable and the results are summed. Therefore, the present value of the

TABLE 4.3 Calculating the Present Value of a Perpetual Periodic Annuity

Year of payment	Amount of payment (a)	Present value $\left(\dfrac{1}{(1 + 0.08)^n}\right)$	Present value (V_0)
25	$500.00	0.146018	$73.01
50	500.00	0.021321	10.66
75	500.00	0.003113	1.56
100	500.00	0.000454	0.23
125	500.00	0.000066	0.03
Total		0.170972	$85.49

perpetual periodic annuity can be written

$$V_0 = \$500.00(A + B + C + D + E)$$
$$V_0 = \$500.00(0.170972) = \$85.49$$

where 0.170972 is the sum of the present value multipliers in column three of Table 4.3.

The present value of a perpetual periodic annuity can be calculated directly by the equation

$$SA_0 = a\frac{1.0}{(1.0 + i)^n - 1.0} \qquad (4.15)$$

where

SA_0 = the present value of the perpetual periodic annuity
a = the amount of the annuity, received n years in the future, and every n years thereafter
n = the number of years between annuity payments
i = the interest rate

The right-hand expression

$$\frac{1.0}{(1.0 + i)^n - 1.0}$$

is the present value multiplier. It may be calculated directly, it may be calculated by obtaining the value of $(1.0 + i)^n$ in Table A.1 and substituting it into Eq. 4.14, or it can often be found in a separate table. Table A.4 in this book contains the present value multipliers for a periodic perpetual annuity. Note that to use this multiplier the first payment must occur n years in the future and the interval between payments must always be the same.

Note also that this is the first time that n has not indicated the unit of time but rather a multiple of the time unit. The student may designate this as n' or some other symbol to remember the difference if it is more convenient.

Remarks

Compound interest techniques are often unpopular with forest managers. Sometimes the managers do not understand them or their calculation and, hence, prefer not to use them. Furthermore, analyses recognizing the time value of money almost always make forestry investments look less desirable than other alternatives and, the higher the interest rate, the less desirable they look. It is often argued that we must leave a legacy to future generations and that there is something inherently good about forestry or resource-based investment. Thus, it is argued, discounted analyses should not be used.

This argument usually indicates incomplete understanding of compounding and discounting. They measure an investment's economic efficiency and are a proper decision guideline. They do not measure nonefficiency items, like how income is distributed among the citizens of a community. Separate analyses should be performed for the nonefficiency items when they are an important part of the decision. On the other hand, some forest managers follow the compounding and discounting techniques too slavishly. It should be remembered that they are guidelines, due to the inability to measure all variables, projection errors in variable estimates, and other reasons discussed above. A judgment must usually be made about each analyses' accuracy and the final decision tempered accordingly.

The preceding pages have removed, it is hoped, some of the confusion about compound interest. Most compounding and discounting formulas flow directly from the basic formula

$$V_n = V_0(1.0 + i)^n$$

The other formulas are simply short-cut methods of making calculations using the basic formula. They are not necessary, strictly speaking, because you can do anything with the basic formula that you can with the others except that it takes considerably longer.

However, the increasing availability at low cost of programmable hand calculators, minicomputers, and remote terminals decreases the likelihood that calculations will be made using multiplier tables or approximations. Tomorrow's forest analyst will probably include the preceding formulas directly in computer programs, which are used to calculate the decision criteria presented in the next chapter. These formulas were developed intuitively rather than mathematically. This approach was believed best for a first exposure. Mathematical derivations can be found in the financial management literature and in the forestry literature (Davis, 1966; Duerr, 1960; and Flick, 1976).

SPECIAL TOPICS

The preceding equations provide the basic tools for making forest investment financial analyses. The coming chapters demonstrate how these tools may be used to provide decision guidelines for the forest manager and landowner. There are many other compounding and discounting formulas that may be useful. Two of these are discussed in this section along with applications to time periods other than a year.

Sinking Fund Formula

Sometimes a firm or individual would like to know how much money it has to save per time period at a known interest rate to obtain a desired amount available at a specified future data. The *sinking fund* formula is used for this purpose.

The sinking fund was originally used by corporations to be sure they saved enough to repay bond issues or other fixed liabilities. An individual may want to use the formula to determine regular savings for retirement or a child's education. Or, a firm may want to create a reserve to purchase a piece of equipment when a piece currently in operation wears out.

For example, suppose a logging truck costs $50,000, will last 5 years, and can be salvaged for $5000. How much must be put in the bank each year at 6 percent interest to replace the truck if the future cost is expected to be the same? Selling the truck at the end of 5 years will generate $5000 cash, therefore, $45,000 ($50,000 − $5000) must be in the bank. What needs to be known is the annual annuity you must pay at 6 percent interest so the future value of the payment series is $45,000.

This is simply a special case of the future value of a terminating annual annuity problem. Equation 4.12 tells us that

$$SA_n = a \frac{(1.0 + i)^n - 1.0}{i}$$

and substituting the term k for the multiplier portion, we have

$$SA_n = ak$$

The future value, SA_n, and the multiplier variables, i and n, are known in the sinking fund problem and the annual annuity must be obtained. This is done by dividing both sides of the equation by k and moving a to the left-hand side so that

$$a = \frac{SA_n}{k}$$

Substituting the values from the problem and Table A.2 yields

$$a = \frac{\$45,000}{5.6371} = \$7,982.83$$

This means that $7982.83 must be put in a 6 percent savings account starting at the end of the first year and for every year thereafter, *including* the fifth year, which will earn no interest, in order to obtain $45,000.

Partial Payment Formula

The partial payment problem is the opposite of the sinking fund problem. The *partial payment* occurs when money has been borrowed and the periodic repayment must be calculated for a specified interest rate and a specified time period. In the sinking fund problem the bank is paying you interest and you are the lender. In the partial payment problem you are paying the bank interest and you are the borrower.

Let's take the preceding problem, only this time suppose the $45,000 has been borrowed at 6 percent interest for 5 years to buy the truck. What is the annual payment needed to repay both principal and interest? This is simply a special case of the present value of the terminating annual annuity. The present value, SA_0, is the $45,000 loan you receive today and the repayment period and interest rate are specified. Equation 4.13 may be rewritten as above, substituting k for the multipler

$$SA_0 = ak$$

dividing both sides by k and moving a to the left-hand side, so that

$$a = \frac{SA_0}{k}$$

and substituting the values from the problem and Table A.3

$$a = \frac{45,000}{4.2124}$$

$$a = \$10,682.75$$

This means that the lender is repaid $10,682.75 beginning at the end of the first year and every year thereafter including the fifth year.

Time Periods Less Than a Year

The time period in the preceding discussions has been 1 year. Each value of n has represented a year so that $n = 1$ represented 1 year and $n = 15$ represented 15 years. There are many applications for which yearly time periods are unrealistic. For example, many loans are repaid and bank deposits made on a monthly basis. A new term, *nominal interest rate*, must be defined and i and n redefined to solve problems for shorter time periods.

The *nominal interest rate* is the quoted yearly interest rate. For example, banks may quote a 6 percent interest rate and then specify the compounding period as daily or quarterly. Another example is the interest rate on the unpaid balance of many credit cards, which is stated as 12 or 18 percent a year.

The variables i and n in the preceding formulas are replaced with i' and n' to solve for time periods of less than a year. The variables i and n have been used to represent the yearly (nominal) interest rate and the number of years. Now they must be redefined to represent the interest rate per time period and the number of time periods. This is done by dividing the nominal interest rate by the number of time periods per year, such as four quarters or 12 months a year, and multiplying the number of years by the number of time periods per year. In formula form

$$i' = \frac{i}{\text{periods per year}}$$

$$n' = n \times \text{periods per year}$$

where

      i = the nominal interest rate
      n = the number of years in the problem

The newly calculated values for i' and n' are then substituted into the formulas already discussed and the answers for time periods shorter than a year are calculated. The main point is that i' is the interest that is actually being charged and, as will be seen in the section on the effective annual rate, can be very different from the nominal interest rate.*

For example, what would be the monthly payment for the preceding loan of $45,000 at 6 percent interest for 5 years? First, i' and n' must be calculated as

$$i' = 0.06/12 = 0.005$$

$$n' = 5 \text{ years} \times 12 \text{ months} = 60$$

then, using Eq. 4.13 and substituting i' for i and n' for n, we obtain

$$SA_0 = \frac{a(1.0 + i')^{n'} - 1.0}{i'(1.0 + i')^{n'}}$$

and

$$\$45,000 = a\frac{(1.0 + 0.005)^{60} - 1.0}{0.005(1.0 + 0.005)^{60}}$$

$$a = \frac{\$45,000}{51.7256} = \$869.98 \text{ monthly payment}$$

---

*Multipliers for continuous compounding are calculated by $V_n = e^{in}$, where e = the base of the natural logarithm; i = the interest rate per unit of time; and n = the number of units of time. This form is often used in theoretical analyses because it is easily differentiable.

Values for the multiplier may be calculated directly or obtained from tables, as before. Using tables sometimes is inconvenient because the values for i' are not always available. Therefore, it is often easier to calculate the multiplier directly, particularly with the ready availability of hand calculators with exponential function keys.

The Effective Annual Interest Rate

Multiple time periods per year can lead to confusion about the true annual interest rate. The true or *effective annual rate* (EAR) is the amount to which $1 would grow at the end of 1 year if the compounding period were 1 year.

The EAR can be calculated by taking the periodic interest rate, i' in the preceding section, and compounding it forward for a year. The formula for this is

$$EAR = (1.0 + i')^{npy} - 1.0 \qquad (4.16)$$

where

$\quad EAR$ = the effective annual interest rate
$\quad\quad i'$ = the nominal annual interest rate divided by npy
$\quad npy$ = the number of payments per year

For example, many credit card statements carry the information on the bottom of the statement that you will pay 1.5 percent interest on the unpaid balance and that the annual rate is 18 percent. What is the EAR of this loan?

$$EAR = (1.0 + 0.015)^{12} - 1.0 = 1.1956 - 1.0 = 0.1956$$

The effective annual rate of interest is 19.56 percent. If you put a dollar in a bank at the interest rate you are paying the credit card company, you would have $1.1956 in the account at the end of 1 year.

DECISION CRITERIA

5

THE ACCOUNTING DEFINITION of an investment is an expenditure for an asset that lasts longer than one accounting period. Projects with costs and revenues that continue for more than one accounting period are also investments. Most forestry decisions are investment decisions because of the long production process or because of the length of the assets' life. For example, campgrounds, stock ponds, and roads all last many years and have benefits flowing from them for many years.

There is a well-established body of knowledge to assist managers in making investment decisions. It is found under the titles of "investments" and "capital theory" in economics books, "engineering economy" in engineering books, and "financial management" and "capital budgeting" in business administration books. The topic has been taught under the title "valuation" in forestry. Valuation is the process of placing a value on something, whether it is the stumpage price for timber or the benefits from a visitor's day of recreation. Valuation allows the forest manager to choose between alternatives by comparing the difference between product value and cost for each alternative.

A forestry investment decision is nothing more than a specialized type of investment decision, and sometimes there isn't any specific distinction. Placing a value on a tract of land with an immature timber stand or determining an optimal rotation age requires special application of general investment analysis. Deciding to purchase road-building or logging equipment is no different for the forester than for the general construction contractor. An example of one of these special applications is known as the Faustmann Formula. However, they still remain simply applications of more general investment analyses.

CASH FLOW ANALYSES

Before proceeding further, we must make the distinction between accounting and cash flow analyses. *Accounting analyses* take data from an organization's financial records. These records are maintained in accordance with the rules of the Internal Revenue Service and standard accounting practices.

One of the basic rules for calculating profit is that a cost is associated with the revenue it produces. This means that a machine that is involved over a period of several years in manufacturing hundreds, or even millions, of products has part of its original cost allocated to each of those products. This is called *depreciation* and it allows for capital consumption during the production process. The cost of a capital asset is not subtracted from profit in the year the asset is purchased. Rather, it is placed in a capital account and appears as an asset on the balance sheet and not an expense on the income statement. Then, at each accounting period, the estimated capital consumption is included as an expense on the income statement and the capital account is reduced accordingly. Both profit and the capital asset account are reduced by the depreciation. Depreciable items in forestry include: equipment such as pickup trucks and tractors; buildings such as district headquarters; permanent roads; and bridges.

Cash flow analyses trace the *actual* movements of cash in the time periods they occur. The total dollar movement and its timing are identified. This is the procedure preferred for investment analysis because it shows the money available for investment.

For example, suppose a logging tractor costing $50,000 was purchased, had a 3-year life, a $5000 scrap value, and that straight line depreciation was used. The two analyses would record this transaction as follows. Annual depreciation for the accounting method is

$$\text{Annual depreciation} = \frac{(\$50,000 - \$5,000)}{3 \text{ years}} = \$15,000$$

Using a time line, we obtain

Year	0	1	2	3
Cash flow	− $50K			$5K
Accounting		− $15K	− $15K	− $15K

The cash flow method records the entire $50,000 as an expense in year zero when the cash was paid for the tractor. It also shows the receipt of $5000 for scrap at the end of year 3 when the tractor is sold. The accounting method, on the other hand, shows only $15,000 a year expenses for the 3 years.

Note that the total expense from both methods is the same, −$45,000. However, the present value of these expenditure streams is different. For example, at 8 percent interest the present value of the cash flow method is −$46,030.84, whereas it is only −$38,656.45 for the accounting method.

There are several methods of calculating depreciation, such as the straight line, declining balance, double declining balance, and sum-of-the-digits methods. The straight line method assumes the asset is consumed in equal amounts throughout its life. It is calculated by dividing the purchase price minus the scrap value by the expected life, or

$$\text{Annual depreciation} = \frac{\text{purchase price} - \text{scrap value}}{\text{expected life}} \qquad (5.1)$$

Purchase price and scrap value are stated in dollars. Expected life is usually stated in a unit of time, such as years or hours of machine operation. The straight line method will be used for examples throughout this book. Other methods will not be discussed. Interested students can find discussions and explanations in accounting books. In practice, firms follow the Internal Revenue Service regulations to determine the type of depreciation and expected asset life.

Depreciation is called a *noncash expense* because profit is reduced by the amount of depreciation but no cash has left the bank account. Depreciation is the major noncash expense in most corporations. Depletion, which will be discussed under taxation, is a second major noncash expense in resource-based organizations.

A good technique to determine the timing of a cash flow payment is to think about a checking account. A positive cash flow occurs when a deposit would occur. A negative cash flow occurs when a check would be written. Remember this technique when trying to place a payment on a time line.

Investment analyses should be made on a cash flow basis rather than an accounting basis because it is the money actually in the bank that is available for operating expense, payments to stockholders, or reinvestment. Paper profits are useless until they are converted to cash. Analyses should also be made on an after-tax basis for the same reason. Tax adjustments will be temporarily ignored to simplify the presentation. However, they are discussed in Chapter 8.

CRITERIA THAT IGNORE THE TIME VALUE OF MONEY

There are two common investment criteria that do not use discounting, the *average rate of return* and the *payback period*. Both methods are commonly used so the student should be familiar with them.

Average Return on Investment

The average return on investment is the ratio of the average annual after tax return, as shown in accounting records, divided by the average annual investment, or

$$AROI = \frac{AAR}{AAI} \qquad (5.2)$$

where

$AROI$ = the average return on investment
AAR = the average annual return after tax, from accounting records
AAI = the average annual investment in the project

The averages are often calculated over the investment's life or for the number of years it takes to completely depreciate the asset. Sometimes, the average annual investment is replaced with the total investment. These differences in calculation make it important to always inquire how the AROI was calculated. Returns on alternative investments are often quoted during discussions or in reports. However, they may have been calculated by different methods and so are noncomparable. Further, the analyst should always know the calculation method so the resulting ratio can be correctly interpreted.

For example, suppose planting with the next larger sized tractor resulted in an after tax savings of $2000 a year because it could operate faster, that it cost $10,000 more than the size tractor currently owned, and that it would be depreciated over 5 years. The AROI of investing in the larger tractor is

$$AROI = \frac{\$2000}{\$10,000 \times 0.5} = 0.40 = 40\%$$

when the average investment is used for the denominator. However, when the total investment is used, the AROI changes to

$$AROI = \frac{\$2000}{\$10,000} = 0.20 = 20\%$$

There are two advantages to the AROI. First, the calculations use accounting data that are usually readily available from an organization's records. Second, the calculations are simple and hence easily understood by decision makers. There are two disadvantages to the ratio. First, it uses an accounting rather than a cash flow analysis and so does not reflect the cash that is actually available for operations. Second, it does not consider the time value of money and so ignores the interest that must be paid or earned by the investment.

Payback Period

The *payback period* is the number of years it takes to recover the cash investment in the project. It is the initial investment divided by the annual cash flow, or

$$PBP = \frac{TII}{ACF} \qquad (5.3)$$

where

$\quad$ PBP $=$ payback period in years
$\quad$ TII $=$ the total initial investment
$\quad$ ACF $=$ the annual cash flow

For example, suppose the preceding planting tractor investment had $2000 a year of noncash expenses to add back. Then, the annual cash flow would be $4000 ($2000 addition to profit plus the $2000 noncash expense) and

$$PBP = \frac{\$10,000}{\$4,000} = 2.50 \text{ years}$$

The payback period ratio has several advantages. First, it is simply calculated and easy to understand. Also, it uses cash flow rather than accounting information and so is an improvement over AROI. Finally, it is a useful ratio when the investment has high risk. Here, the investor may want to know how quickly his initial investment will be returned because of concern about changing market or manufacturing conditions or the ability to project other variables into the future.

However, the ratio also has several disadvantages. First, it can give the wrong answer if the cash flows are uneven each year. For example, suppose the cash flows over the life of the tractor investment were $10,000, $4000, $2000, $2000, and $2000 in the respective 5 years. The annual cash flow would still average $4000, but the investment pays back in 1 year, not $2\frac{1}{2}$ years. A second disadvantage, shared with AROI, is that the time value of money is not considered.

PRESENT NET WORTH

The present net worth criterion is one of two widely used and accepted investment criteria recognizing the time value of money. It can have several names, as is the case with many criteria, including net present value and discounted cash flow. It may be referred to by any of these names, or their initials PNW, NPV, and DCF. Present net worth or PNW is the term used throughout this book.

The PNW is the algebraic sum of the discounted costs and revenues at a specified interest rate. In formula form

$$PNW = \sum_{t=0}^{n} [R_t - C_t] \frac{1.0}{(1.0 + i)^t} \qquad (5.4)$$

where

PNW = the present net worth
R_t = the revenues or positive cash flows in year t
C_t = the costs or negative cash flows in year t
t = the year in which the cash flow occurs
i = the interest rate, usually the alternative rate of return or the cost of capital

The far right-hand term is simply the present value multiplier from Eq. 4.8.

Equation 5.4 can be rewritten in several different forms but the critical steps in calculating PNW remain the same. They are: (1) identify the year in which each revenue and cost occurs; (2) multiply each revenue and cost by the present value multiplier for that year; and (3) add the results for each year algebraically.

For example, suppose you had the opportunity to invest in a loblolly pine plantation where you would have to purchase the bare land at $150 per acre, incur regeneration costs of $75 an acre and annual management and property tax costs of $2 an acre per year. The returns occur at the end of a 25-year rotation when you sell 50 cords an acre for $15 a cord.

The details of this investment are outlined in Table 5.1. The first column shows the type of expenditure, the second column the year in which it occurs, and the third column the before-tax cash flow. The fourth, fifth, and sixth columns are the present values of the cash flows. They are, with one exception, the product of the before-tax cash flow column and the present value of a single payment multiplier. They are calculated using Eq. 4.8.

Annual management costs and property taxes is the one exception. It is a terminating annual annuity; therefore, Eq. 4.13 is used to calculate it. The sum of these columns is the PNW at the specified interest rate, namely, $16.16 at 5 percent; −$36.62 at 6 percent and −$77.57 at 7 percent.

The PNW is interpreted as the present value of the investment's gain or loss at the specified interest rate. The investor can earn 5 percent on this investment and *still* have $16.16 more in today's dollars, while a 6 percent interest on this investment is missed by $36.62 in today's dollars. Six percent could have been earned if the investment returned an additional $36.62 at present value. Restated another way, a $36.62 opportunity cost would be incurred for each acre purchased if the alternative rate of return is 6 percent.

TABLE 5.1   Investment Analyses of Loblolly Pine Plantation on 25-Year Pulpwood Rotation

Item	Year	Before-tax cash flow	Present value (V_0) 5%	6%	7%
Purchase land	0	− $150.00	− $150.00	− $150.00	− $150.00
Site preparation and planting	1	− 75.00	− 71.43	− 70.75	− 70.09
Annual management costs and property taxes	1 – 25	− 2.00	− 28.19	− 25.57	− 23.31
Harvest 50 cords — $15.00 @	25	750.00	221.48	174.75	138.19
Sell land	25	150.00	44.30	34.95	27.64
Total		$625.00	$16.16	− $36.62	− $77.57
Total without land		$625.00	$121.85	$78.43	$44.79

Note:

$$PNW = \$16.16 \,/\, acre \,@\, 5\%$$

$$= -\$36.62 \,/\, acre \,@\, 6\%$$

$$IRR = 5\% + \frac{16.16}{(16.16 + 36.62)}$$

$$= 5\% + 0.306$$

$$= 5.31\%$$

$$L_e 5\% = \$121.85(1.05)^{25}\left(\frac{1.0}{(1.05)^{25} - 1}\right)$$

$$= \$121.85(3.38635)(0.41905)$$

$$= \$172.91 \,/\, acre$$

$$L_e 7\% = \$44.79(5.42743)(0.22586)$$

$$= \$54.91 \,/\, acre$$

where

L_e = land expectation value

An investment is acceptable if the PNW is positive and is not acceptable if it is negative. This is so because the investment is earning more than the alternative rate of return when PNW is positive. The investment earns less than the alternative rate of return when PNW is negative. It is better to invest in your alternative with a negative PNW because you will earn more money.

Another way of looking at PNW is that all costs are charged interest from the time they are incurred until the end of the investment and all revenues earn interest from the time they are received until the end of the investment. The

TABLE 5.2   Alternative View of PNW

Year	Before-tax cash flow	Future value at 5%[a] (V_{25})
0	− $150.00	− $507.95
1	− 75.00	− 241.88
1–25	− 2.00	− 95.45
25	750.00	750.00
25	150.00	150.00
Total	$625.00	$ 54.72

$$^{a}V_0 = \$54.72 \times \frac{1.0}{(1.05)^{25}} = \$54.72 \times 0.29530 = \$16.16\,/\,\text{acre}$$

algebraic sum of the costs and revenues, with interest, is then discounted to year zero. This is the PNW.

For example, Table 5.2 contains the cash flows from Table 5.1. The first column shows the year the cash flow occurs, the second column the amount before tax, and the third column the future value at 5 percent. The third column is calculated using Eq. 4.7. The future values in column 3 are then summed and the present value is taken using Eq. 4.8. This is the PNW and is equal to the value found in Table 5.1.

The alternative view shows the large amount of interest that is charged to investments when they continue over long time periods, even at modest rates such as 5 percent. The $75 regeneration cost has grown to $241.88 by harvest. This is a $166.88 interest charge on this part of the investment ($241.88 − $75). This also shows the importance of keeping regeneration and other initial costs as low as possible.

INTERNAL RATE OF RETURN

Recall that the PNW is the present value of the *gain* or *loss* at the specified interest rate. This means that if there is a gain, the investment is earning more than the interest rate and if there is a loss, the investment is earning less than the interest rate. It follows that the investment is earning exactly the interest rate used to calculate the PNW if the PNW is zero.

This interest rate is called the internal rate of return (IRR) and is the second major investment criterion. It too has several names, which include *return on investment* (ROI) and *rate of return* (ROR). We use here the term internal rate of return (IRR).

IRR is the interest rate that equalizes the present value of the costs and revenues. It is the value of i that causes the following equation to be true

$$\sum_{t=0}^{n} R_t \frac{1.0}{(1.0 + i)^t} = \sum_{t=0}^{n} C_t \frac{1.0}{(1.0 + i)^t} \qquad (5.5)$$

where

IRR = the internal rate of return
R_t = the revenues or positive cash flows in year t
C_t = the costs or negative cash flows in year t
t = the year in which the cash flow occurs
i = the interest rate when Eq. 5.5 is true and is the IRR

In practice the IRR is calculated by an iterative process. For hand calculations, the PNW is first calculated for an interest rate that is estimated to be close to the IRR. The PNW is then calculated for the next highest interest rate if the first answer was positive or the next lowest rate if the answer was negative. This continues until both a positive and a negative PNW have been obtained. The actual IRR is then estimated by interpolating between the positive and negative PNW. This is only an approximation because the interest rate formulas are nonlinear but the interpolation is linear.

Computer programs that calculate IRR are also available. They too use an iterative process except they bracket the positive and negative interest rates and calculate PNW by one-half the difference until they converge on a zero PNW. A tolerance level is usually specified for the departure from zero because it is approached but never reached.

Table 5.1 contains an example of a hand-calculated IRR. Suppose calculations started at 7 percent interest. The PNW is negative, so 6 percent, the next lowest interest rate, is tried. It too is negative, so once again the next lowest rate is used and the PNW becomes positive at 5 percent.

The IRR must lie between 5 and 6 percent because the PNW is positive at 5 percent, negative at 6 percent, and the IRR is the interest rate where PNW is zero. Graphically,

PNW	$16.16	$0.00	− $36.62
	/	/	/
i	5%	IRR	6%

The IRR is estimated by interpolating the distance to the zero PNW from the PNW at 5 percent and then adding that amount to the 5 percent as shown in the footnote to Table 5.1.

The IRR is compared to the alternative rate of return or the cost of capital. An investment is indicated if IRR exceeds the comparison rate and is not indicated if IRR is less than the comparison rate. This is so because the investor will incur a cost if the IRR is less than the comparison rate and make more than the next best alternative (or cost) if it is greater than the comparison rate.

Examination of the present value columns in Table 5.1 indicates why the PNW will eventually become negative as the interest rate is increased. Compare the change in regeneration costs to the change in revenue from the land sale in year 25 as the interest rate increases. The value in the earlier years decreases at a slower rate than those in the later years. This also reinforces the earlier observations about the importance of timing the cash flows. The less money that has to be invested in the early years of an investment and the sooner revenues can be generated, the higher will be the return and the more attractive the investment.

This can have several implications for the land manager. First, projects developing early income, for example, hunting leases or thinnings, are desirable if they are possible. Their desirability must be weighed against the increased risk of having hunters on the land or introducing disease into the stand by thinning. Second, land with standing timber ready for harvest is better than bare land because it is cut sooner. But this is traded off against a higher selling price. Third, seeding is sometimes preferred to planting because lower capital investment in earlier years bears less interest. But this is traded off against lower stocking and hence yield and a longer investment period.

ADVANTAGES AND DISADVANTAGES OF PNW AND IRR

Both of these criteria have their proponents and, at one time, there were lengthy discussions about which was superior. These discussions had more practical significance in the days of hand calculations when time and accuracy considerations may have precluded calculating both criteria. Currently, however, calculations are made quite easily, so the simple solution is to provide both criteria in an analysis. However, it is important to know the advantages and disadvantages as an aid to interpretation.

The major practical disadvantage of the IRR is that the calculations implicitly assume that revenues are reinvested at the IRR in the year they are received and that costs bear interest at the IRR from the year they are incurred. This, of course, is usually not the case, particularly if the IRR is much higher than the next best alternative. This could be illustrated in Figure 3.1(b) if the return on Investment A were, say, twice as large as the return on Investment B.

A major theoretical disadvantage of IRR is that it may, but does not necessarily, have a different root each time there is a change in the sign of the cash flow. This means that more than one IRR can exist, and the analyst does not know which one to choose. Further, none of the multiple roots are "wrong." The problem, as stated, simply has more than one correct answer. Building in a multiple root search routine should be an easy matter for those wishing to

TABLE 5.3 Hypothetical Cash Flows Illustrating Increasing,
Decreasing, and Multiple Root Cash Flows

	Investment		
Year	A	B	C
0	$1,000	−$1,000	−$31,273
1	−1,100	1,100	73,491
2	0	0	− 43
Total	−$100	$100	−$732
Percent IRR	10	10	10 and 25

examine their existence in a particular investment. All that needs to be done is to program the computer to calculate the PNW from 1 to, say, 100 percent. Then, a multiple is identified each time PNW equals zero.

For example, consider the investments in Table 5.3. The PNW of investment *A* is −$100 at zero interest, becomes zero at 10 percent, and is positive at greater than 10 percent (Figure 5.1). Investment *B* is the opposite; it starts from a positive $100 at zero interest, is negative at 10 percent, and becomes more negative as the interest rate increases. Investment *C* illustrates the multiple root disadvantage. It starts as a negative investment, becomes positive at between 10 and 25 percent interest, and turns negative again above 25 percent. Thus, the IRR is both 10 and 25 percent.

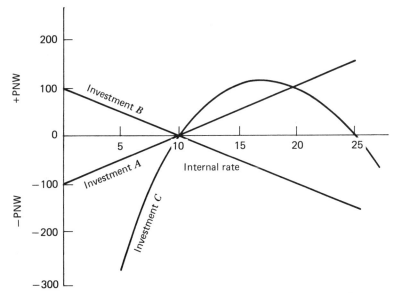

FIGURE 5.1 *Hypothetical investments with increasing, decreasing, and multiple internal rates of return.*

An advantage of the IRR is that it provides an answer in the form of an interest rate. This figure is often more easily interpreted than a PNW. For example, a 20 percent IRR may be considered a good return if the ARR is 10 percent, but it is more difficult to judge how much better than the alternative is an investment with a PNW of +$20,000. The size of the investment can determine the size of the positive present value, rather than the relative superiority of the investment.

A disadvantage of PNW is that it is sometimes difficult to determine which interest rate to use. For example, the alternative investment approach to interest rate determination would require that the firm know all its alternative investments. This is unlikely, or at the least, a very time-consuming and difficult process because of the many analyses that must be made. Further, multiple rather than single cutoff values would be needed as the organization progresses through its alternatives.

Perhaps the greatest advantage of PNW is that it gives an unambiguous answer when maximizing returns from investments. Investments with returns early in the project life can have a higher IRR and a lower PNW than projects with late returns. This means that choosing projects on the basis of the highest IRR can result in a lower total PNW.

As stated earlier, the obvious solution in this age of ready computer availability is to calculate both criteria to use as a decision guideline. Further, PNWs can be calculated at several interest rates to examine the sensitivity of the results. In fact, several canned computer programs do all of this and more in an effort to provide more complete analyses.

LAND EXPECTATION VALUE

Land expectation value is another criterion that is known by several names. The most well known is the Faustmann Formula, but the names land rent and soil expectation value are also used (Davis. 1966). We will use the term Land Expectation Value and the symbol L_e.

Discussions of land expectation value often contain long and complicated formulas that are, as Davis (1966, p. 362) says "...chiefly useful to frighten students." Land expectation value is nothing more than a special case of PNW that has certain restrictive assumptions made about it. These are: (1) land value is zero; (2) the land has no residual stand; (3) the land will be forested in perpetuity; and (4) the cash flows from the forest will be the same in perpetuity.

The reasons for these assumptions come directly from the primary use of the criterion, determining the land's value for producing timber. The first assumption, zero land value, allows calculating land value by PNW. The PNW shows the present value of how much is left over after the investor's money has earned the specified interest rate. The present value of costs could be increased by the amount of the PNW, thereby earning exactly the stated interest rate. The PNW will indicate how much one can spend on a cost category and still earn the desired interest rate if that cost is left out of the PNW calculation and all others are included. Therefore, if the investor wants to know how much he or she can pay for land and still earn 5%, land value is simply left out of the PNW calculation and the residual, the PNW, is what the investor can afford to pay for land. Thus, L_e assumes zero land cost or leaves it out of the calculation. This technique is useful not only in calculating land value but can also be used to estimate other allowable expenditures, for example, maximum regeneration costs.

The second assumption, no residual stand, assures that the regeneration costs for establishing the stand are included in the calculations. The third assumption, perpetual forests, is probably institutional. Foresters probably visualized that once land was put into forest, it would not be taken out. This may not be a bad assumption either for Germany at the time the formula originated or for managed industrial and federal forests in the United States today. This is true particularly when, as was shown in Table 4.3, you need only assume two to three rotations to find an answer equivalent to perpetuity.

The final assumption, that of the same cash flows, is a simplifying assumption. First, it simplifies the calculations since there is a lack of different cash flows to discount. The flows to be discounted at each rotation are the same. Second, it simplifies projecting the costs and revenues in the future rotations. The cash flow is estimated for the first rotation only. This is not a bad assumption because it maintains the same *relative* costs and revenues in the future. The effects of inflation and procedures for adjustments are discussed in Chapter 7.

L_e's utility, as that of any technique, depends on how realistically the assumptions fit the problem being analyzed. The technique should not be used if the assumptions are bad. It should be used if they are close or reasonably close. However, these judgments are usually made by the analyst when the facts of the particular problem are known.

Calculating Land Expectation Value

Land expectation value can be calculated by modifying a regular PNW for the special assumptions. As with any PNW, the first step is to choose an interest rate, for example, 7 percent. The second step combines the first two assumptions. That is, calculate the PNW without land value and with regeneration costs. The last column of Table 5.1 contains cash flows with regeneration costs included and has been summed without land value. This sum is $44.79 per acre at 7 percent interest.

The third step combines the third and fourth assumptions: perpetual forests and equal cash flows. The example in Table 5.1 indicates that the investor expects to receive $44.79 per acre, present value, every 25-year rotation. This is a perpetual periodic annuity, discussed in conjunction with Eq. 4.15, except that the first payment has been calculated as of year zero instead of year 25. This difference in timing is adjusted by compounding the present value forward for 25 years at 7 percent interest

$$V_{25} = \$44.79 \times (1.07)^{25} = \$243.09/\text{acre}$$

or, on a time line

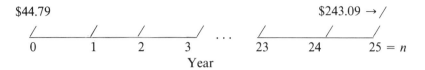

The present value of the entire series is then calculated using Eq. 4.15, or looking the multiplier value up in Table A.4, so that

$$SA_0 = \$243.09 \times \frac{1.0}{(1.07)^{25} - 1.0} = \$243.09 \times 0.22586 = \$54.91/\text{acre}$$

This is the land expectation value of the investment in Table 5.1. Its interpretation is that the investor can pay only $54.91 an acre for the land if 7 percent is the desired earning and if the cash flows remain as predicted. This is an income value of the investment. This income value is then compared to the market price of the land and the decision whether or not to buy is made. The land is not bought if market price is *greater* than $54.91 because the investor would then be earning less than 7 percent and would have incurred an opportunity cost for the difference. The land is bought if market price is *less* than $54.91 because the investor will be earning more than 7% and would incur an opportunity cost for the difference if he or she did not buy. A $54.91 market price is a break-even point, and the investor may either buy or not buy.

The preceding calculations are summarized on the bottom of Table 5.1. Note the strong effect the interest rate has on the price the investor can pay for land. The land expectation value at 5 percent is $172.91, over three times more than the value at 7 percent.

Note again that the same technique can be used to calculate the amount of money that can be spent for any management practice in one year. Simply omit the cost of the practice from the cash flow and calculate PNW. Then compound PNW forward to the year the practice will occur. This is the maximum amount that can be spent in that year while still obtaining the chosen interest rate.

Land expectation value also provides a method of calculating the "bare land value" that foresters often quote. It provides a value estimate of the land as if there were no trees on it because the regeneration costs are included in the calculations. Thus, the value of the bare land is calculated at the interest rate specified.

The preceding steps can be written together in formula form as

$$L_e = V_0 \times (1.0 + i)^n \times \frac{1.0}{(1.0 + i)^n - 1.0} = V_0 \times \frac{(1.0 + i)^n}{(1.0 + i)^n - 1.0} \quad (5.6)$$

where

L_e = the land expectation value
V_0 = the present value of a perpetual periodic annuity that will be received every n years
n = the number of years between annuity payments
i = the interest rate

The right-hand expression

$$\frac{(1.0 + i)^n}{(1.0 + i)^n - 1.0}$$

is the land expectation value multiplier. It may be calculated directly, or by looking up the values in Tables A.1 and A.4 and dividing.

VALUATION OF TIMBERLAND

The preceding discussion has examined land purchases that are devoid of timber. This is seldom true, so the question arises about how to value land with an existing timber stand. This question is conveniently discussed by examining two examples, even and uneven aged timber stands.

Valuation of Even-Aged Timber Stands

Even-aged timber stands are valued in exactly the same manner as bare land except the rotation is entered somewhere *after* stand establishment instead of *at* stand establishment. The current year is year zero, instead of the year the stand was established, and all calculations are made as before.

For example, suppose the investment in Table 5.1 was a 10-year-old stand and all other costs and revenues were the same. The end of the 10th year now becomes year zero and all other cash flows occur 10 years sooner. This happens because we assume the rotation age remains the same; hence, there are only 15 years until harvest. Note that the annual management costs are now incurred only for a 15-year period.

The analysis for this investment is presented in Table 5.4. The IRR has increased from 5.31 percent to 12.04 percent because the revenues are received 10 years sooner, there are no regeneration costs, and the annual management costs

TABLE 5.4   Investment Analysis for 10-Year-Old Loblolly Pine
Plantation

| Item | Year | Before-tax cash flow | Present value (V_0) | |
			12%	13%
Purchase land	0	−$150.00	−$150.00	−$150.00
Annual management cost and property taxes	1−15	−$2.00	−$13.62	−$12.92
Harvest				
50 cords — $15.00	15	$750.00	$137.02	$119.92
Less land	15	$150.00	$27.40	$23.98
Total			$0.80	−$19.02

PNW = $0.80 / acre at 12%

    = $19.02 / acre at 13%

IRR = 12% + $\dfrac{0.80}{(0.80 + 19.02)}$

and property taxes are paid for 10 years less. The example is unrealistic in that
the land purchase price would probably rise with the presence of a 10-year-old
plantation. However, the figures were kept the same for illustrative purposes.

Valuation of Uneven-Aged Stands

Uneven-aged stands are valued using PNW and two special assumptions: (1)
that the land is perpetually in timber, and (2) that the cash flows from the forest
will be the same in perpetuity. These are the same as the third and fourth
assumptions for land expectation value. Two situations may then be identified:
those stands having yearly incomes and those having recurrent incomes for
periods greater than a year.

The valuation of the yearly net income case directly parallels the calculation
of a perpetual annual annuity, that is, Eq. 4.14. Assume, for example, that a stand
will yield 200 board feet (bf) a year, that the stumpage price is $75 per thousand
board feet (mbf), that annual management costs, including marking for a selection cut and property taxes, are $5 an acre, and that the alternative rate of return
is 8 percent. Then

Net yearly income = (0.200 mbf × $75.00/mbf) − $5.00

= $10.00 per acre per year

and using Eq. 4.14, yields

$$V_0 = \frac{\$10.00}{0.08} = \$125.00/\text{acre}$$

This is another income value calculation that indicates $125.00 would have to be invested at 8 percent interest in order to generate $10 income a year. The $125 is the maximum amount that could be paid for the land while still earning the 8 percent interest with the projected cash flows. The $125 is the minimum sales price the investor would accept for the land, because that is the amount needed to reinvest at 8 percent interest to duplicate the $10 a year income derived from the land.

The valuation of incomes occurring at periods greater than a year requires bringing all incomes to a common time period and then calculating the present value of a periodic perpetual annuity, Eq. 4.15. Assume, for example, that the above stand has a 1000 bf harvest every 5 years and that all other costs are the same. The costs are first compounded forward to year 5 using Eq. 4.12; the future value of a terminating annual annuity is

$$SA_5 = \$5.00 \times \frac{(1.08)^5 - 1.0}{0.08} = \$29.33 \text{ per acre}$$

The net income in year 5 is then calculated by

$$\text{Net yearly income} = (1.0 \text{ mbf} \times \$75.00/\text{mbf}) - \$29.33$$
$$= \$45.67 \text{ per acre every 5 years}$$

Equation 4.15, the present value of a periodic perpetual annuity, is then used to calculate the present value of this income stream as

$$SA_0 = \$45.67 \times \frac{1.0}{(1.08)^5 - 1.0} = \$97.31 \text{ per acre}$$

This is an income value and indicates that $97.31 must be invested at 8 percent interest to generate $45.67 income every 5 years. The sales and purchase price indicated can be interpreted exactly as in the yearly income case. Note that the delay of revenues for 5 years and the compounding of costs for 5 years have caused a $27.69 decrease in the land's value. Note also that these techniques may be used to evaluate any cost or income that occurs annually or with a regular periodicity.

Valuation of a Forest

A tract of land being valued will probably not be divided neatly into single stands. It is more likely to be a "forest" in that it is composed of several stands. These may all be even-aged stands of varying ages, they may all be uneven-aged stands with different age structures and/or species compositions, or they may be some combination of even- and uneven-aged stands.

The approach to valuation is simple and direct. Each stand is valued independently using the preceding techniques and the sum of all the stand values is the value for the forest. Note, however, that all stands must be valued as of the same year before they are summed.

Valuing the whole forest may require taking the weighted average of all the stands. That is, the per acre value for each stand is multiplied by the number of acres in the stand before summing, if a total value is desired. The sum is divided by the total number of acres in all stands if a weighted average value per acre is desired.

The revenue received for a timber stand generally increases as the stand becomes older. This can happen for both even- and uneven-aged stands although it is most easily visualized in even aged-stands. Revenue is the product of both price and quantity. Quantity (timber yield) increases with age, as demonstrated by a yield table. However, price can also increase as a stand follows a progression from less valuable to more valuable products, for example, from commercial thinnings through pulpwood to sawtimber or veneer logs. Care must be taken, however, to be reasonably sure there is a strong market for the next highest valued product in the locale of the stand being analyzed. For example, the cubic foot price of pulpwood and sawtimber can be very close in some areas where there is high pulpwood demand and low sawtimber demand.

The increase in stand revenue caused by increases in product value can cause "jumps" in stand value. For example, the PNW calculated for a stand at different ages and plotted over stand age can form a step function, or approximate step function, as the stand grows into different higher-valued products. This step function effect becomes less pronounced the older the stand and the higher the discount rate. The step function may also be visible in valuing a forest depending on the age distribution of its individual stands.

INCLUDING LAND VALUE

Some analysts may want to exclude land value from PNW and IRR analyses. Arguments are presented that (1) the land is already owned so therefore money will not have to be paid for it, and (2) inclusion of a "large" payment for land early in the investment lowers the PNW or IRR.

Land value should be included except in very unusual instances. PNW and IRR are predicated on opportunity costs. In almost all cases the alternative of selling the land and reinvesting the funds *exists*; therefore, the landowner can incur an opportunity cost by not selling land whose market price has risen and reinvesting those funds at the alternative rate of return. Inclusion of land value in the analyses evaluates this opportunity cost and indicates whether land value has risen high enough to make sale and reinvestment worthwhile.

The phenomena of rising land values and sale can be observed in some land-based resource corporations where rising real estate values have caused sale of land to developers or development by the corporation itself. The land value included in the analyses should be the estimated current market value minus any costs of completing the transactions.

It is true that including land values reduces the PNW or IRR. However, this is a fact of forestry investment and the professional forester has a moral obligation to make the facts known. Exclusion of land value simply to improve PNW or IRR is unethical. However, there may be some cases in which land value is legitimately excluded.

One case is when the land, for some reason such as a legal constraint, is in fact unsaleable. For example, a tract of land may have been willed to an individual or institution with the proviso that it never be sold. A second example is when a marginal analysis is made for an additional investment and the land value is not part of the additional investment. For example, a thinning operation may be under consideration. Here, only the added cost of thinning and the added yield resulting from that thinning need be included.

Finally, remember that PNWs and IRRs are *guidelines*. A negative PNW including land value does not always mean the investment is ill advised. There may be nonquantifiable benefits flowing from the investment but excluded from the analysis. For example, the investment may include a second home that can be used for vacations and the land may provide desired hunting acreage. These "nonquantifiables" may provide enough incentive to make the investment despite a negative PNW. However, the PNW should be calculated so that the decision maker will known what losses might be incurred to obtain these nonquantifiable benefits.

VALUING STUMPAGE

6

STUMPAGE IS DEFINED as the trees, standing in the forest, unsevered from their stump. The stumpage price is the price paid for the right to sever the trees from their stumps and remove them from the forest. Stumpage is valued by estimating its market value.

Stumpage valuation may be abstracted into two parts. The first part is to estimate the volume of timber in the proposed sale. This can include estimates of volume by species and size or quality classes. The second step is to estimate the market price per unit of volume. As will be seen below, this may be based on field estimates of the sale's logging costs. The total sale value is the product of the volumes and their estimated market prices. Most of this chapter is devoted to discussing market price estimation because volume estimation is covered in mensuration or biometrics courses.

Both the buyer and the seller want market value estimates. The buyer does not want to pay more for the timber than he could purchase it for elsewhere, and the seller wants to be sure he is paid at least as much for the timber as he can get elsewhere. The buyer may also want to estimate his cost of converting the timber to a merchantable product to be sure that his costs, including the stumpage price, do not exceed the selling price of the merchantable product. The market price is then determined by the buyer's and seller's interactions.

For example, the seller of stumpage may estimate the price the potential buyer will receive for harvested pulpwood delivered to a mill. He may also subtract the cost to harvest and transport the pulpwood including an allowance for profit. The seller does this because he would prefer to make any excess profits that exist. The buyer might make similar estimates to be sure he doesn't lose money on the transaction.

The two estimates may be different for several reasons. The estimates may be erroneous; for example, the seller just doesn't know the buyer's costs. Or, the buyer may have some special advantage that makes him better (or worse) than the average, for example, a more aggressive and efficient harvesting crew. The differences between the two estimates are then settled in the market. In economic terms, the estimates place the buyer and seller on the contract or conflict line and their relative bargaining strengths determine where they end up on that line.

Another important reason to study stumpage valuation, or timber appraisal as it is sometimes called, is because the federal government, and often the state governments, use this method to set a *minimum* price on their timber sales. The government agency for example, the USDA Forest Service, is not allowed to sell timber at less than the appraised price. The agency makes a timber appraisal, advertises the sale, and then receives written or oral bids at or above appraised value.

In some instances there may be only one bid and the timber is sold at that price. The bid price may be the appraisal price, so the appraised price turns out to be the market price. In other cases sales may be advertised but no bids are received. The buyer has in effect made his own appraisal and decided that the appraised price is higher than the market price.

Two methods of estimating market stumpage price predominate. The first is to compare a prospective sale directly to the current market price and the second is to calculate an income value for the sale and estimate the likely market price from that calculation. These are called the direct and analytical approaches by Davis (1966) and the direct and indirect approaches by Duerr (1960).

MARKET COMPARISON

This method is widely used in the southern United States and in the private sector. Briefly, an individual observes the current market price for similar timber, compares the sale to be evaluated to that observed, and estimates the market price of his sale based on the comparison.

The first step is to determine the current market price. Stumpage prices for privately owned timber are difficult to observe because there are seldom public records of the transactions. Furthermore, the private individuals may feel that the price they received or paid for their timber is "no one's business but their own." Timber buyers may be even more circumspect about sales that were purchased for higher than the current market price because they do not want other timber owners to learn about the higher price and withhold their timber from sale in anticipation of a price increase.

Persons who buy and sell private timber, such as procurement men for mills, county agents, consulting foresters, or pulpwood dealers, can usually quote a current market price for stumpage despite lack of documentation. This price varies with time of year, location of the sale relative to the mill, other sale characteristics such as volume per acre and logging difficulty, and other general timber supply and demand determinants that are discussed in forest economics texts. Price also depends on buyer expectations of future market conditions because timber bought today may not be cut for five or more years. Some extremely long timber sales allow for stumpage price increase or decrease depending on changes in the economy. These are usually called escalation clauses and are often based on some of the price indices discussed in Chapter 7.

Information on timber sales from national forests, state forests, and other public holdings is usually public information. Most agencies cooperate fully with requests for current sales data if they are made in person at the office where records are kept. Often, current price and volume data will have to be copied personally. Older data, for example 1 or 2 years old, may be already tabulated and reproduced. Requests for these data can often be filled by mail. However, the data may not reflect the current market because of their age. Other differences in public data may make them less desirable than private observations.

Sale comparison, the second step, is accomplished with varying degrees of formality. It usually requires a mental picture or description of an "average" sale's characteristics. This might include an idea of distance from the mill, slope, underbrush, volume per acre, and so on. The sale being valued is then compared to this "average" and the stumpage value increased or decreased accordingly.

This procedure can occur informally when the buyer has a good personal knowledge of the local market. He has the average prices, logging conditions, and distances to the mill or shipping point well in mind. This man simply goes out and inspects the tract in question, mentally compares it to his intuitive knowledge of the "average," and adjusts the stumpage price up or down accordingly. There is no formalized written assessment or, if there is some report, it is seldom highly specific. This procedure is used very often by procurement men working for large pulp mills or dealers and by the dealers and producers themselves when they are buying a tract of timber. The larger the sale, the less likely they will rely on judgment. However, sales worth tens of thousands of dollars are bought regularly on this basis.

There are several reasons for this informal procedure. On smaller sales a more formalized procedure just is not worth the expense. The average error from the informal method is less than the cost of making formal appraisals. And large buyers purchase enough timber so this average can occur. Another reason is that often the buyer or seller may not have the expertise to make a formal appraisal. For example, a producer may not know how to lay out cruise lines, measure $\frac{1}{5}$ acre plots, and calculate standard errors but he knows the difference between 20 and 25 cords per acre when he sees it.

More formal comparisons are made in writing and vary in degree of formality depending on the sale size and the organization. Davis (1966) reports a rather detailed procedure used by the State of Wisconsin in appraising its timber sales.

Most formal comparisons consider differences in (1) logging difficulty, (2) transportation costs to the mill, and (3) timber quality, including the volume per acre. Logging difficulty differences may include assessments of steepness, ground cover, road building, and length of skid.

Transportation costs to the mill may include not only the distance but also the type of roads and highways that must be used because cost per mile varies by type of road. Details on rail transportation, if needed, can include freight rates, number of different rail lines traversed, frequency of car pick-up at the loading point, and so on. Differences in transportation costs may be reflected in observed market price differences if these prices are for small enough geographical areas.

Timber quality estimates can vary from a simple estimate of "below-average-above" to tallies of log grades. The importance of quality varies with the final product being manufactured. For example, quality is more important in veneer logs than in pulpwood. Volume per acre is sometimes assessed under logging difficulty.

Detailed comparisons may itemize each of the above characteristics and require an individual judgment about them. For example, the State of Wisconsin's procedure reported by Davis (1966) requires the appraiser to estimate proportionate deviation from average for individual logging costs and then sum them to obtain a weighting factor for the observed market price. USDA Forest Service regional appraisal manuals often contain regional adjustment factors for individual logging costs.

INCOME VALUE

The income value calculation of stumpage price is well documented and in forestry is called the conversion return method.* *Conversion return* is the money remaining after production costs are subtracted from a product's selling price. Conversion return includes the raw material cost plus the manufacturer's "margin" for profit and risk. This can be expressed as

$$CR = P - C = M + S \tag{6.1}$$

where

CR = the conversion return
P = the product selling price at the first established market
C = the production costs, including fixed costs, for the product at the first established market
M = the margin for profit, risk, return to capital, and income tax
S = the stumpage price

P is the selling price of the product at the first established market. It could be dollars per cord of pulpwood, fob (free on board) the rail car, or it could be dollars per thousand board feet of number one common, fob the sawmill. The important point is that there be a well-established market so that the observed prices are valid. It is also important that the market be as close as possible to the stumpage in the chain of products produced from the stumpage. This decreases

---

*This section closely follows Davis' (1966) presentation.

the number of costs that must be estimated and thus the work and also decreases the chances of estimation and other errors.

C is the production cost. Costs include the felling, bucking, limbing, transportation, and all costs of getting the product to the point of sale. Note that fixed production costs are included. In theory, the wages of the entrepreneur should also be included. Both the fixed and variable production costs are included because the seller who owns the stumpage, in many cases the mill, does not want to drive the producer or buyer out of business. Stumpage prices that are too high could cause the buyer to leave the industry in the long run and there would be no one to buy stumpage in the future.

M is the margin for profit and risk. In contains four elements: entrepreneurial profit, return to invested capital, uninsurable business risk, and income taxes. Entrepreneurial profit is the profit in addition to wages that induces the entrepreneur to use expertise in organizing a business operation. Return to invested capital is not the interest paid but rather the return to the capital the entrepreneur may invest here rather than in the next best alternative, as discussed earlier. Uninsurable business risks are risks that the buyer may encounter, for example, the risk of the selling price P decreasing before the timber sale is cut out. Inclusion of income taxes places the calculations on an after-tax basis. S, the last variable in the equation, is stumpage price and the variable to be estimated.

The preceding discussion of conversion return is implicitly couched in terms of dollars per unit of volume, such as costs per thousand board feet or price per cord. This is the common usage. Obviously, all variables must be measured in the same unit of volume. However, confusion sometimes occurs because some values are expressed in log scale and others in mill scale. The analyst must adjust these values so all are on the same volume basis. Conversion return and the other variables can also be expressed as the total dollars for the sale.

For example, consider the calculations for a timber sale consisting solely of slash pine pulpwood (Table 6.1). The product selling price is relatively easily determined by observation or requesting the information from a mill procurement man. The production costs are estimated by logging function. The fixed costs for

TABLE 6.1   Calculating Conversion Return per Cord for a Slash Pine Pulpwood Sale

Southern pine pulpwood delivered fob car at rail siding	
Price per cord (P)	$32.00
Production costs per cord	
Fell, limb, buck	$8.00
Skidding	3.00
Load on truck, unload on cars	3.00
Truck haul to rail siding	6.00
Total (C)	20.00
Conversion return per cord (CR)	$12.00

each function are included in the rate per cord. Production costs can be changed from sale to sale to reflect the difficulty of the specific sale being appraised. Large sales may require estimating costs for geographical subdivisions of the sale that reflect changing logging costs. The sale average or total may be calculated by weighing by the estimated timber volume in each subdivision.

The conversion return is the difference between the selling price and the costs, or $12 a cord in the example in Table 6.1. This $12 contains the margin for profit, risk, capital returns, and tax and also the stumpage price. The conversion return (CR) must now be divided between the margin (M) and the stumpage price (P).

CALCULATING THE MARGIN AND STUMPAGE PRICE

Davis (1966) suggests four ratios to calculate the margin (M) which can then be subtracted from the conversion return (CR) to obtain the stumpage price (S). These ratios are the overturn, the profit, the selling value, and the operating ratios. All may be calculated from information contained in a firms' income statement. In practice, a seller, and particularly if it is a government agency, may make surveys to estimate the industry averages for calculating the ratios. A prospective buyer may use his past accounting records, a goal or target, or an industry average, if it is known. The ratios may be calculated from data stating costs and revenues either in total or per unit of volume harvested.

The Overturn Ratio

The overturn ratio calculates M as a proportion of production costs, C, or

$$\text{Overturn} = \frac{M}{C}$$

Note that the overturn ratio, as all other ratios, is calculated as an industry average or organization average, or is set arbitrarily by a firm's managers. The variables M and C used to calculate overturn are thus industry-wide or organization averages and not those estimated for a specific sale, as shown in Table 6.1. The margin is calculated by multiplying both sides of the equation by C so that

$$M = \text{overturn} \times C \tag{6.2}$$

The overturn ratio is first determined as discussed above, for example, from industry averages. C, for use in Eq. 6.2, has been calculated for the sale already to determine CR. Overturn is then multiplied by C to determine M for the sale. M, when calculated, is subtracted from the conversion return to estimate stumpage price.

For example, suppose it were determined by taking an industry average that the overturn ratio should be 0.15 and that we wanted to calculate stumpage price for the example in Table 6.1. Using Eq. 6.2, we obtain

$$M = 0.15 \times \$20.00 = \$3.00 \text{ per cord}$$

and from Eq. 6.1

$$S = \$12.00 - \$3.00 = \$9.00 \text{ per cord}$$

A disadvantage of this ratio is that it does not consider the selling price of the converted product, P. Fluctuations in this price could cause risk to the stumpage buyer. Perhaps more seriously, industry-wide costs to calculate overturn are not always available with the stumpage costs excluded.

The Profit Ratio

The profit ratio, π, is the margin, M, calculated as a proportion of production costs, C, and stumpage price, S, or

$$\pi = \frac{M}{C + S}$$

Then, by algebraic manipulation*

$$M = \frac{\pi P}{1.0 + \pi} \tag{6.3}$$

The profit ratio, as the overturn ratio, is calculated as an industry average or organizational average, or is set arbitrarily as a target.

For example, suppose it were determined from industry averages that the profit ratio should be 0.15 and that the stumpage price for the example in Table 6.1 was desired. Then, using Eq. 6.3 and the estimates from Table 6.1, we set

$$M = \frac{0.15 \times \$32.00}{1.0 + 0.15} = \$4.17 \text{ per cord}$$

and, from Eq. 6.1,

$$S = \$12.00 - \$4.17 = \$7.83 \text{ per cord}$$

An advantage of this method is that the profit ratio, π, can be calculated directly from published income statements because the denominator, $C + S$, is simply the total cost, including stumpage. This figure is almost always available.

---

*The derivation is found in Davis (1966, p. 398).

The Selling Value Ratio

The selling value ratio is simply the margin, M, taken as a proportion of the converted product's selling price, P. This is a common ratio used by financial analysts to assess a firm's profitability and is sometimes called the "profit margin on sales" ratio. In formula form

$$\text{Selling value ratio} = \frac{M}{P}$$

and multiplying both sides of the equation by P yields

$$M = \text{selling value ratio} \times P \tag{6.4}$$

where the ratio is calculated from industry-wide or other data exogenous to the sale being valued.

For example, suppose it was determined that the selling value ratio should be 0.15 and the stumpage price for the example in Table 6.1 was desired. Then using Eq. 6.4, we obtain

$$M = 0.15 \times \$32.00 = \$4.80 \text{ per cord}$$

and

$$S = \$12.00 - \$4.80 = \$7.20 \text{ per cord}$$

This ratio has several advantages. First, the industry average ratios are usually well-known among financial analysts. Second, it is easily calculated from an income statement because net profit (M) and sales (P) are almost always shown.

The Operating Ratio

The operating ratio is the ratio of total costs, $C + S$, to the sales price, P. It is the cost of the converted product stated as a proportion of its sales price. Therefore, 1.0 minus the operating ratio is the proportion of the sales dollar remaining for the margin, M. Stated algebraically,

$$\text{Operating ratio} = \frac{C + S}{P}$$

where all variables are exogenous and as defined in Eq. 6.1, and

$$M = (1.0 - \text{operating ratio})P \tag{6.5}$$

The selling value ratio and the operating ratio are directly related because their sum is 1.0 as demonstrated by the following:

$$\frac{M}{P} + \frac{C + S}{P} = \frac{M + C + S}{P}$$

and from Eq. 6.1 we have

$$P = M + C + S$$

Therefore,

$$\frac{P}{P} = 1.0$$

and

$$1.0 - \text{operating ratio} = \text{selling value ratio}$$

or

$$1.0 - \text{selling value ratio} = \text{operating ratio}$$

Suppose it were determined exogenously that the operating ratio should be 0.85 and that the stumpage price for the example in Table 6.1 was desired. Then, using Eq. 6.5 yields

$$M = (1.0 - 0.85)\$32.00 = \$4.80 \text{ per cord}$$

and from Eq. 6.1

$$S = \$12.00 - \$4.80 = \$7.20 \text{ per cord}$$

The operating ratio gives the same answer as the selling value ratio because of the preceding relationship. Therefore, they may be used interchangeably.

Using these financial ratios to divide conversion surplus between the margin and stumpage price is arbitrary because there is no "correct" ratio to use. Using a particular ratio often depends on data availability to calculate it or sometimes on a general consensus of what is an equitable margin. Equity is a matter of judgment and existing social values and hence is arbitrary, as is data availability. All the financial ratios have the disadvantage that they do not reflect the amount of capital funds invested to generate the margins. Perhaps the best that can be said for them is that they are a convenient, empirical way to determine the margin and hence to estimate the market price of stumpage.

ADJUSTING FOR INFLATION 7

PREVIOUS CHAPTERS IGNORED inflation's effect on decision guide-lines and adjustments to account for it. Considering inflation in decision guide-lines is increasingly important because the inflation rate has increased from a tolerated 3 or 4 percent to monthly highs of over 13 percent on an annual basis.

Inflation is important in investment analysis because the dollars providing the investment return are different from those that paid for the investment. They are not comparable because, during inflation, dollars received in later years will not buy as much as dollars received today. This inflation effect becomes more serious the greater the inflation rate. For example, in 5 years a dollar is worth $0.86 at 3 percent inflation but only $0.54 at 13 percent inflation. The seriousness of this inflation effect is increased in forestry investments because they take many years to complete. In the United States even the shortest common rotation age in the Southeast is over 20 years and in the West rotations range from 60 to 120 years and longer.

Inflation is a continuous long-term increase in the general level of prices. Inflation requires that the general or overall price level increase. It is not sufficient for just the price of food, or housing, or clothing to increase. The average of all prices must increase. The price increase must also cause a net increase. Increased general prices followed by decreased general prices would not be considered an inflationary period. The general price level at the end of the period must be higher than at the beginning. The time period needed to consider a period as inflationary is not strictly defined but is usually understood to be several years. An increase for 6 months followed by constant or decreasing prices is not considered an inflationary period.

MEASURING PRICE CHANGES

Price changes are measured by price indices. The price index is simply the ratio of the price in a time period to the price in a base time period. Algebraically,

$$PI_n = \frac{P_n}{P_0} \times 100 \qquad\qquad (7.1)$$

where

PI_n = the price index in year n
P_n = the price in year n
P_0 = the price in year zero, the base year

For example, suppose the price of Doublas-fir veneer logs, delivered fob the mill, rose from \$95 in 1960 to \$295 per MBF in 1975. The 1975 price index is

$$PI_{75} = \frac{\$295.00}{\$95.00} \times 100 = 310.53$$

Any year can be chosen as the base year and sometimes the average prices for several years are taken as the base. The base year in the above example is 1960. Indices can be used for any time series, not just prices. For example, production can be measured by an index. Here, the production in future years is measured relative to a base year.

The price increase shown by the index is interpreted as the percentage increase. Free on board veneer log prices increased 310.53 percent between 1960 and 1975 as shown in the above example. This is the percentage increase over the entire time period and not the annual compound increase. The annual compound increase is

$$\sqrt[15]{310.53} - 1.0 = 0.07847 = 7.847\%$$

The price index in Eq. 7.1 may be fine for a single commodity but inflation is defined in terms of the general price level. Price indices measuring inflation must therefore reflect prices in the whole economy. This is accomplished by devising a "market basket" of individual goods, services, and/or commodities that are priced every time period. The market basket defines those prices that the index measures. The three major price indices are the Gross National Product (GNP) Deflator, the Consumer's Price Index (CPI), and the Producer Price Index (PPI). Each of these indices has subindices that measure more specific items. For example, the CPI has subcategories of services, food, and housing. There are even indices for individual goods or services within the index.

The GNP Deflator is the most general of the price indices. It is the ratio of the nominal GNP in any year to the real GNP in the same year, or

$$\text{GNP Deflator}_n = \frac{\text{Nominal GNP}_n}{\text{Real GNP}_n}$$

Nominal GNP is the gross national product calculated in the prices in effect in year n. Real GNP is the gross national product in year n but valued at the prices in some base year. Current year (year n) prices are changed to base year prices by multiplying by the GNP Deflator's reciprocal. The GNP Deflator is the most general price change indicator and can be used if a specific index is unavailable or if no other index seems to apply.

The Consumer's Price Index (CPI) is designed to measure price changes in the goods and services purchased by urban consumers or urban wage earners and clerical workers. Over 200 sets of goods and services are included in a market basket chosen to reflect items "purchased for daily living." Thus, the index is designed to measure the cost of living for the urban wage earner and clerical worker.

The CPI is the ratio of the market basket items valued at the current year (year n) prices divided by the market basket items at the base year prices. The reciprocal of the CPI can be used to change current year prices to the base year prices or constant dollars. The CPI can be used for adjusting prices of items sold at retail or those used in day to day personal consumption.

The Producer Price Index (PPI) is designed to show price changes for finished, intermediate, and crude goods and also for individual or groups of commodities in their primary markets. The markets are those where "the first important commercial transaction" occurs and are for "sales in large lots." The PPI used to be called the Wholesale Price Index (WPI). The name was changed in March 1978 to reflect actual data coverage. The data analysis was shifted at the same time to focus on "stage-of-process" indices, such as the Finished Goods Price Index, and place less emphasis on the commodity groups.

The PPI is a weighted average of price changes. Over 2800 items are included. The weights represent the "total net selling value of commodities...into primary markets."

The PPI reciprocal can be used to change current year prices into base year prices just as with the CPI. It can be used to adjust prices of commodities used in manufacturing processes and industry and so is the index most generally used in forestry. Individual time series are available for many wood products, including such specifics as All Douglas Fir Lumber, No. 3 Southern Pine Boards, No. 1 Common Gum, and $\frac{3}{8}$-in. A-C Grade Exterior Softwood Plywood. However, care is needed in using the index because some of the more aggregated commodity indices, such as the All Commodities Price Index, can double count price changes. The stage-of-process indices usually do not have this problem.

The "correct" price index depends on the use to which the analyst wants to put the index. Any serious analyst should obtain copies of the indices and become familiar with their components, calculation, and subcategories before making a final choice.

DEFINITIONS

Several definitions have been implicit in the preceding discussion. They are now presented explicitly.

Current or *nominal* prices are prices in the current time period. They are the price found in the market in year zero, 10, 20, 50, or whenever a transaction is made. They contain inflation.

Constant or *real* prices are prices stated in terms of a base year. This may be year zero in an investment analysis or a price index base year; 1967 is the base year currently used in the CPI and WPI. Constant prices are obtained by multiplying current prices by deflator. Constant prices are usually stated in terms of the base year, for example, 1967 prices.

Current or *constant dollars* are the product of current or constant prices and the quantity of the good, services, or commodity changing hands in the transaction. For example, the revenue from a timber harvest is the product of the stumpage price and the volume harvested. It may be reported in either current or constant dollars.

A *real price change* occurs when a price changes relative to all other prices in the economy. The price must change at a rate different from that of the general level of prices. For example, the price of hand calculators has been decreasing while all other prices have been increasing; thus, there has been a real price decrease in hand calculators. Even a constant price during an inflationary period would be a real price decrease.

Real price changes can be calculated for a single commodity by converting the current price to the constant price using a general price index, for example, WPI or CPI, and then calculating the constant price index from the constant prices. For example, the constant price of lumber in year 1 (Table 7.1) is $78.57 ($82.50/$105) and the real price change is +$3.57 ($78.57 − $75) or a 4.76 percent ($3.57/$75) increase.

Alternatively, the current price index for the single commodity can be deflated by the general price index to show real price changes. For example, the current dollar lumber price index in year 1 is 110 ($82.50/$75) and the constant dollar price index is 104.76 (110.0/105.0). This is a 4.76 percent real price increase, the same as the above example.

The constant dollar price index can be calculated by dividing real prices ($78.57/$75 = 104.76). Alternatively, the current price index can be deflated by the general price index (110.0/105.0 = 104.76).

TABLE 7.1   Hypothetical Lumber Price Changes

Year	General price index	Current lumber price	Constant lumber price	Current lumber price index[a]	Constant lumber price index[a]
0	100.0	75.00	75.00	100.0	100.0
1	105.0	82.50	78.57	110.0	104.0
2	109.0	90.00	82.57	120.0	110.1
3	115.0	100.00	86.96	133.3	115.9

[a]Year 0 = 100.

The indices are interpreted as follows. The current price of lumber increased from \$75 to \$82.50 in year 1. This was a current lumber price increase of 10 percent (current lumber price index = 110) of which 5 percent was inflation (general price index = 105.0) and 4.8 percent a real price increase (constant lumber price index = 104.8). The real price increase shows that the price of lumber increased 4.8 percent relative to all other prices in the economy (as measured by the general price index). Thus, the real price change is sometimes called the relative price change. The inflationary and real price increases are not additive (5.0 + 4.8 ≠ 10.0) but multiplicative (1.05 × 1.048 = 1.100).

There are three kinds of interest or discount rates used in inflation calculations: the current rate, the inflation rate, and the real rate. The *current interest rate* is also called the nominal or the market interest rate. It is the interest rate currently used in money markets or quoted by banks. (Remember, this can actually be many different rates.) The current interest rate contains both the real interest rate and an adjustment for expected inflation.

The *inflation rate* is the rate at which prices are generally rising. The inflation rate is measured by the change in the general price index. The *expected inflation rate* is the inflation rate that people expected to occur in the future. This may or may not be the same as the current inflation rate. The *real rate* of return is the rate people expect to earn on an investment or to pay for their loans after inflation is deducted.

DEFINING RELATIONSHIPS ALBEGRAICALLY

Many of these ideas were expressed algebraically by Hanke, Carver, and Bugg (1975). This section closely follows their paper and the relationships they presented. Given the following notation

D_0^{con} = one constant dollar in year zero

D_n^{con} = the constant dollar value in year n

D_n^{cur} = the current dollar value in year n. Note when $n = 0$, $D_0^{cur} = D_0^{con}$ because constant dollars are by definition the dollars used in the base period

$R = (1 + r)^n$, where r is the real average interest rate for the period ending at year n

$F = (1 + f)^n$, where f is the expected average inflation rate for the period ending at year n

$M = (1 + m)^n$ where m is the average market interest rate, including inflation, for the period ending at year n

the following relationships hold.

The constant dollars at the end of the period equal the constant dollars at the beginning of the period compounded forward by the average real interest rate, or

$$D_n^{con} = D_0^{con} \times R \tag{7.2}$$

The current dollars at the end of the period equal the constant dollars at the end of the period compounded by the inflation rate, or

$$D_n^{cur} = D_n^{con} \times F \tag{7.3}$$

The current dollars at the end of the period equal the constant dollars at the beginning of the period compounded forward by the average market interest rate, or

$$D_n^{cur} = D_0^{con} \times M \tag{7.4}$$

The current dollars at the end of the period equal the constant dollars at the beginning of the period compounded forward by the real and the inflation rates. Algebraically, Eq. 7.2 is substituted for D_n^{con} in Eq. 7.3 to obtain

$$D_n^{cur} = D_0^{con} \times R \times F \tag{7.5}$$

The average market rate of interest equals the average real rate of interest plus the average expected inflation rate plus the product of the real and inflation rates. Algebraically, Eq. 7.4 is substituted for D_n^{cur} in Eq. 7.5 to obtain

$$D_0^{con} \times M = D_0^{con} \times R \times F$$

Then, divide both sides by D_0^{con} and substitute the exponential expressions for M,

R, and F

$$(1 + m)^n = (1 + r)^n \times (1 + f)^n$$

Then take the nth root of both sides, multiply the right-hand terms, and simplify to obtain

$$m = r + f + rf \tag{7.6}$$

EFFECTS ON BEFORE-TAX PNWs

Inflation's effects on before-tax PNWs were discussed by Howe (1971) in the context of benefit–cost analyses for water resource projects. These analyses were before tax because they were made for the public sector that does not consider federal income tax. Howe's conclusion was "...in the case of general inflation, it makes no difference whether we use (1) benefits and costs all stated in construction period (*base year*) prices and a discount rate containing no inflationary premium, or (2) benefits and costs in the prices of the period in which each is incurred (*current dollars*) and a discount factor that fully compensates for the rate of inflation."

This conclusion can be restated as: Make before-tax PNW analyses using either current dollars and a current interest rate or constant dollars and a real interest rate. The answer is the same regardless of the technique used. This conclusion *does not hold* for after-tax analyses, which are discussed below.

Howe's conclusion can be demonstrated algebraically, following Howe (1971) and Klemperer (1979). From Eq. 7.2 we have

$$PNW = \frac{D_n^{con}}{R} \tag{7.7}$$

which would give the PNW in an economy without any inflation. The constant dollars would have to be compounded forward at the expected inflation rate if inflation were present, thus using Eq. 7.3 for D_n^{cur}

$$PNW = \frac{D_n^{con} \times F}{R}$$

but, current dollars must be discounted by the current or market rate, M, where $M = RF$, so

$$PNW = \frac{D_n^{con} F}{RF} \tag{7.8}$$

and the inflation multiplier, F, cancels to obtain

$$\text{PNW} = \frac{D_n^{\text{con}}}{R} \tag{7.9}$$

which is equal to Eq. 7.7 where constant dollars were discounted by the real interest rate.

Gregersen (1975) has pointed out that forestry investment analyses often projected costs and revenues in constant dollars but used a market discount rate, including inflation, instead of a real discount rate. This has resulted in a bias against forestry investment because the PNW is understated.

This can be demonstrated using the above notation and letting PNW′ be the erroneous PNW so that

$$\text{PNW}' = \frac{D_n^{\text{con}}}{RF} \tag{7.10}$$

and comparing Eq. 7.10 with Eq. 7.7,

$$\frac{D_n^{\text{con}}}{RF} < \frac{D_n^{\text{con}}}{R} \tag{7.11}$$

or

$$\text{PNW}' < \text{PNW}$$

because the denominator on the left-hand side of Eq. 7.11 is always greater than the denominator on the right-hand side. The left-hand denominator is greater because it includes both the real and inflation rates.

The bias will be greater the higher the inflation rate, particularly since the denominator is multiplicative. Thus, the problem has been more serious in the 1980s than it was a decade or two before when inflation rates were generally lower. The magnitude of this effect can be demonstrated by examining the impact on revenue assessment. Suppose that a pulpwood investment yielded 30 cords at the end of a 25-year rotation, that the market price were projected to be $15 per cord, that the real interest rate were 3 percent, and that the inflation rate were 10 percent. Then, the unbiased PNW of this revenue is

$$\text{PNW} = \frac{30 \text{ cords} \times \$15.00}{1.03^{25}} = \frac{30 \text{ cords} \times \$15.00 \times 1.10^{25}}{1.03^{25} \times 1.10^{25}}$$
$$= \$214.92 \text{ per acre}$$

whereas the biased PNW is

$$\text{PNW}' = \frac{30 \text{ cords} \times \$15.00}{1.03^{25} \times 1.10^{25}} = \$19.84 \text{ per acre}$$

The net effect of this bias depends on the amount and year that the positive and negative cash flows occur and on the actual difference between the real and market interest rates. This example examines only revenue, and not costs that would also be understated. However, most forestry costs usually occur in the early years of the investment when they would be less understated.

EFFECT ON AFTER-TAX PNWs

PNWs cannot be calculated in constant dollars when income taxes are levied on net income and when, in the same analysis, capital account expenses are deducted from sales to obtain taxable net income. This can be demonstrated by considering the correct PNW for any one year where

$$\text{PNW}_n = \frac{R_n^{con} - C_n^{con} \times (1 - t)}{R} \tag{7.12}$$

where

R_n = the revenue in year n
C_n = the cost in year n
t = the tax rate

Equation 7.12 cannot be used when the cost in year n is wholly or partially a capital account cost, such as depreciation on equipment or depletion on timber. Here federal and state laws require that taxable income be calculated as the difference between *current* revenues and the cost of the capital asset in the year of its purchase. This means that part of the calculation is in current (year n) dollars and part of it is in dollars from an earlier year. The cost dollars are in year zero, or constant dollars, in the special case where the capital asset was purchased in year zero. In this special instance we have taxable income represented by the equation

$$\left(R_n^{con} \times F \right) - C_0^{con} = R_n^{cur} - C_0^{con}$$

and undiscounted income after tax represented as

$$\left(R_n^{cur} - C_0^{con} \right) \times (1 - t) \tag{7.13}$$

Thus, income after tax is understated when calculations are made in constant dollars because the numerator in Eq. 7.12 will always be smaller than the actual numerator (Eq. 7.13). This happens because R_n^{con} is smaller than R_n^{cur} by the amount of the omitted inflation (F). The effect is that PNW is understated because income is understated and that there is a bias against investment in the project being analyzed.

This effect becomes less the closer in time the purchase of the capital asset is to the revenue receipt, if we assume a fairly constant inflation rate. This is true because the asset's price is carried in the capital accounts in current dollars. These current dollars will be closer in value to the revenue dollars the fewer the years separating them.

One correct method to calculate PNW after tax is to work in current dollars because those are the dollars that the tax will be applied to and that will actually describe the cash flows of the investment. Thus, PNW after tax net income can be calculated

$$\text{PNW}_n = \frac{(R_n^{\text{cur}} - C_n^{\text{curc}} - C_n^{\text{curo}}) \times (1 - t)}{M} \qquad (7.14)$$

where

PNW_n = the present net worth of the net income in year n
R_n^{cur} = the revenue in current dollars in year n
C_n^{curc} = the capital asset account costs in current dollars, or the dollars in the year the assets were purchased, which are written off in year n
C_n^{curo} = the costs from ordinary expense accounts incurred in year n
t = the tax rate

The present net worth in Eq. 7.14 is not on a cash flow basis. It still *must be adjusted* for the cash flow effects of depreciation and/or depletion. Care must be taken in evaluating Eq. 7.14 to include only those costs charged against income for the tax rate, t, being used. For example, only costs written off against capital gains income should be included if the capital gains tax rate is being used and only costs written off against ordinary income should be included if the ordinary tax rate is being used.

PNWs can be calculated in either current or constant dollars where costs are only ordinary and not capital because then there is no legal requirement that a combination of current and constant dollars be used to calculate taxable income. Taxable income must be calculated in current dollars the year it is incurred, but it is easily demonstrated that Eq. 7.12 is equal to

$$\text{PNW}_n = \frac{[(R_n^{\text{con}} \times F) - (C_n^{\text{con}} \times F)] \times (1 - t)}{RF} \qquad (7.15)$$

which converts Eq. 7.12 to current dollars. The key point is that both revenue and cost are expressed in either constant or current dollars. Then, either a market or a real interest rate may be used to discount the cash flows.

Klemperer (1979) has pointed out that yield and property taxes are in this category and may be discounted on either a constant or current dollar basis. This is because the yield tax is levied in current dollars against the current dollar value of stumpage revenue and because the property taxes are levied in current dollars and hence the same as any ordinary expenses. These statements implicitly assume that the same average inflation rates apply to these costs and revenues if inflated rather than constant dollars are being used.

Nelson (1976) has shown that the ranking of two mutually exclusive investments having different depreciation expense configurations will have different rankings, after tax, depending on the inflation rate. More specifically, the project with the larger initial investment will tend to be ranked first at the lower inflation rates and the project with the smaller initial investment will tend to be ranked first at the higher inflation rates. Nelson (1976, p. 928) states: "The variation across rates of inflation is entirely due to variation in the capitalized value of future tax savings from depreciation charges. These savings are realized more slowly under...(the project with the larger initial investment)...and therefore their present value is eroded more severely by higher rates of inflation." This, again, biases investment against forestry projects that usually require high initial investment.

Nelson (1976) also found that projects whose cash flows deteriorate more rapidly will tend to be ranked higher than others at higher inflation rates. This, again, is a matter of recouping the investment in earlier years when the value of the cash flows is not eroded by inflation.

CORRECTING PNW FOR INFLATION

There are several ways in which cash flows can be corrected for inflation. In the method presented cash flows are originally stated in year zero or constant dollars, inflated to current dollars in the year they occur, and are then discounted back to present value using the market interest rate.

One advantage of this method is that year zero prices and interest rates are better known than those occurring many years in the future. Thus, better estimates of the relative price of the various goods and services needed for the investment analysis are more likely. Another advantage is institutional. It will probably be much easier to justify using a current market discount rate of, say, about 10–15 percent than a real rate of about 3–6 percent, even though either is equally correct. Using the real rate with constant dollars may make it appear that the investor is biasing the analysis in favor of his or her project. On the other hand, projecting the inflation rate by year over the investment's lifetime is difficult.

Calculating the cash flow after tax for ordinary income is accomplished by Eq. 7.15, simply by noting that C_n^{con} should only include ordinary expenses. Further, this equation can be modified to include real price changes by rewriting it as

$$PNW_n = \frac{\left[\left(R_0^{con} \times PI_{in}\right) - \left(C_0^{cono} \times PI_{in}\right)\right] \times (1 - t)}{RF} \quad (7.16)$$

where

PI_{in} = the price index for the ith good, service, or commodity in year n

Calculating the cash flow after tax for capital gains income is accomplished by Eq. 7.14, modified by adding back the capital costs to place it on a cash flow basis. This equation can also be modified to include real price changes by rewriting it as

$$PNW_n = \frac{\left[\left(R_0^{con} \times PI_{in}\right) - \left(C_0^{cono} \times PI_{in}\right) - C_n^{conc}\right] \times (1 - t) + C_n^{conc}}{RF}$$

$$(7.17)$$

REMARKS

Calculating the price index for individual goods, services, or commodities may be more easily stated than accomplished. One rudimentary approach is to simply fit a time trend to past indices and project them into the future. A more complex method is to use a multivariate analysis relating causal variables to the price index. However, one then must project the causal variables into the future in order to estimate the price index.

Determination of the market interest rate is fairly simple because current rates are regularly published in newspapers. However, choosing an expected average market rate to extend over the analytical period is a matter of judgment and subject to controversy. Determination of the current inflation rate is also fairly simple because of regularly published data. However, once again, the expected average rate for the analytical period is more difficult to estimate and often depends on the analyst's judgment. The real interest rate can be determined by calculation using Eq. 7.6 and solving for r once the market and inflation rates for the period have been chosen.

The preceding equations adjust for real price change and inflation. These adjustments must be combined with those that adjust for income taxes to obtain the cash flow after tax. Needless to say, these calculations become complex before a final answer is obtained.

ADJUSTING FOR TAXES

8

$\mathbf{F}$OREST MANAGERS HAVE traditionally been concerned about three taxes; inheritance and estate taxes, property taxes, and federal income taxes. The first two are discussed briefly and the major part of this chapter is spent on federal income tax, its effects on PNW and IRR analyses, and methods for calculating the analyses "after tax."

All taxes are constantly revised by the legislature imposing them; therefore, the specifics of any tax may change from year to year or by the state that imposes it. Practitioners should consult a tax expert or subscription service for current regulations. The *Timber Tax Journal* is also a good reference. Generalities that can be used to analyze specific cases are discussed. Specifics in force at the time of writing are used to illustrate the analyses and provide an impression of tax effect magnitudes.

ESTATE AND INHERITANCE TAXES

An *estate tax* is a tax levied against the estate of a person who has died. An *inheritance tax* is a tax levied on the person receiving an inheritance. These taxes are levied to gain revenue and to prevent the accumulation of large estates and economic power in the hands of a few people.

The federal estate tax has been selected for discussion because it is found in all the states. Olson, Haney, and Siegel (1981) discuss death taxes in general terms and list taxes levied in the 50 states.

The 1976 Tax Reform Act combined federal estate and gift taxes and phased-in new tax rates over a 5-year period. The Economic Recovery Tax Act of 1981 (ERTA) further liberalized these estate and gift taxes. ERTA also has some provisions scheduled to become effective in 1987.

Gifts and estates are taxed at the same rate. The taxes are levied on the value of the gift or the estate. For example, $125,000 in taxes would be paid if an estate were valued at $500,000 and the average tax rate were 25 percent. Similarly, taxes must be paid on gifts made to people during the year if the gifts exceed certain values. For example, a $10,000 gift at a 25 percent average tax rate requires $2500 taxes. Total gift and estate taxes in the example are $127,500 ($125,000 + $2500).

The law provides for a unified gift and estate tax credit. The credit is applied to reduce taxes levied on taxable gifts made during a lifetime. The unused remainder of this credit is then applied to the tax on a person's estate.

For example, suppose a person had a taxable estate and had made a gift to one recipient as in the above example and that the unified tax credit was $150,000. Then, $2500 of the $150,000 credit is applied to taxes due for the gift and another $125,000 of the credit is applied to the value of the estate. Thus, no taxes would be paid because the $150,000 unified credit exceeds the amount of the taxes by $22,500 ($127,500 to $150,000). And another $90,000 ($22,500/0.25) of gifts could have been given to use the remaining tax credit. In this example, estates of $600,000 or less pay no taxes if there have been no taxable gifts to which the unified credit was applied. This $600,000 is called an *exemption equivalent*. In fact, a $600,000 exemption equivalent based on a unified tax credit of $192,800 will be allowed in 1987 when all ERTA provisions become effective. This compares to a $175,625 exemption equivalent before. There are also several gift exclusions. An *exclusion* is the amount excluded from the taxable amount. For example previously there was a $3000 per recipient annual gift tax exclusion that is now $10,000. Thus, in our example, $1750 tax would be paid under the old law (($10,000 − $3000) × 0.25), whereas no tax would be paid under ERTA (($10,000 − $10,000) × 0.25). Other important exclusions are that parents may make unlimited gifts to their children for educational and medical expenses and the gross estate may be reduced by the full value of bequests to a surviving spouse or the gifts to that spouse during one's lifetime.

Foresters have long been concerned about estate and other death taxes because of the large amounts of money that may have to be paid soon after a forest owner's death. The effects are difficult to predict and can be harmful or beneficial to forestry, depending on which scenario is chosen. The harmful scenario visualizes the well-managed and regulated forest sold under duress to satisfy the estate taxes to someone who cuts the trees, builds a subdivision, and withdraws the land from forestry forever. In the positive version a poorly managed, understocked, overmature forest is sold to a large corporate or private owner who cuts the overmature timber, establishes fully stocked plantations, and manages it intensively for timber in perpetuity.

The correct scenario obviously depends on the specific case although the seller is under some pressure to sell in order to pay taxes. However, in certain circumstances the government will allow an extension so that only the interest on the taxes needs to be paid during the first 5 years. Then, the taxes may be paid in installments during the next 10 years. This can remove some of the pressure to sell.

PROPERTY TAXATION

Property taxes are almost always levied by the county and sometimes, in addition, by municipal governments. These "local" governments prefer property taxes because they are easier to administer than sales or income taxes, because they tend to fluctuate less with changes in the economy, thereby providing a steady income, and because they are difficult to avoid.

Two major classifications of property are usually identified, real property and personal property. Real property is immobile property such as land, buildings, and other permanent assets. Trees are considered real property because most laws define them as part of the land. Personal property is property that is mobile. It is usually divided into two categories, tangible and intangible. Tangible personal property is an asset that the taxpayer has under his direct control, such as autos, household furnishings, and the like. Business inventories, such as pulpwood or logs in a woodyard, are tangible personal property and may be taxed. Intangible personal property is a claim on an asset, such as a bank account or security.

Real property is almost always taxed and personal property is sometimes taxed, depending on the particular state. Personal property is only sometimes taxed because it is difficult to inventory and difficult to value once the inventory is taken. Foresters are primarily concerned with real property taxation that occurs as taxes on the forest lands. They may also be interested in personal property taxes levied on wood inventories or equipment found on the district.

Taxation Procedure

The taxation procedure consists of inventory, valuation, appeal, setting the levy, setting the mill rate, collection, and delinquency actions.

Inventory

The county assessor, who may be an elected official, first inventories the items to be valued. The land inventory is taken and maintained from court records of deeds and land sales. The land may be classified by use, depending on the valuation method. Classification may require field inspection, aerial photo interpretation, or some combination.

Valuation

Most states require that property be valued at the "fair market value" for its highest and best use. Fair market value is often defined as what a willing buyer would pay a willing seller, both reasonably informed of the facts, and neither

under duress. This is why property taxes are sometimes called "*ad valorem*" taxes
—they are assessed "to value." In many cases the assessed value is a proportion
of the fair market value, such as one-half or one-third. The sum of all the assessed
values in a county is the *tax base*. The tax assessor places an assessed value on the
property and notifies all property owners of their assessment.

Appeal

Property owners who do not like their assessment may appeal it to a local
board, which often consists of elected local officials. These are variously called
Board of Appeals or Board of Equalization.

Most appeals are made on either horizontal or vertical inequities. A horizontal inequity occurs when the same property is assessed at different values; for
example, your neighbor's land is assessed at $15 per acre while yours is assessed
at $120 per acre. A vertical inequity occurs when higher-valued property is
assessed at the same or lower value than the lower-valued property; for example,
when both farm land and forest land are valued at $100 per acre.

Setting the Levy

The county commissioners determine the budget for operations for the
coming year while property is being assessed. The budget applies to the whole
county. It is sometimes complicated by special tax districts, for example, school
districts. These districts also make their budgets. The sum of the budgets is the
amount of the *tax levy*.

Setting the Mill Rate

A mill is $1/10$ of a cent or $1/1000$ of a dollar. Taxes are the assessed value
multiplied by the mill rate. A tax rate of 20 mills means you pay 20 mills tax for
each dollar of assessed value or $20 per $1000 of assessed value. The mill rate is
obtained by dividing the tax levy by the tax base and multiplying by 1000. For
example,

District	Tax base	Tax levy	Mill rate ($ / M)
County	10,000,000	$500,000	50.0
School A	7,000,000	70,000	10.0
School B	3,000,000	60,000	20.0

Everyone in the county pays 50 mills tax for operating the county government
and services. In addition, people living in school district *A* must pay 10 mills to
operate their schools, while people living in school district *B* must pay 20 mills.
The total tax is 60 mills (50 + 10) in district *A* and 70 mills (50 + 20) in district *B*.

Collection

The assessments and mill rates, both independently determined, are sent to the tax collector who multiplies the two to determine the tax and mails the tax bills. Taxes are paid to the tax collector who then distributes the funds back to the county and to the various districts.

Delinquency

The system must have a penalty to make it work. This penalty is the county's ability to take property if taxes remain unpaid and sell it for the back taxes. Again, systems will vary by state, but in general, taxes may be delinquent for several years before action is taken. Delinquency is published in the county newspaper each year. Finally, the notice that the property will be sold for taxes is also published. A tax deed to the property is then sold by auction, sometimes literally on the courthouse steps. The landowner then has several years to purchase back the deed from the buyer, with interest, before the deed becomes final.

Many state forests were created in the 1930s when landowners felt taxes were too high, relative to current sales price, and did not pay the taxes. These lands were auctioned; however, in many cases, people did not buy them due to lack of money. The lands then reverted to the county or state and were eventually made into state forests.

System Deficiencies

There are several deficiencies in the property tax, the first of which is bad assessments. There are, in turn, several reasons for bad assessments. First, the assessor, who is often an elected official, may lack the personal knowledge and/or an adequate staff to make good assessments. Some assessors, because they want to be reelected, try to please everyone so personal differences may ensue. In addition, some assessments are just simply difficult or impossible to make. For example, assessed value may vary by forest age and composition; thus, the county's entire forest ownership must be cover type mapped. Or, the market price of a 10,000-acre forest block is hardly ever observable but may have to be estimated.

A final reason for bad assessments is that reassessments are made infrequently. Their expense is one deterrent and the citizens' dissatisfaction over new assessments is another. Thus, a flat percentage increase is often applied to previous assessments and labeled a reassessment. However, property values change at different rates. Trees grow or are harvested, people or corporations build additions to their property, and market values change at differential rates over the years. Thus, a reassessment that performs new inventories and studies new market values is needed.

A second difficulty is that property taxes are not general—that is, they do not fall evenly on all property owners. This is because several categories of property are often tax exempt. Personal property exemptions have already been discussed. In addition, property owned by government, religious, and charitable organizations is also often exempt. Several states also have homestead exemptions. Here, property value up to a specified dollar amount is exempted from taxation if the property is used as a homestead. Finally, special tax concessions may be given to industry to attract a manufacturing plant to the county. For example, property taxes may be waived for 10 or 15 years. All these exceptions reduce or "erode" the tax base and mean that fewer people must pay the taxes and that the taxes are not evenly distributed over all property owners.

A final deficiency is that property taxes may not be a good way to judge who should pay taxes. Two principles are often cited as criteria for making this judgment. The first is the "benefits received principle," which states that those benefiting from government services should pay for them according to the amount of those benefits that are received. The other is the "ability-to-pay principle," which states taxes should be paid according to a person's ability to pay the tax. Property taxes may reflect neither the ability to pay nor the benefits received. Consider, for example, a retired couple who purchased a home during their working years. The home is taxed as before but their children are grown, so they no longer benefit from the county schools and their income is reduced so that they are now less able to pay. Other examples can be cited.

Property taxes may be considered ordinary expense for federal income tax. Thus, income is reduced in the year they are paid by the amount of property tax before calculating the federal income tax payment. Property tax is often combined with annual management cost estimates in PNW analyses for ease of estimation. However, there is no reason why they cannot be shown as a separate item.

FEDERAL INCOME TAX

The federal income tax affects almost every person and organization in the United States, both in their individual decisions and collectively through its effects on the economy. The tax laws change periodically through new Congressional legislation and new interpretations by the Internal Revenue Service (IRS) and the courts of new and old laws.* This section focuses on the corporate income tax structure. However, the principles apply to individuals once their specific tax status is established. The principles also apply to state income taxes, which must be considered in those states that levy them.

Income is divided into two tax categories, ordinary income and capital gains income. This division is significant because capital gains income is taxed at a

---

*See USDA Forest Service (1982) for an alternative discussion of federal income taxes.

lower rate than ordinary income. Ordinary income arises from the sale of a final product of economic activity. The current maximum tax rate on corporate ordinary income is 46 percent. Capital gains income arises from the increased market value of capital assets realized when they are sold. The length of time an asset must be held to be considered a capital asset is defined by the IRS regulations and laws. The current maximum tax rate on corporate capital gains income is 28 percent, while that for noncorporate taxpayers is 20 percent.

Timber income has always qualified as capital gains income *if*: (1) it was owned over six months; (2) it was not held for sale in the ordinary course of business; and (3) it was sold "lump sum," that is, the owner received a fixed dollar amount for all the timber on a specified area. Timber income was taxed as ordinary income *if*: (1) is was cut for use in the owner's business or for resale or (2) it was sold on a cutting contract and the owner was paid per unit volume of timber cut.

This treatment had two negative effects. First, timber industries were discouraged from owning and managing their own timberlands because timber income was taxed at the higher ordinary income tax rate. Industry timber income was considered ordinary income because timber was held for sale in the ordinary course of business. A second negative effect was the fact that any timber owner was discouraged from making thinnings or improvement cuttings because this type of cut prior to the harvest cut was interpreted as putting the owner into the business of selling timber. Thus, ordinary rather than capital gains tax rates were again applied to timber income.

These regulations were modified in 1954 by sections 631(a) and 631(b) of the Internal Revenue Code. The intent of this modification was to give timber preferential treatment in order to increase investment in timber and increase the United States' timber growing potential.

Section 631(b)

Section 631(b) allows net revenues from the sale of timber to qualify as capital gains income if: (1) the timber was owned for more than 1 year prior to cutting and (2) the owner maintained an economic interest in the timber cut. This means that the owner *cannot* sell the timber in a lump sum sale but has to be paid on the basis of what is cut. For example, the owner could agree to be paid a fixed stumpage price per thousand board feet or cord for each unit of volume scaled at the mill. Thus, this section covers the organization that sells stumpage.

This section is important because the owner can be in the regular business of selling timber and still be eligible for the capital gains rate. The owner can run a tree farm and be in the business of selling timber and still qualify for capital gains as long as he or she sells the timber with a retained economic interest. However, the owner must pay tax at the ordinary rate if the timber is sold for a lump sum.

The term "owner" is broadly interpreted and it is applicable to a person who has purchased the right to cut timber but does not own the land on which it is growing. Therefore, a person may lease land and grow timber or purchase the rights to cut timber, called a timber right, hold that right for 1 year, and still qualify for capital gains treatment.

The amount of taxable capital gain is the difference between the sale price and the sum of cost or other basis of the timber plus the expense of the sale. For example, suppose you buy a timber right for stumpage at $8 a cord, sell 10,000 cords at $10 a cord, and have sale expenses of $1000. Then,

$100,000 = Sales ($10 × 10 Mcords)

− 80,000 = Cost of timber right ($8 × 10 Mcords)

−1,000 = Sales expenses

$19,000 = Taxable capital gains income

Section 631(a)

Section 631(a) allows capital gains treatment for timber that is cut for sale or use in the owner's business if: (1) the timber was owned for 1 year before it was cut and (2) the timber was cut for sale or use in the business. Thus, this section covers the organization that owns timber that is harvested and converted into another product by that organization before being sold. For example, a lumber company may own timber that it cuts and brings to its mill to be sawed into lumber. The lumber, rather than the stumpage, is then sold in the regular course of business. Two special terms must be defined before taxable capital gains income can be calculated, *depletion allowance* and *fair market value.*

Depletion allowance is like depreciation of timber. It is the capital expenses connected with the purchase and growing of timber. The total dollars in the depletion account are divided by the units of wood that generated the cost to obtain a *depletion rate* per unit volume of wood cut. For example, an acre costing $80 to site prepare and plant and that yields 40 cords of pulpwood has a depletion rate of $2 per cord. The depletion allowance is $80 if all 40 cords are harvested. Depletion rate calculation is discussed in greater detail below.

The fair market value is defined as before; what a willing buyer would pay a willing seller, both reasonably informed of the facts and neither under duress. The fair market value of the stumpage must be estimated. It can usually be established by: the expert testimony of a consulting forester; the original cost adjusted for changes in price, quality, and quantity of timber since purchase; or transactions evidence, that is, observed actual sales. Note in all these cases a market value is being estimated.

The taxable capital gains income under Section 631(a) is the difference between the fair market value and the depletion allowance. This difference is taxed at the capital gains rate and the fair market value is then charged against ordinary income, in the year the timber is cut, as an expense of the product sold.

For example, suppose a sawmill cuts 2 million bf from its own land and elects Section 631(a) treatment. Suppose further than its depletion rate was $10 per mbf, that it had established a fair market value of $55 per mbf for the stumpage, sold the lumber for $160 per mbf, and had incurred manufacturing costs, including logging costs, of $70 per mbf. Then, capital gains tax:

$55.00 = Fair market value

−10.00 = Depletion

$45.00 = Taxable capital gains income

×0.28 = Capital gains tax rate

$12.60 = Tax

and ordinary income tax:

$160.00 = Sales

−55.00 = Fair market value

−70.00 = Manufacturing costs

$ 35.00 = Taxable ordinary income

×0.46 = Ordinary tax rate

$16.10 = Tax

The total tax is $12.60 + $16.10 = $28.70 per mbf. The tax would have been calculated as follows if all income were ordinary:

$160.00 = Sales

−70.00 = Manufacturing cost

−10.00 = Depletion

$80.00 = Taxable ordinary income

×0.46 = Ordinary tax rate

$36.80 = Tax

Note that in both cases tax is paid on $80 income but $8.10 ($36.80 − $28.70) less tax is paid with the capital gains treatment.

Capital gains savings can be calculated by taking the difference between the ordinary and capital gains tax rates and multiplying it by the amount of taxable gains income. Algebraically,

$$S_c = (T_o - T_c)Y_c \tag{8.1}$$

where

S_c = capital gains savings
T_o = the ordinary income tax rate, expressed as a decimal
T_c = the capital gains income tax rate, expressed as a decimal
Y_c = the income which would be taxable as capital gains

The preceding $8.10 tax decrease can be calculated using Eq. (8.1) as

$$S_c = (0.46 - 0.28)\$45.00$$
$$S_c = \$8.10$$

The movement of taxable income from ordinary to capital gains thus provides a real increase in the cash flow because fewer dollars are paid in taxes. There is, therefore, a strong incentive to have as many sales dollars as possible reported as capital gains rather than as ordinary income.

Accounting for Timber Costs

The procedures required by the IRS in accounting for the timber growing costs are rather strict. The distinction must be made between ordinary expense and capital expense because taxes will be greater or smaller depending on whether a particular expense is written off against ordinary or capital gains income. Therefore, the IRS establishes recommendations and regulations about which expenses are ordinary and which are capital.

Ordinary expenses are those that are ordinary and necessary in carrying out a trade or business and that are paid or incurred during the year. These are intended to be expenses needed in the daily conduct of business and that are spent on items whose consumption will not last longer than a year. Some times items that last longer than a year may be expensed if their cost is relatively low. Here, it is judged that accounting for these low cost items is not worth the trouble.

Ordinary expense items in forestry include: tools lasting less than a year or tools with a small cost, such as shovels and axes; repair and maintenance of mechanical equipment and buildings, such as maintenance of trucks and tractors —but not expenditures on capital improvements; and salaries, wages, and other labor payments, as long as they are not related to the acquisition or establishment of capital assets. Other expenses include some taxes, road maintenance, interest payments, insurance, logging costs, and protection costs.

Capital expenses are expenses for those items whose consumption lasts longer than a year. These are items that are, perhaps, purchased in 1 year and then consumed over several years during the production process. The cost of the forester's pickup truck, which may last several years before it must be replaced, is an example. Some times it may not even be consumed at all; an example would be the land on which the forest grows.

More specific examples of forestry capital expense include: land and land acquisition costs, such as cruising, surveying, and legal fees; all equipment, such as trucks, tractors, and power saws; improvements to the forest property, such as roads, culverts, bridges, and buildings; the value of standing young growth and timber when land is purchased; and regeneration costs, such as site preparation, planting, and the cost of trees.

Some expenses are optional and the owner may choose whether to treat them as ordinary or capital expenses. These include: property and yield taxes; interest payments on forest land mortgages; and carrying charges such as insurance premiums on timber or fire and insect protection expenses. Most landowners find it more financially desirable to declare these items as ordinary expense instead of capital expense, as explained below.

Capital Expenses

The IRS requires that capital accounts be established for three general types of forestry expenses; equipment, land, and timber. Several accounts may be established under each of these categories depending on the complexity of the forest organization and its accounting practices.

The Equipment Account. The cost of a piece of equipment is placed in a capital account for equipment at the time of purchase. Then, each accounting period, the capital account is reduced by the amount of the depreciation as the equipment is used and this amount is counted as an expense of current sales. Sales are reduced by the amount of depreciation, and other expenses, to calculate taxable income. This is an accounting basis, not a cash flow basis. Note also this capital expense reduces ordinary rather than capital gains income.

For example, consider a pickup truck purchased for $9500 that has a $500 scrap value, an expected life of 3 years, and straight line depreciation. At time of purchase $9500 is placed in the capital account and each year $3000 is taken out to write off against current income. Finally, the remaining $500 is written off against income when the pickup is sold.

The Land Account. The land account contains that portion of the purchase price that is attributable to the land as opposed to other assets on the land, such as timber or buildings. Proportionate land purchase expenses such as attorney or surveying fees must also be included. The account is not depletable but is reduced by the land costs at the time the land is sold.

For example, suppose 100 acres is purchased at $300 per acre and that it also costs $300 to appraise the land and another $200 in legal fees. It is established that there is $200 per acre worth of timber on the land. Then, land value = $300

− $200 = \$100$ per acre and this is charged to the land account. Also, one-third ($100/$300) of all costs must be included, so $0.333 \times \$500 = \$167.00$ is added. The total entries are

$10,000.00 = Land value ($100 × 100 acre)

_166.67_ = Purchase costs

$10,166.67   Total

The land cost per acre is $101.67 ($10,166.67 ÷ 100). If at some time later 1 acre is sold for $200, capital gains taxes are paid on $200.00 − 101.67 = $98.33 and the land account is reduced by $101.67.

The Timber Accounts. The timber accounts are divided into three categories: tree planting and seeding, young growth, and merchantable timber. The tree planting and seeding account and the young growth account hold nondepletable expenses. The expenses of growing trees become depletable as the trees grow and become merchantable; thus, the expenses in these accounts are moved to the merchantable timber account when timber becomes merchantable. The merchantable timber account is reduced by the depletion rate for each unit of volume that is cut and this amount is written off against capital gains income. That is, taxable capital gains income is reduced by the depletion on the timber cut to generate that income.

Tree Planting and Seeding Account. The tree planting and seeding account carries regeneration costs. For example, suppose the above 100 acres is regenerated and site preparation costs $40 per acre, planting costs $20 per acre, and 800 seedlings are planted per acre at a cost of $10 per thousand. Entries into the account are

$4,000.00 = Site preparation ($40 × 100 acres)

2,000.00 = Planting ($20 × 100 acres)

_800.00_ = Seedlings ($10 × 100 acres × 0.8)

$6,800.00 = Total

Young Growth Account. The young growth account is used only for new purchases, whereas the tree planting and seeding account is used any time regeneration costs are incurred—on either old or new land. This young growth account contains that part of the purchase price from a land purchase that is attributable to the existing trees, which are not yet merchantable and hence nondepletable. The $200 per acre timber value and the $333.33 expense in the above example would be entered into this account if the timber were nonmerchantable.

Merchantable Timber Account. The merchantable timber account contains the value of merchantable timber on all lands. The $200 an acre timber value would have been entered into this account if the timber was merchantable. The

$333.33 in expenses would also have been entered. The total entry to the account would have been ($200 per acre × 100 acres) + $333.33 = $20,333.33.

Suppose 5 years later the land were clear-cut and 50 mbf per acre were sold for $75 per mbf. Then the cost of the purchase is written off against the income and the taxable capital gains income is

$375,000.00 = Sales (50 mbf × 100 acres × $75.00)

$\underline{-20,333.33}$ = Depletion allowance

$354,666.33 = Taxable capital gains income

Calculating Depletion

The preceding example was oversimplified because there was only one timber stand and all revenues from the stand were reduced by its cost. Usually, many stands are being cut and depleted and a timber inventory account must be established to record changes in volume due to growth, cut, and mortality.

Practices vary widely by company depending on their needs and the individual case. However, there is always at least one volume account and there may be more. For example, only cubic foot volume may be recorded or both cords and board feet may be recorded.

Merchantable timber volume is added to the volume account when timber is purchased, annual growth is added each year, and cut and mortality are subtracted as they occur. The account may be periodically adjusted to agree with continuous forest inventory (CFI) results.

The merchantable timber account is receiving parallel dollar additions for new purchases and in-growth from the tree planting and seeding and young growth accounts and dollar subtractions for cutting and mortality. The merchantable timber account, with these dollar adjustments, is called the *adjusted basis* for depletion.

A merchantable timber account in dollars is maintained for each timber inventory account. For example, two merchantable timber accounts would be maintained if there were both cord and board foot timber inventory accounts.

The *depletion rate* is the adjusted basis divided by the volume in the corresponding timber inventory account. There would be two depletion rates if both cords and board feet were accounted for in the volume accounts. The depletion rate for the preceding example is

$$\text{Depletion rate} = \frac{\$20,333.33}{50 \text{ mbf} \times 100 \text{ acres}} = \$4.067 \text{ per mbf}$$

The *depletion allowance* is the depletion rate multiplied by the volume of timber cut. The depletion allowance is subtracted from the merchantable timber account and shown as a capital gains expense in generating timber income.

Timber depletion allowances can never exceed the original costs entered in the accounts. The depletion allowance in the preceding example was

Depletion allowance = $4.067 × 50 mbf × 100 acres = $20,335.00

The two figures differ due to rounding.

The Importance of Expensing

Placing costs into capital accounts and removing them gradually, or in a lump sum as the asset is used, is called *capitalizing*. This is one of several definitions of the term and so its use is ambiguous. Reducing current revenues, either ordinary or capital gains, by a current cost is called *expensing*. Most corporations prefer to expense a cost because of the time value of money. Expensing allows the corporation to use its funds for a longer time period than capitalizing would allow. This occurs because the firm will pay less tax in earlier years and therefore have the use of the funds.

Assume, for example, sales of $100,000 a year, ordinary expenses of $50,000 a year, and one capital expense of $30,000. Assume further than the capital expense has no scrap value, that it is completely depreciated over 3 years on a straight line basis, and that the income tax rate is 46 percent. The advantage of expensing rather than capitalizing the capital cost is then demonstrable (Table 8.1).

TABLE 8.1   Example of the Importance of Expensing

	Year			
	1	2	3	Total
	Capitalizing			
Sales	$100,000	$100,000	$100,000	
Costs	50,000	50,000	50,000	
Depreciation	10,000	10,000	10,000	
Taxable income	$40,000	$40,000	$40,000	$120,000
Tax (46%)	$18,400	$18,400	$18,400	$55,200
PV 10% of tax				$45,758.08
	Expensing			
Sales	$100,000	$100,000	$100,000	
Costs	50,000	50,000	50,000	
Depreciation	30,000	0	0	
Taxable income	$20,000	$50,000	$50,000	$120,000
Tax (46%)	$9,200	$23,000	$23,000	$55,200
PV 10% of tax				$44,652.14

The taxable income and tax paid are the *same* under each method. However, a difference in cash flow timing occurs. Tax of $18,400 is paid each year with capitalizing, whereas the tax is only $9200 in the first year with expensing. The difference in these cash flows can be seen by taking their present value at 10 percent. The value of the expensing cash flow is $1105.94 *less than* the capitalized cash flow ($45,758.08 − $44,652.14), indicating the firm incurred opportunity costs of that amount. The amount of the opportunity cost will differ with each situation. The greater the proportion of costs in capitalized expenses, the higher the interest rate, and the longer the time periods, the greater will be the opportunity cost.

This also demonstrates the advantage of accelerated depreciation rates. The accelerated rate reduces taxes in the earlier years, although the same amount of tax is eventually paid, and allows the firm to invest the tax savings in those years and earn interest on them.

The effect of shifting expense dollars from capital gains expenses to ordinary expenses is sometimes confused with the expensing effect just discussed. A cost, once incurred, is expensed rather than capitalized in the situation discussed above. Here, however, the incurred cost is written off against ordinary expenses as opposed to capital gains income. It is advantageous for the firm to increase ordinary expenses rather than capital gains expenses because the ordinary tax rate is higher and hence the tax reduction greater.

Suppose, as a simplified example, a firm has $10,000 in sales in both ordinary and capital gains items and $1000 in expenses that it could charge against either ordinary or capital gains income (Table 8.2). A total tax of $6940 results when the expense is charged to ordinary income versus a total tax of $7120 when the expense is charged to capital gains income, a difference of $180. This is a direct tax savings and is money that the firm will never have to pay in taxes. The $180 tax savings in Table 8.2 can be calculated as

$$S_o = (0.46 - 0.28) \times \$1000.00 = \$180.00$$

The amount of the savings can be calculated by the formula:

$$S_o = (T_o - T_c)E_o \tag{8.2}$$

where

S_o = the tax savings due to ordinary versus capital gains expensing
T_o = the ordinary income tax rate, expressed as a decimal
T_c = the capital gains income tax rate, expressed as a decimal
E_o = the expenses charged against ordinary rather than capital gains income

This indicates the desirability, whenever possible, of shifting expenses from capital gains to ordinary income. This effect and the preceding effect of expensing

TABLE 8.2　Example of the Effect of Charging Expense against Ordinary Income versus Capital Gains Income

	Ordinary income	Capital gains income	Total
	Cost Charged to Ordinary Income		
Sales	$10,000	$10,000	$20,000
Expense	−1,000	−0	−1,000
Taxable income	$ 9,000	$10,000	$19,000
Tax rate	×0.46	×0.28	—
Tax	$ 4,140	$ 2,800	$ 6,940
	Cost Charged to Capital Gains Income		
Sales	$10,000	$10,000	$20,000
Expense	−0	−1,000	−1,000
Taxable income	$10,000	$9,000	$19,000
Tax rate	×0.46	×0.28	—
Tax	$4,600	$2,520	$7,120

versus capitalizing are often combined, for example, if a firm can shift costs from a depletable capital account to an ordinary expense account.

Adjusting Cash Flow Analyses for Taxes

Cash flow analyses, such as PNW, must be adjusted to an aftertax basis to show funds actually available for other investment. Analyzing income changes due to tax will indicate the procedure.

The marginal tax rate is used for calculations rather than the average tax rate because it is the rate that will apply to the new investment. It is assumed in this discussion that no shift is made from one marginal tax rate to another. This is a good assumption for large corporations because they are usually well entrenched in the 46 percent bracket. However, tax bracket shifting can be important when analyzing either personal taxes or those for a small corporation.

Ordinary Income

Ordinary income is income arising from the sale of a final product of economic activity and is taxable at the ordinary rate. Fishing or hunting leases are examples of ordinary income items in forestry. Adjusting ordinary income for taxes is demonstrated by the following example.

Suppose that there were $10 of ordinary income that was increased by $1, that there were no expenses, and that the marginal tax rate was 46 percent. Then, the tax and the income after tax on the first $10 is

Tax $= \$10.00 \times 0.46 = \$4.60$
Income after tax $= \$10.00 - \$4.60 = \$5.40$

The tax and income after tax with an extra dollar of income, generated by the proposed investment, is

Tax $= \$11.00 \times 0.46 = \$5.06$
Income after tax $= \$11.00 - \$5.06 = \$5.94$

And, the increase in total income after tax from the investment is the difference between these two incomes, or

Increased income after tax $= \$5.94 - \$5.40 = \$0.54$

The dollar increase in income is worth only $0.54 after tax because $0.46 in ordinary tax had to be paid out of the $1 increase in income.

The value after tax of an increase in ordinary income can be calculated by

$$\text{VAT} = Y_o(1.0 - T_o) \tag{8.3}$$

where

VAT = the value after tax
Y_o = the increase in ordinary income, before tax
T_o = the marginal ordinary income tax rate, expressed as a decimal

The increased income after tax can be calculated for the preceding example as

$$\text{VAT} = \$1.00 \times (1.0 - 0.46) = \$0.54$$

The value after tax, VAT, is the value used in the after tax cash flow analyses. The term $(1.0 - T_o)$ in Eq. 8.3 is a multiplier to make the adjustment. The multiplier is used for any ordinary income items before they are discounted.

Ordinary Expenses

Ordinary expenses are analyzed and adjusted in the same manner. When an ordinary expense dollar is spent the tax paid is reduced; therefore, the cash flow is reduced by something less than $1. For example, assume that the 46 percent marginal tax is applicable and that there were $10 taxable income from an investment. Then, tax and income after tax are

Tax $= \$10.00 \times 0.46 = \$4.60$
Income after tax $= \$10.00 - \$4.60 = \$5.40$

The tax and income after tax with an extra dollar of expense are

Tax = $10.00 − $1.00 = $9.00 × 0.46 = $4.14
Income after tax = $9.00 − $4.14 = $4.86

And, the change in income after tax from spending $1 extra is the difference between the two incomes, or

Change in income after tax = $4.86 − $5.40 = $0.54

The dollar increase in expenses only caused a $0.54 decrease in profits because the income tax that would have been paid was decreased by $0.46.

The value after tax of an increase in ordinary expenses can be calculated by Eq. 8.3 if the ordinary expense, E_o, is substituted for Y_o. Using the preceding example, we obtain

$$VAT = \$1.00(1.0 - 0.46) = \$0.54$$

The value after tax, VAT, is the value used in the after tax cash flow analyses. As above, the adjustment multiplier $(1.0 - T_o)$ is calculated and used on all regular expenses before discounting or compounding them. The general principle expressed in Eq. 8.3 may be used for any type of revenue or cost as long as the corresponding marginal tax rate is used to calculate the multiplier.

Capital Gains Income and Expenses

The calculations become more complex for capital gains costs that are capitalized and for either ordinary or capital gains incomes that have depreciation or depletion rates applied against them. The full amount of a capital expenditure must be shown as a negative cash flow the year it is made because no part is written off against taxes. For example, a $6000 truck takes $6000 out of the bank account but there is no change in taxes. Now, $2000 a year is written off against income on an accounting basis if the full amount is depreciable, straight line, over 3 years. However, the full $6000 dollars is deducted in year zero on a cash flow basis, and a cash flow basis should be used for PNW and IRR analyses. Comparing the two on a time line, we have

Cash Flow
− $6,000

| 0 | 1 | 2 | 3 |
| Accounting | − $2,000 | − $2,000 | − $2,000 |

The $2000 depreciation in deducted each year and taxes are lower by that amount.

The easiest way to calculate cash flow is to simply calculate the taxes as they would occur and add back the depreciation. For example, assume $10,000 income, $3000 ordinary expense, and the $2000 depreciation from above. Then,

Taxable income = $10,000 − $3,000 − $2,000 = $5,000

and

Tax = $5,000 × 0.46 = $2,300

The cash flow in that year is the taxable income minus the tax, plus the noncash expenses (depreciation), or

$5,000 − $2,300 + $2,000 = $4,700

And if this happens for each of the 3 years, the cash flow time line would be

− $6,000	$4,700	$4,700	$4,700

Total = $8,100

whereas the accounting time line is

0	$2,700	$2,700	$2,700

0
Total = $8,100

In summary, capitalized costs are shown as a negative cash flow in their full amount in the year they are incurred. No reduction is made for taxes because they do not affect taxes in that year. Income against which the capital costs are charged in future years, usually as depreciation or depletion, should be calculated for each year, after tax. The amount of the capital cost must be added back to the cash flow in these future years because it is a noncash expense. The full amount of the capital cost was already subtracted in the year the capital asset was purchased. These principals apply both to capital gains income, such as that generated by the sales of timber or land, and also to ordinary income that has capital expenses charged against it.

PNW Example
The investment contained in Table 5.1 is adjusted to an after tax basis as follows (Table 8.3).

Purchase Land. Land is placed directly in the capital account and is not charged against income until the land is sold. Therefore, there is no effect on taxes in the year it is purchased and the cash flow is reduced by $150. In effect, a $150 check is written for the land and the bank account is reduced by that amount with nothing offsetting it.

Site Preparation and Planting.   The full amount of this cost is entered into the cash flow for the same reasons as the land purchase. In practice, the full amount would be placed in the tree planting and seeding account and then moved to the merchantable timber account for depletion. However, a proportionate amount of this cost is depletable before the end of the investment if the stand is commercially thinned.

Annual Management Cost and Property Tax.   These are ordinary expenses and taxable at the 0.46 rate; therefore, the annual cost, after tax, with Eq. 8.3 is

$$VAT = \$2.00(1.0 - 0.46) = \$1.08$$

Harvest.   The harvest income of $750 is a capital gain income. The depletion allowance is the $75 site preparation and planting costs incurred in year 1 of the investment. The cash flow after tax is

$$
\begin{aligned}
\text{Sales} &= \$750.00 \\
\text{Depletion allowance} &= -75.00 \\
\text{Taxable income} &= \$675.00
\end{aligned}
$$

And, using Eq. 8.3, we obtain

$$VAT = \$675.00(1.0 - 0.28) = \$486.00$$

However, the depletion allowance is a noncash expense and must be added back, so that

$$\text{Cash flow} = \$486.00 + \$75.00 = \$561.00$$

TABLE 8.3   Cash Flow Analyses Adjusted to an After-Tax Basis

Item	Year	Cash flow Before tax	Cash flow After tax
Purchase land	0	-$150.00	-$150.00
Site Preparation and Planting	1	-75.00	-75.00
Annual Management Cost and Property Tax	1-25	-2.00	-1.08
Harvest			
50 cords — $15.00 @	25	750.00	561.00
Sell land	25	150.00	150.00
Total		$625.00	$459.00

The depletion allowance was calculated by using the entire $75 in the merchantable timber account. Alternatively, a depletion rate could have been calculated as

$$\text{Depletion rate} = \frac{\$75.00}{50 \text{ cords}} = \$1.50 \text{ per cord}$$

Then, the depletion allowance is the product of the volume cut and the depletion rate, or

$$\text{Depletion allowance} = 50 \text{ cords} \times \$1.50 \text{ per cord} = \$75.00$$

This calculation can be repeated for any number of intermediate cuts, always reducing the merchantable timber account in proportion to the then existing volume.

The depletion allowance for an intermediate cut is calculated by dividing the merchantable timber account dollars (adjusted basis) by the volume on the stand at the time of intermediate cut to obtain a depletion rate. The volume removed in the intermediate cut is then multiplied by the depletion rate to obtain the depletion allowance for the intermediate cut.

Suppose that in the preceding example, stand volume in year 15 were 25 cords per acre, that 10 cords per acre were thinned, and that the final harvest were 40 cords per acre. Then,

$$\text{Depletion rate}_{15} = \frac{\$75.00}{25 \text{ cords}} = \$3.00$$

$$\text{Depletion allowance} = \$3.00 \times 10 \text{ cords} = \$30.00$$

$$\text{Adjusted basis} = \$75.00 - \$30.00 = \$45.00$$

and in year 25, at harvest

$$\text{Depletion rate}_{25} = \frac{\$45.00}{40 \text{ cords}} = \$1.125$$

$$\text{Depletion allowance} = \$1.125 \times 40 \text{ cords} = \$45.00$$

$$\text{Adjusted basis} = \$45.00 - \$45.00 = \$0.00$$

Note that the procedure causes a higher depletion rate at the intermediate cut than at harvest. This is an added advantage of intermediate cuts. Not only is revenue received earlier but depletion, a noncash expense, it taken at an accelerated rate.

Sell Land. The sale of land is also capital gains income. The capitalized purchase price is subtracted from the sale price and the difference is the taxable income. The cash flow is calculated as

$$
\begin{aligned}
\text{Sales} &= \$150.00 \\
\text{Land cost} &= -\underline{150.00} \\
\text{Taxable income} &= \$\ \ 0.00
\end{aligned}
$$

Using Eq. 8.3, we obtain

$$\text{VAT} = \$0.00(1.0 - 0.28) = \$0.00$$

and adding back the land cost, which is a noncash expense,

$$\text{Cash flow} = \$0.00 + \$150.00 = \$150.00$$

The sales price of the land could have been more than the purchase price, in which case there would have been income tax paid.

ADJUSTING FOR RISK

9

WE STARTED WITH the discounted cash flow model, and the various criteria derived from it, to provide decision guidelines. Next, we learned how to modify the model to account for both inflation and income taxes. The final modification that we study is that for risk and uncertainty.

Cash flows in the previous models have all been treated as if they were known with complete certainty. A point estimate was made of the amount of a cost or revenue and also of the year in which it would occur. Calculations then proceeded as if that estimate would occur precisely as made. However, most analysts readily admit that they do not expect their estimates to occur as precisely as they are stated. Some difference from the estimate is always expected. This difference may be due both to the natural variability of the systems with which a forest manager deals and also to the errors that enter the estimates.

However, the point estimate is often treated as if it were expected to occur. This is because it is usually the best *single* estimate that can be made. It is the value believed most likely to occur of all other possible values. The arithmetic mean is often used as the point estimate. There are many other values distributed around the mean but the mean remains the best estimate if only one estimate is allowed. For example, yield tables contain a single value that is used to estimate the volume of timber that will grow in a certain number of years. Few foresters expect each acre to yield exactly that amount because the yield table cannot account for all the site differences and because the yield table may not precisely apply to all the acres that are being examined. However, it is expected that the average yield on all these acres will be close to that contained in the yield table.

A single estimate is often all that a superior, who is the decision maker, desires from an analyst. In fact, the superior may exhibit impatience if the analyst spends too much time qualifying and explaining the analysis. The decision maker may just want the "best" information available and this is the point estimate. In other cases, the decision maker may want some indication about "how good" the analysis is. Sometimes a subjective indication such as "pretty good" or "not too tight" will suffice. In other cases, a more quantitative assessment, such as those discussed below, may be desired.

The terminology used in analyzing risk and uncertainty can be defined by expanding on the decision making model in Figure 1.1. More specifically, the "Alternatives," "Constraints," and "Decision" boxes can be rewritten as in Figure 9.1.

We begin with the decision maker perceiving the need to make a decision. This may be in response to a new objective or goal but more often it results from comparing a functioning system to some standard. For example, weekly pulpwood receipts, when compared to the budgeted receipts, may show that too much wood is being received. This alerts the manager that some action may be needed.

The second step is to identify the alternatives. These are the different courses of action that can be taken to reach the objective. They are the different things the manager might do to reduce the amount of pulpwood being received. The alternatives for decreasing the woodyard inventory might include: locking the woodyard gate and refusing further deliveries; notifying the dealers and producers to reduce their cut by 10 percent; doing nothing this week but reducing dealer quotas next week. The outcome of each alternative is then predicted. The

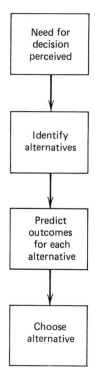

FIGURE 9.1 *Restatement of decision-making model.*

preceding models we discussed contained just one outcome, the point estimate. However, each alternative can have several outcomes. For example, locking the woodyard gate may (1) anger the producers so that they will slow down deliveries next week, resulting in a wood shortage; (2) have no effect other than to reduce this week's wood receipts; or (3) make the producers increase their cut next week to make up for lost income and thereby shift the oversupply forward by 1 week.

Each of the above outcomes is possible. The outcome that does in fact occur will depend on the *state of nature*. The state of nature is the environment surrounding the decisions that condition the outcome and causes it to occur. These ideas are formalized in a *decision matrix* which contains the alternatives in the rows, the states of nature in the columns, and the outcomes as the elements of the matrix (Table 9.1).

Alternative 1 has three possible outcomes, O_{11}, O_{12}, and O_{13}, depending on which state of nature prevails. Similarly, the other alternatives each have three outcomes and each outcome is dependent on the state of nature. The outcome that finally occurs depends on both the alternative chosen and the state of nature that occurs. For example, outcome O_{11} will prevail if state of nature S_1 occurs and the first alternative course of action is followed but outcome O_{21} will prevail if alternative 2 is followed. Outcome O_{32} will prevail if alternative 3 is followed and state of nature 2 occurs. The decision matrix often contains the outcomes stated as the losses incurred for one combination of alternatives and states of nature. A *payoff matrix* states the outcomes in terms of benefits, incomes, or payoffs.

There are three different conditions under which decisions are made. These are *certainty*, *risk*, and *uncertainty*. Certainty exists if there is only one outcome for each alternative. Stated differently, the outcome for each alternative is known; thus, choosing the alternative automatically defines the outcome. Risk exists if a probability distribution can be attached to the different states of nature and hence to the different outcomes. The state of nature cannot be predicted for each occurrence but the number of times each state of nature will occur if the decision is made frequently can be predicted. The probability distributions can come from different sources. They may be based on historical evidence and records or they may be obtained subjectively by asking experts for their opinion about the likelihood of states of nature occurring.

Uncertainty exists if there is *no* information about the probability distributions of the states of nature. This means that not even a subjective estimate of the

TABLE 9.1   A Decision Matrix

	States of nature		
Alternatives	S_1	S_2	S_3
A_1	O_{11}	O_{12}	O_{13}
A_2	O_{21}	O_{22}	O_{23}
A_3	O_{31}	O_{32}	O_{33}

probabilities can be made by experts. Many people believe that uncertainty does not exist under this strict definition. These people believe that subjective probability distributions can be assigned if the analyst knows enough about the system to identify alternatives and states of nature and to predict outcomes for them. They feel it is highly unlikely that all this information is known but that, at a minimum, subjective probabilities are not. Decision guides for uncertainty are briefly discussed because they include models and terms frequently heard, although it is unlikely that any of the models will be applied in practice. The decision models are discussed in reverse order, namely, uncertainty, risk, and certainty.

DECISION MAKING WITH UNCERTAINTY

Decision models for decision making with uncertainty usually require developing a decision or payoff matrix. We will use the decision matrix in Table 9.2, which contains the outcomes for several alternatives and states of nature. The matrix indicates that if alternative 1 is chosen a loss of 12 units will occur for state of nature S_1, a loss of 8 units for S_2, and a loss of 2 units for S_3.

The *minimax* criterion, also called the maximin criterion, takes a pessimistic view of life and seeks to avoid the most objectionable circumstances. The criterion is called minimax because it minimizes the chance of the maximum loss. It has been called a coward's criterion by at least one author, however, circumstances can be thought of where the worst results may be so distasteful that they are to be minimized in any circumstance. The criterion is to choose the *worst* possible outcome under each alternative and to choose the least objectionable alternative from among these. The worst possible outcomes in the decision matrix (Table 9.2) are: S_1 for A_1 (loss = 12); S_1 for A_2 (loss = 7); and S_3 for A_3 (loss = 15). The criterion instructs you to choose A_2 because this is where the possible loss is minimized.

The *minimin* criterion, also called the maximax criterion, takes an optimistic view of life and seeks to obtain the highest payoff from those available. The criterion is called minimin because it minimizes the minimum payoff. It implicitly assumes only the best possible outcomes will occur and picks the best among them. The criterion is to choose the best possible outcome for each alternative and

TABLE 9.2 Hypothetical Decision Matrix

	States of nature		
Alternatives	S_1	S_2	S_3
A_1	12	8	2
A_2	7	5	5
A_3	0	10	15

Source: Thompson (1970).

then to choose the alternative with the best among these. The best outcomes in the decision matrix (Table 9.2) are S_3 for A_1 (loss = 2); S_2 and S_3 for A_2 (loss = 5); and S_1 for A_3 (loss = 0). The criterion instructs you to pick A_3 because this has the least loss that is the highest payoff.

The *minimax regret* criterion incorporates the idea of opportunity cost into the decision-making process. The decision matrix is recalculated to show the amount of "regret" that would occur in each state of nature if the wrong alternative were chosen. The alternative with the minimum loss in each state of nature is chosen as the most desirable and subtracted from all other outcomes for that state of nature. The resulting decision matrix is then minimaxed. For example, if S_1 in Table 9.2 prevailed, the best alternative is A_3 because that has the least loss. This loss value is then subtracted from all other outcomes in S_1 to show the amount of "regret" (Table 9.3). The rationale is that the decision maker would have no regret if he chose A_3 and S_1 prevailed because that is the best he could do. The difference between A_3 and the other alternatives is the amount of regret incurred if one of these alternatives were chosen instead of A_3. The procedure is repeated for the other states of nature, S_2 and S_3. The maximum amount of regret for each alternative is identified in the matrix by asterisks. A_2 is chosen as the course of action because it has the minimum amount of regret.

The *principle of insufficient reason* states that you should assign equal weight to each state of nature and choose the alternative with the highest payoff if you know absolutely nothing about the probabilities of occurrence. The criterion requires taking the mean payoff for each alternative, which in Table 9.2 is $A_1 = 7.333$; $A_2 = 5.667$; and $A_3 = 8.333$. A_2 is chosen because it has the highest payoff (least loss). This criterion is very close to placing a subjective probability distribution on the states of nature. As such, it is almost a criterion for decision making under risk. In fact, many people believe that it should be categorized that way.

DECISION MAKING WITH RISK

The riskiness of an investment is the amount of certainty with which the return on that investment, including recouping the initial investment, can be

TABLE 9.3   Decision Matrix for Minimax Regret Criterion

	States of nature		
Alternatives	S_1	S_2	S_3
A_1	12 − 0 = 12*	8 − 5 = 3	2 − 2 = 0
A_2	7 − 0 = 7*	5 − 5 = 0	5 − 2 = 3
A_3	0 − 0 = 0	10 − 5 = 5	15 − 2 = 13*

*Maximum amount of regret for each alternative.

predicted. The return on a certificate of deposit (CD) is certain and risk-free. The bank issuing the CD issues a federally insured contract to the depositor. This contract promises to repay the principal plus a stated amount of interest at defined time periods. There is no variability in the outcome or the return on this investment and no risk. Riskiness, then, is defined as the variability of the returns from a proposed investment. It is measured by either the variance or the standard deviation of a probability distribution of the returns on that investment. The distribution may be either empirically or subjectively determined. Some evaluation techniques use simulation based on very limited subjective data.

The distributions of expected returns for four investments are shown in Figure 9.2. These are normal distributions and the only type we will discuss. Nonnormal distributions, with skewness, often occur but are not discussed in this text. The investment return is measured on the x axis by present net worth (PNW). The high points of the distribution are the mean and provide the "best" estimate (the point estimate) of the investment's return. The y axis measures the probability that the indicated investment return will occur. The point estimates for Investments A and B (left diagram, Figure 9.2) are both $5000. The investor would be indifferent between these two investments if risk were not considered. However, the distributions show that Investment A is far less risky than Investment B. Investment A will never be less than about $4000 nor more than about $6000, while there is a chance that Investment B will return zero dollars. Ordinarily, the investor is assumed to be a risk averter and would choose Investment A rather than Investment B. The investor who was not a risk averter —that is, was a gambler—might choose Investment B because of the chance of receiving a return as high as $10,000.

The returns for Investments C and D (right diagram, Figure 9.2) are different. The point estimate for Investment C is $4000, while that for Investment

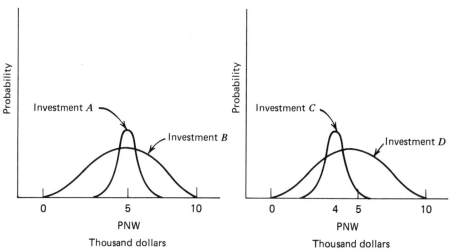

FIGURE 9.2 *Probability distributions of investment returns.*

D is \$5000. Investment *D* would be chosen if risk were ignored; however, the distributions show that Investment *C*, with the lower return, is less risky than Investment *D* with the higher return. However, the decision is ambiguous because the higher return is for the riskier investment.

The standard deviation or variance for each distribution could be calculated and used as a quantitative guideline of each investment's riskiness. This would allow calculating the size of the difference between their riskiness. Alternatively, the probability of each investment returning greater than a specified dollar amount, say \$3000, could be calculated and the decision based on that guideline. However, even these calculations do not provide a final answer. The choice between these investments depends on how much risk the individual investor is willing to take. A very conservative person, or firm, might choose Investment *C*, whereas a less conservative person might choose Investment *D*.

The distributions, or their means and standard deviations, can be estimated either empirically or subjectively. Empirical estimation is based on actual observations of past investments. Studies can be made and means and variances calculated. Usually, however, there must be many investments with similar characteristics for the empirical estimates to be valid. Furthermore, the underlying characteristics of the proposed investment should be similar to those on which the calculations were based. This may be true for such investments as land or timber purchases but will probably not be true for investments such as opening a new woodyard, building a new sawmill, expanding existing capacity of an old mill, or purchasing a newly developed piece of equipment.

Subjective estimates by the managerial personnel familiar with the proposed investment may be possible if a normal distribution of returns can be assumed. A "best estimate" of cash flow is obtained and used as the distribution mean. Variability can be estimated by obtaining judgmental estimates of the likelihood of the cash flow being more or less than the mean. For example, the executive or group of executives in charge might be asked "What is the likelihood that the cash flow will be half as much of your best estimate?" An answer of "50/50" would establish the dollar value at about 0.68 standard deviations. Dividing one-half of the "best estimate" by 0.68 will give the value of one standard deviation (Figure 9.3). Subjective estimate questions can be phrased in any manner that is most comfortable for the executives as long as they establish a dollar return and probability level on one side of the mean and as long as a normal distribution can be assumed.

Conditional Cash Flows

The preceding techniques have implicitly assumed that the cash flows occurring in one time period are independent of the cash flows that occur in another time period. This means that the cash flow in the 10th year would not be affected if the cash flow in the 5th year did not occur at the predicted mean. This might not be too bad an assumption for some forestry investments such as a land purchase or plantation regeneration. Here, the cost categories such as purchase price, site preparation cost, and timber harvest may well be independent of each other. For example, increased site preparation and planting costs due to increased labor and equipment costs would probably not affect the biological processes determining timber yield at the end of the rotation. On the other hand, some classes of investments would not have independent cash flows. For example, reduced wood flows to a new woodyard in the first and second year of an investment might well indicate a weakness in the procurement system that will cause reduced wood flows in future years as well. Similarly, higher maintenance costs in the first year for a new piece of equipment may indicate that the equipment was not as reliable as hoped and will require more maintenance throughout its life.

For example, consider the hypothetical investment in Table 9.4. Two events can occur in year 1; the cash flow will be either $2000 or $10,000. The probabilities of these events are 0.25 and 0.75, respectively. Five events are possible in year 2. These are cash flows of −$2000, $1000, $10,000, $15,000, and $20,000, respectively. However, these cash flows depend on what happens in the first year. The first two events, event Nos. 1.1.0 and 1.2.0, can occur only if the $2000 cash flow, event 1.0.0, occurs in the first year. These events could occur if there were a deteriorating market for the investment's product as reflected by the lower cash flow in year 1. The probability of these events occurring, if event 1.0.0 occurs, is 0.33 and 0.67, respectively. The last three events, events 2.3.0, 2.4.0, and 2.5.0, cannot occur unless event 2.0.0 occurs in the first year. The probability of these events occurring, if event 2.0.0 occurs, is 0.50, 0.35, and 0.15, respectively. Eleven events are possible in the third year, each of these depending on which event occurs in the second year. The event numbers indicate the preceding event(s) on which the current event depends. For example, event 1.1.1, the first event in year 3, depends on event 1 in year 2 and event 1 in year 1. The ninth event in year 3, event 2.4.9, depends on event 4 in year 2 and event 2 in year 1.

The probability of an event occurring is the product of the individual event probabilities. The probability of event 1.0.0 is 0.25; the probability of event 1.1.0

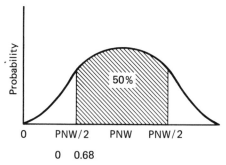

FIGURE 9.3 *Subjective estimate of mean and standard deviation of proposed investment.*

TABLE 9.4   Investment with Conditional Cash Flows

Year 1			Year 2			Year 3		
Event No.	Prob- ability	Cash flow ($)	Event No.	Prob- ability	Cash flow ($)	Event No.	Prob- ability	Cash flow ($)
1.0.0	0.25	2,000	1.1.0	0.33	−2,000	1.1.1	0.25	−5,000
						1.1.2	0.75	−2,000
			1.2.0	0.67	1,000	1.2.3	0.50	1,000
						1.2.4	0.50	2,000
2.0.0	0.75	10,000	2.3.0	0.50	10,000	2.3.5	0.50	10,000
						2.3.6	0.50	12,000
			2.4.0	0.35	15,000	2.4.7	0.33	12,000
						2.4.8	0.33	15,000
						2.4.9	0.33	17,000
			2.5.0	0.15	20,000	2.5.10	0.75	20,000
						2.5.11	0.25	25,000

is 0.0825 (0.25 × 0.33); and the probability of event 1.1.1 is 0.020625 (0.25 × 0.33 × 0.25). These are joint probabilities and the probability of any one series of conditional events may be more formally stated as

$$PJ_i = \pi_t P_{ti} \qquad (9.1)$$

where

PJ_i = the joint probability of event i occurring
P_{ti} = the probability of event i occurring in time period t where event i consists of two or more conditional events occurring in different time periods

The expected value for this series of conditional probabilities is the product of the total cash flows for any event multiplied by the joint probability of that event occurring and summed over all the events. The total undiscounted cash flow for event 1.1.1 is −$5000 ($2000 − $2000 − $5000). The probability of the event's occurring is 0.020625 (0.25 × 0.33 × 0.25) and the product is −$103.13 (Table 9.5). The product of the other cash flows is similarly calculated and their sum is the expected value of the investment. In this example the present value is

TABLE 9.5   Expected Value and Standard Deviation of Investment with Conditional Cash Flows

Event (*i*)	Total cash flow $(\Sigma_i CF_{ti})$	Joint probability $(\pi_t P_{ti})$	Expected value (Columns 2 × 3)	Weighted squared deviations $[\Sigma_i CF_{ti} - E(V)]^2 PJ_i$
1.1.1	− $5,000	0.020625	− $103.13	$22,911,919
1.1.2	− 2,000	0.061875	− 123.75	56,918,913
1.2.3	4,000	0.083750	335.00	49,575,231
1.2.4	5,000	0.083750	418.75	45,583,726
2.3.5	30,000	0.187500	5,625.00	522,994
2.3.6	32,000	0.187500	6,000.00	2,525,584
2.4.7	37,000	0.087500	3,237.46	6,577,461
2.4.8	40,000	0.087500	3,499.96	11,916,774
2.4.9	42,000	0.087500	3,674.96	16,351,316
2.5.10	50,000	0.084375	4,218.75	39,622,002
2.5.11	55,000	0.028125	1,546.88	20,005,180
Sum		0.999997	28,329.80	$272,511,100

$$E(V) = \sum_i \left[\sum_t CF_{ti} \times PJ_i \right] = \$28,329.88$$

$$\sigma = \sqrt{\Sigma_i \left[\sum_t CF_{ti} - E(V) \right]^2 PJ_i} = \sqrt{\$272,511.100} = \$16,508$$

$28,329.88. These calculations may be more formally expressed as

$$E(V) = \sum_i \left[\sum_t CF_{ti} \times PJ_i \right] \qquad (9.2)$$

where

$E(V)$ = the expected value of the conditional cash flows
CF_{ti} = the cash flow for the *i*th event in time period *t*
PJ_i = the joint probability of event *i* occurring

The standard deviation can be calculated using the formula

$$\sigma = \sqrt{\Sigma_i \left[\sum_t CF_{ti} - E(V) \right]^2 PJ_i} \qquad (9.3)$$

The last column in Table 9.5 contains the squared deviations ($[\Sigma_t CF_{ti} - E(V)]^2$) multiplied by the joint probabilities (PJ_i). For example, the value for event 1.1.1 is $22,911,919 ($[\$5000 - \$28,329.88]^2 \times 0.020625$). The sum of the last column, $272,510,700, is the variance and its square root, $16,508, is the standard deviation of the expected value of the cash flows. The expected value, $28,330, and its standard deviation, $16,508, can then be compared to other potential investments. The expected value is a measure of profitability and the standard deviation is a measure of risk. Alternatively, the probability distribution can be plotted by using the joint probabilities (Table 9.5, column 3) and total cash flows (Table 9.5, column 2). In practice, the total cash flows would be discounted values rather than simply the sum of the annual cash flows.

The conditional probability procedure presented above applies to those cases where there are varying degrees of correlation between events occurring in different time periods. These events will occur regardless of the decision maker's actions. A procedure has been developed by Hillier (1963) for those cases where cash flows are either perfectly correlated or completely independent. The Hillier technique calculates the expected value using the usual formulas. That is, point estimates are made of the cash flows in each year and their present net worths are obtained. The major difference is that cash flows in each year are categorized by whether they are completely independent of the preceding year's cash flows or whether they are perfectly correlated with the preceding year's cash flows. Hillier presents a formula for calculating the standard deviation of the probability distribution around the expected value. The formula may be obtained from Hillier (1963) or Van Horne (1977). Further discussion of this technique is not presented because it appears to have limited applicability to forestry investment decisions.

Decision Trees

Decision trees deal with sequential decisions where the outcomes depend on the preceding decision. However, the technique has no requirement of complete independence or perfect correlation as does that of Hillier. Rather, it allows for several different events after each decision. Decision trees have been present in forest investment literature for some time. An early presentation was made by Bentley and Kaiser (1967), while a more recent presentation was made by Talerico, Newton, and Valentine (1978).

A decision tree is composed of a series of chance events, usually represented by circles, and a series of decision points, usually represented by boxes. The probabilities of each chance event occurring and the associated cash flow are estimated. The expected value of the present net worth for each decision point is then calculated. The decision rule is to follow the decision path with the highest expected value.

For example, suppose a company was opening a new pulpwood procurement area and wanted to decide between building one woodyard or several. The

TABLE 9.6   Projected Wood Flow

Woodyards constructed	Supply level	YEAR (thousands of cords) 1	2	3	4 – 10	Present net worth,[a] (thousands of $)
One	High	20	20	20	20	464.5
	Low	5	5	8	10	106.3
Two	High	30	30	30	30	621.7
	Low	10	10	16	20	207.2
Three	High – High	45	45	45	45	946.2
	High – Low	35	35	38	40	741.7
	Low – High	20	20	32	35	497.5
	Low – Low	15	15	20	25	226.2

[a]Cash flow discounted at 0.10. For example, three woodyards: High – High cash flow = (2 yards × − $150) + (1 yard × − $150 × 0.90909) + (45 × $5.00 × 6.14457) = $946.20.

company would build either one or two yards currently (time period zero, decision 1) and then decide after 1 year whether to build a third (time period 1, decision 2) if it had previously built two yards. Pulpwood will be supplied in the new area at either a high or low level. Further suppose that the supply quantities could be predicted (Table 9.6) that woodyards cost $150,000 each to build, that the net contribution per cord of new pulpwood is $5, that the company's objective is to maximize this net contribution, and that the discount rate is 10 percent. A decision tree may be formed (Figure 9.4) showing these relationships and the probabilities of either high- or low-level supply. The probabilities may be either empirically or subjectively estimated. The decision tree indicates that three woodyards should be constructed because that gives the highest expected value ($664,500).

Calculating the decision tree requires working from right to left across the tree. The first step is calculating the PNW. This is simply the annual wood flow multiplied by the value per cord minus the woodyard construction costs, all discounted at 10 percent. For example, the PNW for one woodyard with the high supply level is

$$\text{PNW} = (20,000 \text{ cords} \times \$5.00/\text{cord} \times 6.14457) - \$150,000 = \$464,457$$

These PNWs are entered in the decision tree at the end of the chain of decisions which generated them. These values are shown in the right column in both Table 9.6 and Figure 9.4. The expected values at each decision point, indicated by a box in Figure 9.4, are calculated next. These are simply the product of the PNWs and the probability of their occurrence. For example, the

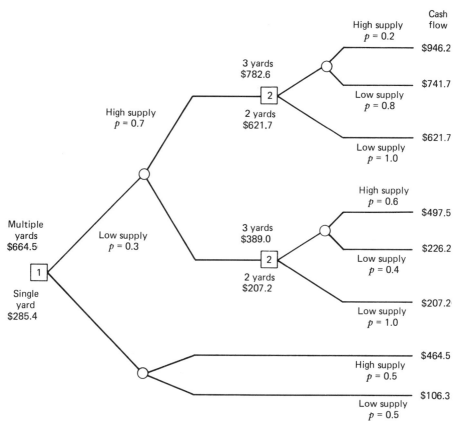

FIGURE 9.4 *Decision tree for single versus multiple woodyards.*

expected value of the high level supply–three woodyard event is

$$(0.2 \times \$946.2) + (0.8 \times \$741.7) = \$782.6$$

Examining these expected values identifies which decision to follow. In both high and low supply the three woodyard alternative is highest ($782.6 > $621.7 and $389.0 > $207.2). Thus, the decision at box 2 is to build three woodyards regardless of whether supply is high or low *if* the multiple woodyard alternative is chosen.* But is that alternative better than building just one yard? The decision is made by choosing the alternative that has the highest expected value for all

---

*The data might have indicated two yards were better than three for the high supply and that three yards were better than two for the low supply.

events. In our example,

$$E(V) \text{ multiple yards} = (0.7 \times \$782.60) + (0.3 \times \$389.00) = \$664.5$$
$$E(V) \text{ single yard} = (0.5 \times \$464.5) + (0.5 \times \$106.3) = \$285.4$$

The decision at box 1, then, is still to build multiple woodyards. The decision would have been to build one woodyard if $E(V)$ single yard had been higher than $E(V)$ multiple yards.

Abandonment Value

Abandonment value examines the riskiness of an investment by including an assessment of the investment's value if it was abandoned and sold during the projected investment life. The basic idea is that investments that can be sold during their life are less risky than those that cannot be sold. Similarly, those that can be sold for a higher price are less risky than those that can be sold for a lower price, all other things equal.

For example, suppose an integrated lumber company could invest in a sawmill located in a small rural town or in a warehouse in a large city. The warehouse would probably be the less risky investment, if we assume that the expected value and variance were equal for both investments, because a warehouse in a big city could be used by many industries, not only the forest products industry. This means the likely resale value of the warehouse would be high if the investment was unsuccessful and the firm sold it before the end of the projected investment. Conversely, an unsuccessful sawmill in a small town can only be used for sawing timber. An unsuccessful sawmill, or even a successful one, is likely to have fewer buyers, hence a lower resale or abandonment value.

These ideas are formalized in an analysis using the expected value–variance criteria. The traditional analysis examines an investment's expected value and variance without considering possible early liquidation. Abandonment value analysis includes the investment's value if it is sold. More specifically, the cash flows in future years are compared to the abandonment value in that year. The investment is abandoned any time the expected value of the cash flow is less than the abandonment value. The investment's abandonment value is then substituted for the cash flow.

For example, consider the cash flows in Table 9.4. The expected values of the undiscounted cash flows at the end of year 1 are $-\$3410$ ($0.33 \times - \$2000 + 0.25 \times - \$5000 + 0.75 \times - \$2000$), \$2170, \$16,000, \$19,770, and \$24,250 for events 1.1.0, 1.2.0, 2.3.0, 2.4.0, and 2.5.0, respectively. Thus, the expected values of the cash flows at the start of year 2 are $-\$1240$ if event 1.0.0 occurred in the first year ($-\$3410 + \$2170$) and \$60,020 if event 2.0.0 occurred in the first year.

Suppose the project had an abandonment value of \$15,000 at the end of year 1. The manager would then abandon the project if event 1.0.0 occurred in the first year because the investment could be sold for \$15,000, whereas \$1240 would be

TABLE 9.7   Expected Value and Standard Deviation of Investment with Conditional Cash Flows and an Abandonment Value

Event no. (i)	Total cash flow	Joint probability	Expected value	Weighted squared deviations
1.0.0	$17,000	0.25000	$4,250.00	$56,649,181
2.3.5	30,000	0.18750	5,625.00	790,377
2.3.6	32,000	0.18750	6,000.00	529
2.4.7	37,000	0.08750	3,237.50	2,141,258
2.4.8	40,000	0.08750	3,500.00	5,525,865
2.4.9	42,000	0.08750	3,675.00	8,657,270
2.5.10	50,000	0.084375	4,218.75	27,176,356
2.5.11	55,000	0.028125	1,546.88	14,809,467
Sum		1.000000	$32,053.13	$110,750,303

$$E(V) = \sum_i \left[\sum_t CF_{ti} - PJ_i \right] = \$32,053.13$$

$$\sigma = \sqrt{\Sigma_i \left[\sum_t CF_{ti} - E(V) \right]^2 PJ_i} = \sqrt{\$110,750,303} = \$10,524$$

lost if it were kept. However, the project would be continued if event 2.0.0 occurred in the first year because the expected value following that event is $60,020, which is greater than the $15,000 abandonment value. Thus, the project is abandoned in the first case because the expected value of future cash flows is less than the abandonment value but retained in the second case because the expected value of the future cash flows is greater than the abandonment value.

The new cash flows, when abandonment value is considered, are shown in Table 9.7. They are the same as in Table 9.5 except the cash flows for event 1.0.0 are replaced with $17,000. This is because the cash flows in years 2 and 3 are replaced by the abandonment value if a $2000 cash flow occurs in the first year. The expected value and its standard deviation for this case are $32,053 and $10,524, respectively.

Comparing these new values to the nonabandonment values of $28,330 and $16,508 shows that the investment is now both more profitable and less risky. Profitability increases because the lower, and in this case negative, cash flows are replaced with the abandonment value. Risk decreases because the variability from three cash flows has been replaced with one cash flow and because the value of that cash flow is nearer the expected value. In general, one would expect that the addition of abandonment value to a cash flow would increase its predicated profitability and decrease its risk. This is a simplified case because abandonment values in year 3, and additional future years if they occur, were not considered. Furthermore, the cash flows were undiscounted to help students duplicate the calculations. In practice all of the cash flows would have been discounted. Abandonment value has been used to examine a proposed new investment. However, it can be used regularly to examine the wisdom of continuing existing investments. This might be particularly true if an investment is becoming more costly or less profitable than expected. There is an obvious limit to the continual reexamination of past investments. This could soon become a preoccupation and divert needed resources from operations.

The CAPM Techniques

The Capital Asset Pricing Model (CAPM) appears frequently in current literature, although its actual use is probably much less frequent. This frequency makes CAPM important enough that the student should at least be acquainted with it.

CAPM was developed and applied to portfolio analysis in securities investments. It allowed assessing whether an individual firm's security, say its common stock, was more or less risky than the securities market as a whole. The application to project analysis requires the view that a firm wants its stock's market price to rise. Investors bidding on the stock in the market determine the stock's price. The amount they are willing to bid reflects the past rate of return and that which they expect in the future. The rate of return can be thought of as the IRR for a single time period.

The rate of return the market expects for the individual firm is considered the risk-free interest rate plus the amount the market requires for the systematic risk that the individual firm bears in relation to the entire market. Systematic risk may, as a first approximation, be defined as risk that cannot be diversified away by either a firm or an investor. This return expected by the market, R_e, is determined empirically and then used as the discount rate, or alternative rate of return, for the IRR and PNW criteria discussed in Chapter 4. The IRR and PNW are calculated for a proposed project or investment. Any proposal exceeding R_e is adopted, if we assume unlimited capital, because the firm will then have its actual return higher than expected by the market. This higher return will then become the expected return and investors will bid more for the firm's stock. Thus, the assumed objective of the firm, increasing its market value per share, is obtained.

These ideas can be expressed more precisely using the formula

$$R_e = R_f + B_i \left(R_r - R_f \right) \tag{9.4}$$

where

R_e = the return expected for the firm in the market
R_f = the risk-free return, that is, the risk-free interest rate
R_r = the return for a portfolio of risky assets traded in the market
B_i = the "beta" for the ith firm

R_e, R_f, and R_r are estimated for several time periods—for example, for 36 or 60 quarters. R_e is the return in each time period for the firm being analyzed. R_f may be estimated by the mean interest rate on short-term government bonds because these are considered risk-free. R_r may be estimated by observing the returns from a group of stocks regularly traded on a major stock exchange, such as the New York Stock Exchange, or perhaps by the returns on stocks in one of the regularly published indices, such as the Dow Jones or Standard and Poor's. The return in all cases is the change in the security price during the period plus any dividends divided by the final security price.

The beta can then be estimated by ordinary least squares regression. In this case, beta is simply the coefficient of the independent variable $R_r - R_f$. Large brokerage firms often will provide beta values for firms whose stocks are regularly traded on the major stock exchanges. Thus, the interested analyst may not even have to calculate the beta value. The beta reflects that firm's systematic risk. A beta equal to 1.0 means the firm is just as risky as the whole market, a value less than 1.0 means it is less risky, and a value greater than 1.0 means it is more risky. This is the systematic risk that empirically moves with the market. Hence, it cannot be removed by diversification.

The beta for an individual firm can be used for projects that are more or less the same as the firm's historical means of production. However, sometimes a firm will diversify and branch into a new line of business, for example, a paper manufacturer deciding to open its first sawmill. Some authorities suggest substituting the beta for a firm already established in the new field to reflect the market's estimate of the riskiness of that line of endeavor.

The CAPM procedure has several practical and theoretical difficulties, not the least of which are the severe assumptions needed to apply the model in its purest form. The student or practitioner interested in applying CAPM should research in greater depth these problems and restrictions before any analysis is made.

DECISION MAKING WITH CERTAINTY

Thus far we have discussed decision making with uncertainty and decision making with risk. The third and final case is decision making with certainty. This case is as unlikely as decision making under the strict definition of uncertainty. Certainty requires that the outcome of each alternative is known. Thus, there is in effect only one state of nature in terms of the decision matrix in Table 9.1. That is the state in which all outcomes are perfectly known. The decision maker can then choose the alternative that best matches his objectives, for example, minimum cost or maximum profit.

Decision making with certainty is probably the most widely used model, or assumption, despite its unrealism. All cash flow projections that have only a single point estimate or yield projections using results from a single table or equation are implicitly using the certainty model. Here, the point estimate and the year in which it occurs are analyzed as if they undoubtedly will occur. Decisions are then made on the basis of these analyses.

The widespread use of the certainty model is probably because it is the easiest assumption to make, the easiest to implement, and the easiest to understand. The model reduces the number of analyses that need to be made and the amount of data required for them. The model may be the most logical one available for use, given the level of data or the analyst's sophistication. However, the decision maker should remember that these decisions are almost always being made in a risky world.

TRADITIONAL
FOREST REGULATION

II
PART

INTRODUCTION TO FOREST REGULATION

10

FOREST REGULATION DETERMINES the what, where, and when of timber harvesting on the managed forest. The regulation decisions indicate what species and how much of them should be cut. They also, in many cases, indicate where on the ground the cutting should take place. Certain specific stands may be designated for cutting in the plan. Alternatively, only the volume and species may be designated and the forest manager must then locate stands in the forest that have the indicated characteristics and designate them for harvest. Finally the when of harvesting is shown in cutting schedules. The heart of any forest regulation plan is to indicate the time period, most commonly the 5-year period, in which the timber should be cut.

Forest regulation decisions are far-reaching and ubiquitous. They determine both the timber and nontimber products obtained from the forest. Obviously, the age at which trees are cut will affect the timber products obtained. The size of harvests, their placement, and the configuration of the cut also can be used to manipulate forest production. For example, several small clearcuts will often produce more game than one large clearcut because of the increased edge effect. Cut configuration greatly affects the aesthetic values obtained from the forest. And road placement, determined in part by which stands are cut, not only affects aesthetic values but also accessibility for hunters, fishermen, and other recreationists.

It almost goes without saying that regulation decisions are long-term decisions. The area cut today takes decades before it is ready to cut again. Different products will come from a stand at different stages of its life; hence, the timing of the cut also determines the sequencing of this product flow. Furthermore, planning the cut decades in the future often requires projecting costs, revenues, and yields for the same time period. All of these interrelated influences must be considered simultaneously when making regulation decisions and are part of the regulation job.

A *regulated forest* is one that yields an annual or periodic crop of about equal volume, size, and quality. This definition implicitly refers to timber but is general enough to cover all forest products if "crop" is defined to include wildlife, recreation, aesthetic values, and other forest products. Thus, forest regulation consists of manipulating forest lands and growing stock to best achieve the forest owner's yield objectives.

Note that the crop may be less than "maximum." The necessary condition for a regulated forest is the periodic yield, not the quantity or degree of site utilization. Thus, maximum timber yield may be given up to increase wildlife production. Note also that both the kind of crop and the desired volume, size, or quality are defined by the owner to coincide with his or her objectives.

Regulating a forest is often a main forest management objective. The regulated forest is desired to obtain a sustained yield of forest crops. However, depending on the current forest condition, sustained yield may not occur for many years. Further, regulating a forest may cause opportunity costs in other management objectives, such as even current wood flow, maximizing PNW, or maintaining scenic vistas. Thus, as will be seen, a forest may not be regulated as rapidly or as completely as is possible.

THE NORMAL FOREST

The normal forest is a conceptual model for forest regulation that was developed in Germany and France during the early period of forest management. The model is predicated on cutting fairly small, uniform blocks of even-aged timber. The management objective was maximum timber production.

The normal forest is defined as one having (1) normal increment, (2) normal age class distribution, and (3) normal growing stock levels. Normal increment was generally considered to be the maximum attainable for a particular species and site. Thus, something more than mere regulation was required. Normal age class distribution occurred when the forest had a series of stands of equal productivity (but not necessarily size) varying in age by equal intervals from the youngest age class to the oldest. The oldest age class was equal to the rotation age. This age distribution caused the periodic even timber harvest. Normal growing stock was automatically obtained when there was normal increment and age class distribution.

The normal forest and its management can be demonstrated by assuming a 25-acre forest on a 25-year rotation with 25 stands, each 1 year older than the next. The site is equal on all stands. Each stand is cut on January 1 of its 25th year and instantaneously regenerated. Figure 10.1 is a map of this forest, over time. Figures 10.1*a*, *b*, *c*, and *d* represent the forest on December 31, 1975, 1976, 1977, and 1999, respectively.

Each cell is a 1-acre stand and is identified by its coordinates. The column coordinates are numbered 1 through 5 and the row coordinates are lettered A

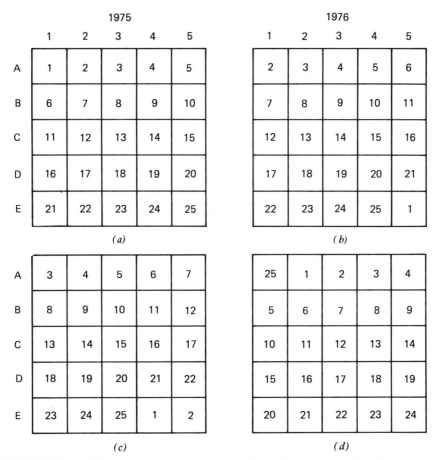

FIGURE 10.1 *Map of a normal forest over time. Numbers in cells are stand age.*

through E. A1 identifies the stand in the northwest corner, A5 identifies the stand in the northeast corner, and so on. The numbers in each cell are the age of the stand on December 31 of the indicated year. For example, stand A1 is 1 year old in 1975 (Figure 10.1*a*), 2 years old in 1976 (Figure 10.1*b*), 3 years old in 1977 (Figure 10.1*c*), and 25 years old in 1999 (Figure 10.1*d*).

The sequence starts in 1975. A normal age class distribution exists because there are 25 stands, each varying in age by an equal interval, the oldest being equal to the rotation age. Their productivity is equal because the site and stocking are equal on each stand.

On January 1, 1976, stand E5 is cut, because it has reached rotation age, and is instantaneously regenerated to normal stocking. Figure 10.1*b* shows the forest on December 31, 1976 when stand E5 is now 1 year old because it has grown for the entire year of 1976. All stands are now 1 year older, so stand A1 is now 2 years old, stand A2 is now 3 years old, and so on. Stand E4 is now 25 years old and will be the next stand harvested. This is shown in Figure 10.1c, where it is now December 31, 1977 and stand E4, which was cut and regenerated on the first day of 1977, is now 1 year old. Stand E3 is the next stand to be cut.

Figure 10.1d shows the forest 24 years after Figure 10.1a. Stand A1 is now the oldest stand and will be cut "tomorrow," on January 1, 2000. The map of 2000 will be the same as that for 1975 (Figure 10.1a). This harvesting sequence continues in perpetuity. The oldest stand is cut each year and regenerated. The flow of wood from the forest is constant and equal because each stand is the same or equally productive.

A normal forest and a regulated forest are not the same thing. The difference is that *all* normal forests are regulated but *not all* regulated forests are normal. Stated differently, a normal forest is a sufficient condition for regulation but it is not a necessary condition. A forest may be regulated but not normal. A normal forest is a maximum concept (maximum increment) and deals with an even-aged forest. A regulated forest may be even or uneven aged and need not produce maximum increment. Thus, a normal forest is a special case of a regulated forest.

The normal forest does not exist anywhere with all its conditions fulfilled because of the diversity in nature. For example, some genetic variation in growing stock would be expected as would variation in site. This could, of course, be rectified by variable-sized stands if the variations were known and the differential yields caused by them could be predicted. A more practical reason for normal forests not existing is that most forests are changing in size over time. New tracts of land are added and old ones are sold. Each one of these changes must be incorporated into the management plans. Finally, normal stocking is difficult to define on a working basis; witness all the spacing and thinning studies both in the past and in the present.

However, the concept of a normal forest still has great value. It is the normative model for even-aged management plans and embodies management principles that foresters currently strive to affect. The idea of a constant yearly wood flow, or a constant flow in small yearly multiples, is basic to all management plans. The idea of maximizing growth (increment) on forest stands is the first approximation of a management objective used in many management models.

Normal stocking, which comes from the normal increment concept, is currently of concern. Foresters are still defining a "fully" stocked stand and discussing the appropriate levels of stocking, usually in terms of basal area per acre. Finally, the concept of a normal age class distribution has been a guiding model for past even-aged management practices. Age class acreage has been manipulated to obtain an even wood flow and many land purchases have been made to "fill in" gaps in age class structure.

The normal forest model is only today being modified by mathematical programming techniques that select stands for harvest on other bases. These techniques will be discussed in a later chapter. However, the normal forest is still important because it provides a theoretical base and because many forests are currently managed using this model.

Implications for Management Practices

The age class distribution and the volume of the preceding example can be represented graphically (Figures 10.2*a* and 10.2*b*). The *x* axes are "acres or age" because the model presented above has only 1 acre in each age class. The cumulative age class distribution is a straight line indicating equal numbers of acres in each age class (Figure 10.2*a*). Here it is seen that 5 acres (*x* axis) are 5 years of age and younger (*y* axis), 10 acres (*x* axis) are 10 years and younger (*y* axis), until all acres are 25 years of age or younger.

This straight line cumulative age distribution becomes a management tool for the forest manager. The straight line is the normative model toward which the manager would like to bring his forest because that will provide the normal age class distribution and, if we assume equal productivity per acre, the constant equal timber flow.

The volume per acre is shown in cords although any unit of measurement can be used (Figure 10.2*b*). Volume is shown on the *y* axis and "acres or age" on the *x* axis. Acres or age can be used because the model has only one acre in each age class.

There is no volume in the first 10 years because it is not yet measurable in cords. The total volume on the forest is the area under the curve or, with calculus,

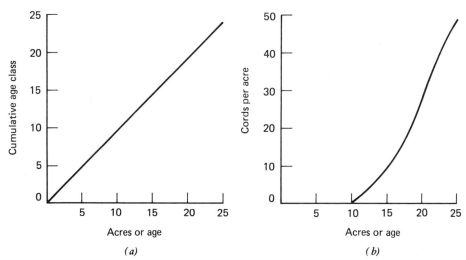

FIGURE 10.2 *Cumulative age class distribution and volume per acre for a normal forest.*

the integral of the function from 10 to 25 years. This volume is sometimes called the growing stock. However, growing stock can include some or all of the trees in the age classes that were below the merchantability limits, those less than 10 years old in Figure 10.2b. Thus, one should always ascertain the definition and diameter limits for "growing stock" volumes.

The curve indicates there will be a periodic (in this case annual) flow of timber of about the same volume (50 cords) if all the conditions hold. And if site and genetic strains of planting stock are equal, it will be about the same size and quality. This is perhaps the classic representation of the regulated forest, 25 acres, each exactly like the other except each is 1 year younger than the preceding. Each year 1 acre is cut and the following year the next youngest group takes its place while the acre cut has a new stand established.

YIELD TABLES AND THE NORMAL FOREST

Growth and yield functions, and the yield tables derived from them, are appropriately studied in mensuration or biometrics classes. However, they are extremely important in forest management because they provide the timber production data on which many management analyses are based. They are discussed here only as they relate to management analyses.

Many yield tables represent a normal forest. Early yield tables assumed "normal" or near maximum stocking and hence were called "normal yield tables." They were also for naturally regenerated stands. These tables are of limited usefulness because most stands do not have "normal" stocking, but rather something less, and because many stands in the United States today are artifically regenerated plantations. In addition, these tables had a tendency to show too dense a stocking in the earlier age classes, resulting in attempts to maintain too much growing stock and reduced yields. Therefore, they really were not "normal." All of these factors made it difficult for a forester to match conditions on his stand, thereby limiting the usefulness of normal yield tables.

Empirical yield tables include stocking as a variable and many have been made for plantations. These are an improvement but in many cases only "normal" yield tables are available and sometimes there are no yield tables that fit the forest being managed.

Yield tables are a necessary forest management tool. They are used for predicting yields, as a standard for stocking, and as a measure of site quality. Yield predictions are used in analyses such as the financial analysis of proposed programs for stands under management or the analysis of proposed purchases. Use as a standard to judge if a stand is under- or overstocked requires comparing stocking on the ground to that producing maximum yield in the yield table. Making this comparison then provides guides for other management decisions. A rough idea of site quality is obtained by comparing your timber volumes to that in the yield table if the stocking is comparable.

RULES OF THUMB FOR ESTIMATING GROWING STOCK AND YIELD

A forest manager often needs to known the growing stock volume and his expected yield from that growing stock, as just discussed. Yield tables and rules of thumb may be used to obtain "quick and dirty" estimates. These are not final or extremely accurate answers; however, information costs money, and sometimes the benefits of more precise information are not worth the cost. In other cases the basic data may be unavailable for a more precise estimate.

Graphical Representation of a Yield Table

A yield table for Douglas-fir with a 180-site index is plotted (Table 10.1 and Figure 10.3) to help explain the rules of thumb. Figure 10.3 shows the volume per acre on each acre along the x-axis if there is 1 acre per age class.

A yield table for Douglas-fir on site index 180 is reproduced in Table 10.1. This same yield table is plotted as a curve in Figure 10.3. Note that the "acres or age" variables have been retained on the x axis, indicating that a normal age distribution is assumed. This means that the curve will show the volume per acre on each acre along the x axis if there is 1 acre per age class.

For example, the 20th acre, which is 20 years old, contains 1100 cubic ft of wood and the 60th acre, which is 60 years old, contains 11,600 cubic ft. The 19th acre shows zero volume, not because there are no trees but because the trees are below the merchantability limits of the table. Figure 10.3 is the same as Figure 10.2b except that it is for Douglas-fir instead of Loblolly pine and the unit of measurement is cubic feet instead of cords.

TABLE 10.1   Douglas-Fir Yield Table for Site 180

Age	Cubic foot volume	Age	Cubic foot volume	Age	Cubic foot volume
20	1,100	70	13,500	120	19,700
30	3,600	80	15,200	130	20,400
40	6,750	90	16,650	140	21,050
50	9,300	100	17,900	150	21,600
60	11,600	110	18,800	160	22,150

Source: McArdle *et al.* (1961).

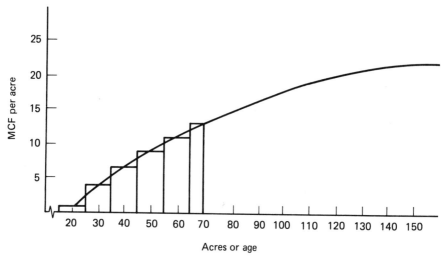

FIGURE 10.3 *Graph of Douglas-fir yield table.*

The equality of acres and age on the x axis, discussed above, can be applied to yield tables to estimate growing stock volume and yield on a forest if that forest approximates "normal forest" conditions.

Estimating Growing Stock Volume — The Summation Formula

Growing stock volume can be estimated using a yield table. The values in the table cannot be directly used because the volume on the acres whose ages are not contained in the table would be omitted. For example, the 21- through 29-year-old acres would be omitted, the 31 through 39 would be omitted, and so forth.

The formula for the yield table or curve could be integrated if it were known and the user remembered the necessary calculus; however, neither may be the case. Another alternative is to carefully draw the curve for the yield table (Figure 10.3) on cross-section paper and then estimate the area under the curve by planimetering, counting squares, or some other method. However, this is time-consuming and sometimes inaccurate.

The summation formula approximates integration using discrete instead of continuous values. The formula is

$$G_r = n\left(V_n + V_{2n} + V_{3n} + \cdots V_{r-n} + \frac{V_r}{2}\right) \tag{10.1}$$

where

r = the rotation age
n = the number of years between yield table entries
G_r = total volume of growing stock on r "acres or years"
V_n = yield table volume per acre at age n, $2n$, and so forth

For example, suppose the Douglas-fir stand was on a 70-year rotation and the yield table in Table 10.1 was the most applicable. Then, $r = 70$, $n = 10$, and

$$G_{70} = 10(1,100 + 3,600 + 6,700 + 9,300 + 11,600 + 13,500/2)$$
$$= 390,500 \text{ cubic feet growing stock on 70 acres}$$

and

390,500/70 acres $= 5,579$ cubic feet per acre average

This figure can then be multiplied by the number of acres in the forest to estimate total growing stock.

The summation equation contains the implicit assumption that the volume in the yield table is the midpoint of the age distribution and that the acres in that age class, on the average, contain the midpoint volume. This implicit assumption is shown by the rectangles in Figure 10.3. The product of the acre or age interval, n, and the volume at the midpoint, V_n, is the area of the rectangle. For example, $10 \times 3600 = 36,000$ cubic feet for the 10 acres centering around age 30.

The volume of the last midpoint, V_r, is divided by 2 in Eq. 10.1 to adjust for the rotation age ending on the midpoint, not to adjust the volume. Stated differently, n is really divided by 2, not V_r. The equation is written with $V_r/2$ as a matter of notational convenience.

There are a few other assumptions that should be made explicit. The acres below the first acre/age category in the yield table are assumed to have zero growing stock volume. In our example, those acres below the 15-year mark are assigned zero volume. However, the mean volume per acre is calculated by dividing by the full rotation age of 70 acres/year. The mean is therefore biased low for those acres containing measurable volume.

Another implicit assumption stems from the estimated growing stock being predicted in terms of the acres or age on the x axis of Figure 10.3. The total and mean estimates are therefore only applicable to forests with age distributions approximating the normal. The further the age distribution is from normal, the less accurate the estimated growing stock will be.

Finally, the yield table is for a fully stocked or normally stocked stand. Therefore, the forest to which it is applied must be fully stocked. Methods to adjust for understocked stands are discussed below.

Estimating Yield — The Yield Table

The forest's annual yield can be estimated directly from the yield table under the special assumptions of the normal forest. The volume per acre is read from the yield table and simply multiplied by the number of acres in the age class.

For example, the yield is 13,500 cubic feet an acre at a 70-year rotation. Total yield would be 135,000 cubic feet a year if there were 10 acres in each age class.

Estimating Yield for "Abnormal" Stocking — Hundeshagen's Formula

Heretofore the forest stands were assumed to have normal or full stocking. This is seldom the case in practice, and therefore yield table estimates must be adjusted for understocked stands. This is accomplished by Hundeshagen's Formula:

$$\frac{Y_a}{G_a} = \frac{Y_r}{G_r} \qquad\qquad (10.2)$$

where

Y_a = actual yield
G_a = actual growing stock
Y_r = yield in a fully stocked forest at rotation age
G_r = growing stock in a fully stocked forest at rotation age

For example, suppose a timber cruise showed the growing stock on the above Douglas-fir tract was 292,875 cubic feet instead of that estimated from the yield table and that an estimate of the annual harvest from the stand was desired. Then, using Hundeshagen's Formula, we obtain

$$\frac{Y_a}{292,875} = \frac{13,500}{390,500}$$

$$Y_a = 13,500 \times \frac{292,875}{390,500} = 10,125 \text{ cubic feet per acre}$$

The total annual yield for the forest is estimated by multiplying by the number of acres in each age class as above. For example, total yield would be 101,250 cubic feet if 10 acres were in each age class.

Hundeshagen's Formula is simply a proportion in which the yield is assumed to have a straight line relationship with the growing stock. This is demonstrated in the preceding example where it can be seen that the actual growing stock is three-fourths of the normal; therefore, the actual yield is estimated as three-fourths of the normal.

Using Hundeshagen's Formula requires a few implicit assumptions. The first, mentioned above, is that a straight line relationship exists between growing stock volume and yield. That is, it is assumed that one-half the normal growing stock volume produces one-half the yield, or 10 percent volume produces 10 percent yield. This assumption may not be bad for slightly over- or understocked stands; however, it becomes poorer the farther away from normal stocking the actual stand is. The second assumption is that the forest has a normally distributed age structure.

Estimating Yield — Von Mantel's Formula

Von Mantel's Formula is sometimes called the triangle formula because of its derivation, which is explained below. It is an extention of Hundeshagen's Formula and eliminates the need for a yield table. Thus, it is perhaps the ultimate simplification for yield estimation.

The basic assumption for this formula is that, in a regulated forest, growing stock increases in a straight line with age. Growing stock can then be expressed as a right triangle. The area under the curve is the growing stock volume and can be estimated by calculating the area of the triangle, where area $\Delta = \frac{1}{2} \times$ base $\times$ height

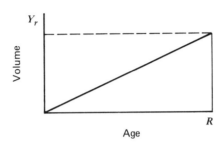

Noting that the base of the triangle is equal to the rotation age, R, and height is equal to the yield at rotation, Y_r, we may rewrite the area formula as

$$G_r = \frac{RY_r}{2}$$

where

      G_r = the volume of growing stock at rotation age
      R = rotation age
      Y_r = the yield at rotation age

This expression is substituted into Hundeshagen's Formula so that

$$Y_a = G_a \times \frac{Y_r}{\dfrac{RY_r}{2}} = G_a \times Y_r \times \frac{2}{RY_r}$$

and canceling Y_r and rearranging the variables, we obtain

$$Y_a = \frac{2G_a}{R} \tag{10.3}$$

Equation 10.3 is known as Von Mantel's Formula, which can be manipulated to solve for any variable, given the other two. The formula allows estimating actual yield by knowing only the rotation age and the actual growing stock. In our example

$$Y_a = \frac{2(292,875)}{70} = 8368 \text{ cubic feet per acre}$$

Note that the estimate using Von Mantel's Formula is lower than the yield table estimate (8368 versus 13,500). One reason for the difference is that measurable volume is assumed to start at age zero, which it doesn't. Graphically, measurable volume actually looks like

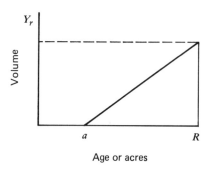

Age or acres

so that

$$G_r = (R - a)\frac{Y_r}{2}$$

and

$$Y_a = \frac{2G_a}{R - a} \tag{10.4}$$

In our example the yield table begins at age 20 but extends by assumption down to the 15th acre so that

$$Y_a = \frac{2(292,875)}{70 - 15} = 10,650 \text{ cubic feet per acre}$$

All the implicit assumptions required for using Hundeshagen's Formula are required for using Von Mantel's Formula. In addition, a straight line relationship between yield and age must also be assumed. Finally, the reader should remember that all these formulas are predicated on the basis of normal forest conditions being present.

Comments on Rules of Thumb

The gross assumptions included in these formulas and the resulting imprecise estimates are readily evident; hence, the student might well question the value of presenting them. The main value of the formulas is their simplicity. They provide a rough estimate from minimum information and it must always be remembered that information costs money.

Another important reason for studying these formulas is that they are still used by some foresters; hence the student should be acquainted with them and their limitations. For example, foresters sometimes estimate annual cut on uneven-aged stands using Von Mantel's Formula. The large potential errors these methods contain should be remembered and decisions tempered accordingly.

REGULATING EVEN-AGED FORESTS

11

THE NORMAL FOREST model has focused attention on the entire forest as the management unit. This is appropriate because the entire forest must be manipulated to acquire management objectives. However, manipulation actually occurs in the stand. The individual stands are cut or not cut or have cultural practices applied or not applied.

Even-aged forests and their management predominate in forestry for two good reasons. First, the most important commercial tree species are generally intolerant and hence are found and best managed in even-aged stands. Second, economies of scale make it less expensive to reproduce and harvest even-aged stands. This, in turn, lowers the supply value (discussed in Chapter 2) of timber and presumably the market price that the consumer must pay for wood products such as paper, lumber, or fuelwood.

There are several terms that should be defined before discussing even-aged management. The *regulatory rotation age* is the number of years between final harvest cuts. This is the number of years that would be used in a cash flow analysis. The *cutting rotation age* is the age of the timber stand when it is cut. This is the number of years that would be used to determine yield from a yield table.

The cutting rotation age may be less than, equal to, or greater than the regulatory rotation age. The cutting rotation age is less than the regulatory age in clearcut management when the harvested area is allowed to lie fallow for 1 or more years before the stand is reestablished. The two ages are equal when the new stand is established immediately after the harvest. The cutting age is greater than the regulatory age when reproduction is established prior to harvest, as in a shelterwood system.

A *stand* is defined as "An aggregation of trees or other growth occupying a specific area and sufficiently uniform in composition (species), age arrangement, and condition as to be distinguishable from the forest or other growth on adjoining areas" (Society of American Foresters, 1958). In practice, many landowners have their own definition for their inventory system. These definitions often depend on the intensity of the owner's management and sometimes on IRS rules for establishing depletion rates. A minimum stand size is often defined. This can be five acres or less or as high as several hundred acres. Stands are also often defined by the volume of wood per acre they contain or some other measure of density. This is important for harvesting decisions.

Area control is a method of determining the annual cut or harvest by specifying the number of acres to be cut each year. These acres are cut and the timber on them is harvested. Area control can be used for both even- and uneven-aged management. The acres to be cut using unmodified area control are

$$\text{Acres cut} = \frac{\text{total acres in forest}}{\text{regulatory rotation age}} \tag{11.1}$$

Application of unmodified area control and clearcutting results in a normal forest at the end of one rotation, if productivity and stocking are the same on all acres in the forest. Unmodified area control requires cutting the same number of acres each year. However, site and stocking on the forest being harvested, or regulated, are seldom equal the first time. Therefore, unmodified area control can cause wide fluctuations in annual volume harvested. This is generally undesirable for the landowner, particularly with mills needing constant raw material supplies.

Volume control is a method of determining the annual cut or harvest by specifying the volume of wood to be cut each year. There are many formulas that can be used to determine volume to cut; for example, Hundeshagen's and Von Mantel's formulas discussed in Chapter 10.

Volume control calculations usually require knowing total growing stock volume and seem better suited to uneven-aged management. The major disadvantage is that unmodified volume control does not specify the location in the forest where the volume should be cut. Actual practice usually combines area and volume control. Cut determination is discussed at greater length in Chapter 14.

EVEN-AGED REGULATION

Forest regulation is, in the final analysis, a tool to achieve management objectives. Therefore, objectives must be specified in order to know how to use the tool. The implicit objectives in most historical regulation schemes were to maximize the volume harvested and to maintain an increasing or, eventually, even wood flow. Maximum wood yield is obtained by choosing the correct rotation age —a topic discussed in Chapter 13. Increasing or even wood flow is obtained by regulating the forest. The normal forest provides maximum yield and even flow once it is attained. Most regulation models and techniques begin with timber regulation. This is subsequently modified for other multiple-use products as discussed in the multiple-use chapter.

A hypothetical 7000-acre Douglas-fir tract, with the age distribution as shown in Table 11.1, is used as an example. Assume that 70 years has been determined as the appropriate rotation age, that cutting and regulatory rotation age are the same, and that the yields at harvest are as shown in Table 10.1.

One hundred acres would be desired in each age from 1 through 70 years if all the conditions of the normal forest discussed in Chapter 10 held. Stated differently, we would like a map of the 7000 acres to resemble the maps in Figure 10.1 or a cumulative age class distribution to look like Figure 10.2a.

One way of analyzing the actual age class distribution to see if it looks this way is to calculate and manipulate proportionate acres. A *proportionate acre* is an acre stated in proportion to the rotation age. The sum of all proportionate acres in all of the age classes equals the rotation age. The "acres or age" on the x axis of Figures 10.2 and 10.3 are, in effect, proportionate acres. That is, they could be proportionate acres if the forests were greater than 25 and 70 acres, respectively.

Proportionate acres are calculated using a simple proportion:

$$\frac{PA_i}{A_i} = \frac{R}{\sum_i A_i}$$

$$PA_i = A_i \times \frac{R}{\sum_i A_i} \qquad (11.2)$$

TABLE 11.1 Age Distribution for Hypothetical Douglas-Fir Forest

Age class (years)	Acres	Proportionate acres	
		Total	One Year Class
1 – 10	750	7.5	0.75
11 – 20	250	2.5	0.25
21 – 30	250	2.5	0.25
31 – 40	750	7.5	0.75
41 – 50	1,250	12.5	1.25
51 – 60	0	0	0
61 – 70	1,250	12.5	1.25
71 +	2,500	25.0	2.50
Total	7,000	70.0	

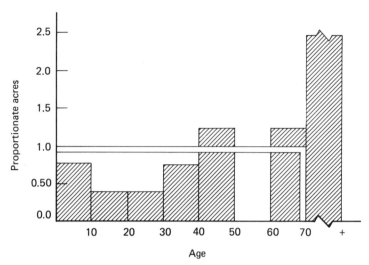

FIGURE 11.1 *Frequency distribution of age classes in proportionate acres.*

where

PA_i = proportionate acres in the ith multiple year age class
A_i = actual acres in the ith multiple year age class
R = rotation age

For example, the total actual acres in the hypothetical forest (Table 11.1) is 7000 acres and the rotation age is 70 years; therefore, the ratio $R/\Sigma_i A_i$ is

$$\frac{R}{\sum\limits_{i} A_i} = \frac{70}{7,000} = 0.01$$

The proportionate acres (Table 11.1, column 3) are obtained by multiplying the actual acres in the age class (Table 11.1, column 2) by the ratio. For example, in the 1–10 age class

750 actual age class acres $\times$ 0.01 = 7.5 proportionate acres

The concept of the normal age distribution may be presented graphically using a frequency distribution of the proportionate acres. One proportionate acre is desired in each yearly age class, as is seen in the map in Figure 10.1. This is a straight line at the 1.0 proportionate acre mark that extends to the oldest desired age, 70 years, and then down to the x axis (double line, Figure 11.1). The rectangle formed by this double line and the x and y axes indicates that 1 proportionate acre is desired in each age from 1 to 70 years. This is needed to perfectly regulate the forest, if we assume equal site and normal stocking.

The distribution of proportionate acres currently found on the forest can be plotted by first calculating the number of proportionate acres in each 1-year age class. This is done by dividing the proportionate acres in the actual age class (Table 11.1, column 3) by the number of years in the actual age class (10 years in our example) to obtain the proportionate acres in 1-year age classes.

The number of proportionate acres in the 1-year age class can then be plotted on the same frequency distribution. For example, the 1- to 10-year age class has 0.75 acres in each 1-year class; the 11–20 year age class has 0.25 acres each year; and so forth (Figure 11.1). The current distribution is cross-hatched to ease comparison.

There is an implicit assumption that the actual acres within a multiple year age class are equally distributed over that multiple year age class. This is a simplifying assumption that is made repeatedly throughout our calculations. Those who feel it is too crude can, in practice, spend the time and money to estimate acres, or other variables, in finer subdivisions, such as 5- or 1-year age classes.

The acres in the final age group (70 +) are assumed to be distributed over 10 different 1-year age classes. This may or may not be true; however, it is likely that, in practice, more detailed information than is presented here would be available because this is the merchantable age class.

The actual and desired age distributions can now be readily compared. There are too few acres in the 1–40 and 51–60 age classes, as shown by the cross-hatched area (Figure 11.1), that is below the double line. There are too many acres in the 41–50 and 60 + age classes as shown by the cross-hatched area that is above the double line.

The regulation objective is to rearrange these age classes to obtain a normal, or near normal, age distribution by manipulating the cutting schedule. This distribution is desired because it will provide the wood flow and volume established as a management objective, not because it is intrinsically good.

The graphic presentation is not necessary. Age classes with too many and too few acres are readily apparent in column 4, Table 11.1. There should be 1 proportionate acre in each yearly age class if the distribution is normal. Those age classes with less than 1 acre have too few acres and those with more than 1 acre have too many acres. The graphic presentation is helpful because it provides a visual impression of desired age class redistribution.

In fact, using proportionate acres is not necessary either and some analysts may prefer not to use them. A comparison between the actual and desired age distributions can be made by noting that seven age classes are desired; therefore, 1000 acres (7000 acres/7 age classes) are desired in each age class. The actual acres (A_i) in each age class (Table 11.1, column 2) can then be compared to this figure.

Regulating the Forest

The normally distributed age class (double line, Figure 11.1) can be obtained fastest by unmodified area control. This requires cutting 1 proportionate acre a year for the next 70 years. The impact of this policy, if it is followed until the timber currently in the 41–50 age class is harvested, is examined by projecting the age distribution.

Projecting the age distribution caused by this cutting policy is accomplished most easily if viewed as two separate cases. The first is when the timber stand is not cut and the second is when the timber stand is cut.

The number of years cutting will occur must be known to determine the age distribution. The number of years cutting will occur is the sum of the total proportionate acres to be cut (Table 11.1, column 3) divided by the number of proportionate acres to be cut each year, or

$$\text{Years to cut} = \frac{\sum_i PA_i}{\text{proportionate acres cut per year}} \tag{11.3}$$

and in this example

$$\text{Years to cut} = \frac{25.0 + 12.5 + 12.5}{1.0} = 50.0$$

Thus, it will take 50 years to cut all the acres from those in the oldest stand back down to those currently in the 41–50 age class.

Calculating the age distribution of uncut stands is uncomplicated. The current age distribution can be thought of as occurring at time period zero ($t = 0$) on a time line. The age class distribution 50 years in the future at $t = 50$ will be examined. Therefore, each uncut stand will be 50 years older than it is at $t = 0$. The number of acres and their age class can be calculated by adding 50 years, or the appropriate age increase, to the $t = 0$ age class.

For example, consider Table 11.2. The first three columns are the same as the first, third, and fourth columns in Table 11.1. They show the age classes and their proportionate acres in total and yearly classes. The fourth column is the age of the stand at $t = 50$ and is simply column 1 plus 50. Therefore, the 1–10 age class becomes

$$(1 + 50) - (10 + 50) = 51 - 60$$

The example has been simplified and so the age classes at $t = 50$ conform with the 10-year age span at $t = 0$. The total and 1 year class proportionate acres remain the same in $t = 50$ because the age class span remains the same.

Calculating the age distribution for the cut stands is more complex. We begin with the assumption that the oldest age class will be cut first. This is usually valid;

TABLE 11.2   Age Distribution Calculations at $t = 50$ with 1 Acre per Year Harvest

| | $t = 0$ | | | | $t = 50$ | | |
| | Proportionate acres | | | | 1-year age class | | |
Age class	Total	In 1 year class	Age class	10-year age class	Number	Prop. A.	Actual acres
1 – 10	7.5	0.75	51 – 60	51 – 60	10.0	0.75	750
11 – 20	2.5	0.25	61 – 70	61 – 70	10.0	0.25	250
21 – 30	2.5	0.25	71 – 80	71 – 80	10.0	0.25	250
31 – 40	7.5	0.75	81 – 90	81 – 90	10.0	0.75	750
41 – 50	12.5	1.25	1 – 12.5	1 – 10	10.0	1.0	1,000
				11 – 20	2.5	1.0	250
51 – 60	0.0	0	—	—	—	—	—
61 – 70	12.5	1.25	13.5 – 25	11 – 20	7.5	1.0	750
				21 – 30	5.0	1.0	500
71 +	25.0	2.50	26 – 50	21 – 30	5.0	1.0	500
				31 – 40	10.0	1.0	1,000
				41 – 50	10.0	1.0	1,000

however, the analyst can make adjustments in projections if there is good reason to believe it is invalid.

The first step is to calculate the number of years it will take to cut the first age class, in this case the 71 + class. Using Eq. 11.3, we obtain

$$\text{Years to cut}_{71+} = \frac{25.0}{1.0} = 25.0$$

The oldest stand at $t = 50$ will be 50 years of age because it was first cut 50 years ago. The youngest stand at $t = 50$ will be 26 years of age because it took 25 years to completely harvest the age class. Therefore, the age class span is 26–50 years at $t = 50$ (column 4, Table 11.2). This span contains the same 25 proportionate acres we started with; only the age of the stands in those acres has changed.

This calculation is confusing because of the natural inclination to subtract 25, the number of years to completely harvest the age class, from 50, the age of the oldest stand. However the oldest stand is one of the 25 stands present in the age class and so it must be counted as well. The easiest way to determine the age class span is to draw a time line and count the number of stands.

The age class span for the other age classes can be calculated similarly. The 61–70 year class at $t = 0$ was cut immediately after the last 71 + stand, hence; its oldest stand is 25 years of age. It took 12.5 years to cut (with Eq. 11.2); hence, the youngest stand is 13.5 years old. Similarly, the age span for the stands in the 41–50 age class at $t = 0$ is 1–12.5 years.

The new age distributions found in column 4, Table 11.2 must now be divided into 10-year age classes to compare them to the age distribution at $t = 0$. This is done by first listing the 10-year-span age classes now present in each of the $t = 0$ age classes (column 5, Table 11.2).

For example, the 71 + age class at $t = 0$ is now 26–50 years of age (column 4). These stands are in the 10-year age classes of 21–30, 31–40, and 41–50 (column 5). The 10-year age classes are calculated similarly for the other cut stands.

The number of 1-year age classes in each of these 10-year age classes is calculated next by counting the number of 1-year age classes, or stands, in each of the 10-year age classes. The 71 + age class at $t = 0$ has five stands in the 21–30 age class at $t = 50$, that is, those 26, 27, 28, 29, and 30 years of age. The 31–40 and 41–50 age classes have 10 stands in each (column 6, Table 11.2). The number of 1 year classes is calculated similarly for the other stands. Note that some cut stands have fractional values.

Calculating the number of proportionate acres in each 1-year age class is the final step. This is 1.0 for the cut stands because that cut was specified to obtain a normal age distribution (column 7, Table 11.2). The proportionate acres in each of the uncut stands is the same as in $t = 0$ because these stands were unchanged by our harvesting activities.

The proportionate acres may be converted back to actual acres in the age class by multiplying the proportionate acres in a 1-year age class by the number of 1 year age classes (column 7 × column 6, Table 11.2). This multiplication calculates the proportionate acres in the multiple-year age class—variable PA_i in Eq. 11.2. The ratio in Eq. 11.2 is known from previous calculations so it is a simple matter to solve the equation for A_i, the actual acres in the age class (column 8, Table 11.2).

For example, the actual acres in the 51–60 age class at $t = 50$ is

$$PA_i = 0.75 \times 10.0 = 7.5$$

$$A_i = \frac{7.5}{0.01} = 750 \text{ acres}$$

The results of the proposed regulatory scheme are examined by inspecting the proportionate acres in column 7 of Table 11.2 and/or by plotting a frequency distribution (Figure 11.2). Column 7 shows 1 proportionate acre in all age classes from 1–50, which results in a well-regulated forest for these age classes. However, the two remaining age classes are overmature (by the definition of 70 years rotation) and most of the stands will be 80–85 years of age when they are cut.

This picture is also evident in Figure 11.2, where the frequency distribution of the age classes has been plotted. The double line once again shows the desired normal distribution and the cross-hatched areas show the actual. The lack of acres in the 50–70 age class is apparent as is the presence of overmature timber in the 70–90 age classes.

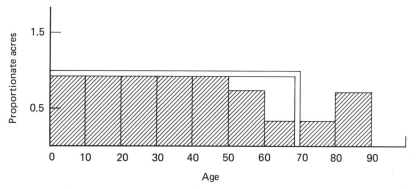

FIGURE 11.2 *Frequency distribution of age classes at t = 50 with 1.0 acres a year harvest.*

There are several advantages and disadvantages to the proposed unmodified area control regulatory scheme. The major advantages are: (1) that a normal age distribution is obtained most rapidly and (2) that growth is being put on older and presumably larger trees and hence might increase the stumpage price. The major disadvantages are that stands are overmature, therefore, (1) growth is decreasing and (2) dollar returns occur further in the future and are worth less when discounted.

Regulating the Forest — A Second Iteration

The weights put on the advantages and disadvantages of unmodified area control depend on the owner and his objectives. Some owners may want to regulate the forest as soon as possible. Others may want dollar returns as soon as possible. In any case, other alternatives are usually examined to assess opportunity costs and to see if the situation can be improved. This is done by an iterative process.

The major objection to strict area control in this forest was that the timber in both the cut and uncut stands would be overmature when harvested. For example, the timber in the 61–70 age class at $t = 0$ will be 95 to 98.5 years of age ($70 + 25 = 95$ and $61 + 12.5 + 25 = 98.5$) when harvested. This can be changed by increasing the rate at which harvest occurs.

Suppose, considering the flatness of growth curves around their maximum and as a matter of judgment, the grower is willing to accept some overmaturity at harvest but not too much. Cutting all of the 71 + age class rapidly probably would not be satisfactory because the poor age distribution would be perpetuated. This is exactly what would happen if, for example, the class were completely harvested in 10 years.

An initial assessment can be made by rearranging Eq. 11.3 to solve for proportionate acres cut per year and varying the years to cut. For example, let us examine the 61–70 and 71 + age classes at $t = 0$. There are a total of 37.5

proportionate acres in these classes (12.5 + 25.0) so that

Years to cut	Proportionate acres cut per year
10	3.750
15	2.500
20	1.875
25	1.500
30	1.250
35	1.070

Cutting the two to age classes in 10 years would worsen the age distribution because each age class would then have 3.75 proportionate acres, whereas they now only have 1.25 and 2.50, respectively. Furthermore, 3.75 is very far from the desired 1.0 proportionate acre per age class needed for a normal distribution.

Willingness to accept some age distribution imbalance to accelerate the cut allows an arbitrary choice of the 30-year cut. This results in 1.25 proportionate acre cut a year.

Table 11.2 is now recalculated, only for $t = 30$, to examine the age distribution for this alternative (Table 11.3). This scheme results in the 71 + age class being cut 2.5 years sooner and the 61–70 age class being cut when it is about 90 years of age (70 + 20 = 90 and 61 + 10 + 20 = 90). Strict area control could then be adopted in year 30 for the remainder of the stands and a normal age distribution would be obtained by the end of the next full rotation.

TABLE 11.3 Age Distribution Calculations at $t = 30$ with 1.25 Acres per Year Harvest

	$t = 0$			$t = 30$			
	Proportionate acres				1-year age class		
Age class	Total	In 1 year class	Age class	10-year age class	Number	Prop. A.	Actual acres
1 – 10	7.5	0.75	31 – 40	31 – 40	10.0	0.75	750
11 – 20	2.5	0.25	41 – 50	41 – 50	10.0	0.25	250
21 – 30	2.5	0.25	51 – 60	51 – 60	10.0	0.25	250
31 – 40	7.5	0.75	61 – 70	61 – 70	10.0	0.75	750
41 – 50	12.5	1.25	71 – 80	71 – 80	10.0	1.25	1,250
51 – 60	0	0	—	—	—	—	—
61 – 70	12.5	1.25	1 – 10	1 – 10	10.0	1.25	1,250
71 +	25.0	2.50	11 – 30	11 – 20	10.0	1.25	1,250
				21 – 30	10.0	1.25	1,250

The results of the 1.25 proportionate acre cut can be shown graphically with the normal distribution outlined in a double line (Figure 11.3). The lack of the 80–90 age class is particularly noticeable. Substitution of the added acres in the 1–30 age class at $t = 30$ for the 80–90 age class at $t = 50$ is evident when the two figures are compared.

As before, there are both advantages and disadvantages to the 1.25-acre cut scheme. The advantages are: (1) the cash flows occur sooner in time and hence have a higher present net worth and (2) the timber is harvested closer to its rotation age which, presumably, was set to maximize timber yield or some other criterion over time. The major disadvantage is that the age distribution is not as close to normal as with unmodified area control.

The choice between the two regulation schemes depends on the assessment of the forest manager, the landowner, and the objectives. Emphasis on financial objectives will almost always increase the number of proportionate acres cut due to the time value of money.

In summary, this is a "cut and try" or iterative method for deciding on the sequence of harvests to regulate the forest. Unmodified area control is a good starting point because it provides a fully regulated forest most rapidly. The results of strict area control are then examined and a judgment made as to whether or not they are acceptable. The sequence of harvests is then changed in a second iteration, based on what was deemed unsatisfactory about the first sequence and based on the analyst's judgment. There are no immutable rules for deciding what changes should be made in a harvest sequence or when a particular sequence is satisfactory. This is left to the judgment of the analyst, the forest manager, and the landowner—a situation that often causes students discomfort.

Many organizations would desire more information than only age class distribution before choosing a harvest sequence. This information would almost always include a wood flow estimate for each alternative. The wood flow estimates should be extended one step further to a present net worth analysis, including the costs and revenues for each alternative.

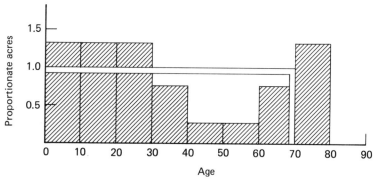

FIGURE 11.3 *Frequency distribution of age classes at t = 30 with 1.25 acres a year harvest.*

CALCULATING WOOD FLOW

There are many alternative ways to estimate wood flow. One of the more rudimentary will be presented because the more sophisticated techniques are beyond this introductory text. Wood flow may be calculated by listing the age class of the harvested stands and estimating the year they are harvested. The years to cut each age class may be calculated using Eq. 11.3 and then allocated to the age class (column 2, Table 11.4). For example, for the strict area control alternative

$$\text{Years to cut}_{71+} = \frac{25.0}{1.0} = 25.0$$

This is the first stand harvested; therefore, harvest will occur between years 1 and 25. The next age class is calculated as

$$\text{Years to harvest}_{61-70} = \frac{12.5}{1.0} = 12.5$$

and the time period of harvest begins 1 year after the last harvest, year 26, and extends 12.5 years (25 + 12.5) to year 37.5. Draw a time line if the calculations are confusing.

The age of the timber at harvest (column 3, Table 11.4) is calculated by adding the year of harvest to the age class extremes. There is an implicit assumption of an even age distribution from 71 to 90 years for the 71 + age class. Then, the first stand is harvested at 91 years of age (90 + 1) and the last stand at 96 years of age (71 + 25).

The mean age at harvest is calculated next. This is 93.5 years ((96 + 91)/2) for the 71 + age class. The actual age at harvest for each stand could be calculated. However, the gross nature of these calculations and data makes this precise an estimate unseemly.

The yield per acre at mean harvest age (column 5, Table 11.4) is obtained from the yield table (Table 10.1). It is then multiplied by the actual number of acres harvested per year (column 7, Table 11.4) to obtain the estimated annual yield (column 8, Table 11.4). The yield for a mean age that does not coincide with an age in the yield table can be estimated by assuming a straight line relationship between ages and interpolating. For example, the yield for mean age 93.5 is estimated as

$$Y_{93.5} = \left[\frac{93.5 - 90.0}{10.0} \times (17,900 - 16,650)\right] + 16,650 = 17,087.5$$

TABLE 11.4 Wood Flow Calculations for 1.0 and 1.25 Acre per Year Harvest Alternatives

Age class at $t = 0$	Year (t) harvested	Age when harvested	Mean harvest age	Cubic foot yield at mean age	Acres per year Propor.	Actual	Estimated annual yield (million cubic ft)
1.0 acre per year harvested							
41–50	38.5–50	91–88.5	89.75	16,650	1.0	100	1.67
61–70	26–37.5	98.5–96	97.25	17,556	1.0	100	1.76
71+[a]	1–25	96–91	93.5	17,088	1.0	100	1.71
1.25 acres per year harvested							
61–70	21–30	91–91	91.0	16,775	1.25	125	2.10
71+[a]	1–20	91–91	91.0	16,775	1.25	125	2.10

[a]Assumes ages evenly distributed over 71–90 age classes.

The total annual yield for the 71 + age class is then estimated by

Annual yield = 17,008 × 100 acres = 1.71 million cubic feet

Estimating acres in the age class has been discussed earlier in this chapter. The wood flows have been estimated for each alternative (Table 11.4).

The final extension of this analysis is to calculate a PNW. This PNW should include any differential costs of the alternatives and allowance for different numbers of time periods in the alternatives. One way to allow for different numbers of time periods would be to project each alternative far enough to obtain full regulation and then end the analysis in the same time period for each alternative.

REGULATING UNEVEN-AGED FORESTS

12

MANY FOREST REGULATION concepts developed for even-aged forests also apply to uneven-aged forests. The concepts of regulating the forest for continuous wood flows, obtaining these by manipulating the age of the trees in the forest, and managing individual stands to obtain overall forest objectives still apply. However, as pointed out by Hann and Bare (1979), the philosophies behind the two systems are different.

Even-aged management has been viewed as more of a science wherein variables affecting management decisions can be quantified and reduced to a series of formulas. These formulas can then be solved to provide strong guidelines for management decisions.

Uneven-aged management, which was developed after even-aged management, has been viewed as more of an art wherein variables affecting management decisions are considered intuitively or judgmentally by the forest manager. This judgment is based on the manager's knowledge of silvics, silviculture, ecology, and the other biological forest sciences. Thus, there is a scientific foundation for uneven-aged management. However, the variables affecting management decisions are viewed as less quantifiable and more emphasis is placed on the forest manager's judgment. Hann and Bare (1979) believe that, although this view has existed in the past, it need not continue in the future. They believe that many of the questions affecting uneven-aged management are quantifiable and that optimal or near optimal uneven-aged management plans may be calculated.

Defining and discussing several terms will help explain uneven-aged management. First, an *uneven-aged stand* is a stand where "...there are considerable differences in the age of the trees present and where three or more age classes are represented" (Society of American Foresters, 1958). A *cutting cycle* is the planned interval between major felling operations in the same stand, and *reserve growing stock* is the growing stock in the forest that is reserved (uncut) to produce the growth for future cuts.

Davis (1966) identifies three kinds of uneven-aged forests. The first is the "true" all-aged forest, where all ages and all sizes of trees are found intermixed in the same stand. This is the classical concept of an uneven-aged stand and is seldom found on the ground. In fact, some foresters believe these stands never existed. They think the small trees, which were thought to be a younger age class, were in reality suppressed trees of the same age as the larger trees. Proponents of this view claim that when the stand was cut, the smaller trees never responded to the release.

The second kind of uneven-aged forest is one composed of small and irregular groups of more or less even-aged trees. These groups are small in size and contain mostly one age class. They can be visualized as a series of $\frac{1}{5}$- or $\frac{1}{10}$-acre plots that blend into one another and are not readily distinguishable along their edges. This is the most commonly found situation on the ground.

The last kind of forest is a mosaic of readily distinguishable even-aged stands spread throughout the forest. All ages and sizes are present but the individual stands are predominantly one age and one size. This and the even-aged forest are simply different points along the same continuum.

The concepts of a cutting cycle and reserve growing stock can be presented graphically (Figure 12.1). The x axis is time in years and the y axis is the volume per acre on the stand. Point a is the volume just before harvest; point b the volume just after the harvest; distance c the amount of harvest; distance d the amount of reserve growing stock; and distance e the cutting cycle.

For example, suppose the growth rate were 5 percent a year; the reserve growing stock, distance d, were 5000 cubic feet; and the cutting cycle, distance e, were 5 years. In 5 years the growing stock would increase to 6381 cubic feet (5000×1.05^5), point a. At harvest, it would be cut back to the original level of 5000 feet (point b), and the harvest would be 1381 cubic feet ($6{,}381 - 5{,}000$), or distance c.

The harvest would be less if the forest manager had decided to increase the growing stock, and the straight line representing growing stock would slope

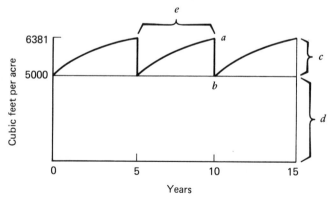

FIGURE 12.1 *The cutting cycle for a single stand.*

upward and to the right. The harvest would be increased if the reserve growing stock were to be decreased, and the straight line would slope downward to the right.

The reserve growing stock over time is represented by the rectangle in Figure 12.1. It can be viewed as the principal amount you deposit in the bank, and the harvest is the interest on that principal. For example, $500 in the bank at 5 percent would grow to $638.14 in 5 years. The $138.14 growth in the account can be viewed as the quantity harvested and the $500 as the growing stock. Also, the reserve growing stock does not consist of the same trees that existed at the beginning of the cycle, just as the principal in the bank is not the same dollars, with the same serial numbers, that were deposited.

REGULATING THE UNEVEN-AGED FOREST—CONCEPTUAL MODEL

Briefly, the conceptual regulation model is a forest divided into a series of stands that are regularly harvested on the cutting cycle. The stands all provide an equal volume for harvest and thus may vary in size depending on site productivity. There are as many stands as there are years in the cutting cycle, in the simplest case, so that one stand may be harvested each year. In practice, there may be several stands, each harvested in the same year, but the sum of the volume harvested from all stands in each year is the same.

This model can be shown graphically as a series of overlapping cutting cycles. One cutting cycle for each stand occurs each year and there is a continuous flow of wood (Figure 12.2). Stands 1 through 5 are shown for a 5-year cutting cycle. Stand 1 is the same as in Figure 12.1 and is harvested in years 0, 5, 10, 15, and so on. Stand 2 is harvested in years 1, 6, 11, 16, and so on. Only the cycle for from year 6 to year 11 is shown in Figure 12.2.

The cutting cycles for the other stands are also shown for only a single cycle, but the student should understand that they would be repeated consecutively, every 5 years. Stand size can be equal if site quality is equal because the volume harvested will then be equal. Alternatively, stand size is varied to provide equal harvests.

Maps of uneven-aged forests might look like those in Figure 12.3 on a 5-year cutting cycle. Map *a* shows five single stands, each of which is cut once every 5 years. Stands 3, 4, and 5 are lower on the slope, border a stream, and are more productive. Therefore, they occupy a smaller area than stands 1 and 2, which are near the ridge top and have lower productivity.

Map *b* (Figure 12.3) is a stylized view of multiple stands. Each cell represents 1 stand and there are 25 stands on the forest. Each is the same size, if we assume there is equal productivity, and 5 are cut every year. The numbers in the cell indicate in which of the 5 years the harvest occurs. The checkerboard configuration is not sacrosanct and the cut might occur across rows or down columns.

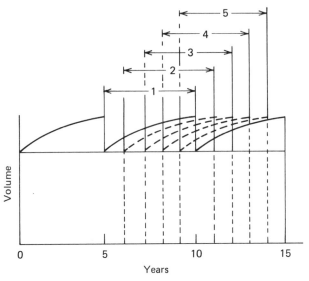

FIGURE 12.2 *Cutting cycle for regulated uneven-aged forest.*

The acres harvested annually are simply calculated if equal site productivity and constant reserve growing stock are assumed:

$$\text{Annual acres harvested} = \frac{\text{total acres in forest}}{\text{years in cutting cycle}} \qquad (12.1)$$

This conceptual model leaves four key questions about the regulated forest unanswered. These are: (1) How much reserve growing stock should be carried?

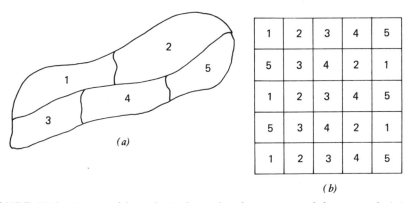

FIGURE 12.3 *Maps of hypothetical regulated uneven-aged forests with (a) one stand harvested per cutting cycle and (b) multiple stands harvested per cutting cycle.*

(2) What should the diameter distribution on the stand be? (3) What should the species composition of the stand be? (4) What should the cutting cycle length be?*

Volume of Reserve Growing Stock

The amount of growth is highly, but not solely, dependent on the reserve growing stock volume. This is demonstrated by the simple equation

$$\text{Growth} = \text{growing stock} \times \text{growth percent} \tag{12.2}$$

or, in the preceding example

$$\text{Growth} = 5,000 \times .05 = 250 \text{ cubic feet per year}$$

Assume, as a first approximation, that the management objective is to maximize growth. Then, the greater the growing stock, the greater the growth because, as indicated by Eq. 12.2, growth percent is multiplied by a larger number. .

However, the growth percent also is a function of growing stock volume because, after a point, the denser the stand, the slower the growth. Thus, beyond a certain point, the larger the growing stock, the smaller the growth percent. The goal, under the first approximation, is to find the growing stock volume in which growth is maximized.

The "proper" level of reserve growing stock will do this because of the above interrelationships. Davis implies that the determinants are almost intuitively obtained by long years of experience and expert judgment. In any event, there is no widely used simple formula to estimate the "proper" level for uneven-aged stands.

Diameter Distribution

A basic premise of uneven-aged management is that the stand contains trees of all, or many, age classes and sizes. The relationship would be a straight line from a purely optimal view (Figure 12.4a). However, many younger trees (those usually with the smaller diameters) do not survive as result of either mortality or cutting.

Thus, many more smaller trees are needed in order to obtain larger ones in the future. This results in the famous J-shaped curve (Figure 12.4b) associated with Meyer (1943, 1952, 1953). That is, the forest manager will attempt to carry more trees in the stand with smaller rather than larger diameters at breast height, so that there will be smaller trees to replace the larger ones that are harvested.

The J-shaped curve is based on on the work of a French forester named de Liocourt. He believed that the desirable diameter distribution in the stand

---

*The discussion of these questions closely follows Chapter 8 in Davis (1966).

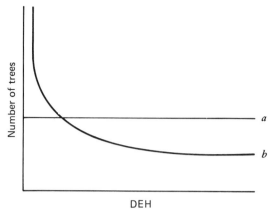

FIGURE 12.4 *Diameter distributions in uneven-aged stand; (a) desired and (b) actual.*

could be described by the relationship

$$X_{td} = qX_{td-1} \tag{12.3}$$

where

X = the number of trees in diameter class d during time period t
q = a constant; $0 < q < 1.0$

This relationship simply states that, in any time period, the number of trees in a diameter class is some constant proportion of the number of trees in the next smaller diameter class. It will result in the J-shaped curve when plotted on a pair of axes.

The value of q is a function of the species present in the forest and of site quality. q can be determined empirically; however, there are obvious limitations to finding a truly optimal q value when all the possible combinations of species and site are considered. This is particularly true in uneven-aged management, where stands containing several species are common. The value of q is important since it obviously make a great deal of difference, as a management guideline, where the curve lies on the axes and how rapidly it drops.

The final configuration of the diameter distribution has other, nonbiological determinants. For example, the desired product or the marketability of different diameters will also affect the distribution that the forest manager attempts to maintain. In fact, Hann and Bare (1979), and others cited in their work, suggest that the J-shaped distribution should be questioned and that some other distribution might be better for a given set of management objectives.

Species Composition

The basic question in species composition is balancing the species that will reproduce and grow well on the site with those that are desirable for reaching the management objectives. There are obvious limitations imposed by the site on which species may be successfully maintained. These include such variables as soil fertility, moisture, and altitude.

The site limitations help define a set of species from which individual species can be chosen to fulfill management objectives. In a practical sense, the choice is often at least partly determined by the species already occupying the site. The forest manager will arrange his cutting, or perhaps even engage in enrichment planting, to favor those species that have been determined as most desirable. Species desirability can be affected by such things as marketability, the owner's aesthethic values, and production of food and shelter for wildlife. However, once again, there is no simple formula or procedure to determine the most desirable species composition.

Cutting Cycle Length

There are also many factors affecting the cutting cycle length. The final choice is a balance of these factors, as weighted by management objectives. Some of the more important factors are species composition, financial needs, and site.

The silvical characteristics of the particular species planted affect the length of the cutting cycle in several ways. For example, shade-tolerant species can have a longer cycle because open stand conditions are not required for successful reproduction. Or, faster-growing species can have a shorter cycle and slower-growing species a longer cycle because less or more time is needed to reach merchantable dimensions. And, in general, the better the site, the faster the growth, the more often cutting is possible, and the shorter the cycle.

The owner's financial needs also can have a large effect, particularly if the forest is not yet regulated. For example, the cycle may be shortened to create an annual income for a small owner to pay taxes, forest management costs, and perhaps some other costs. On the other hand, the owner may have less demanding financial needs so that income can be postponed, the cycle lengthened, and perhaps, reserve growing stock increased. Other objectives, such as maintaining den trees for wildlife, can also affect cycle length.

Once more, the forest manager is left to determine the most desirable condition by intuitively integrating several variables. Further, as the above discussions shown, there are also interactions between the four key questions that must also be integrated. For example, species composition affects cutting cycle length and diameter distribution, but cutting cycle length also affects the planted species and the diameter distribution.

In general, shorter cutting cycles allow better biological control because diseased or infested trees can be cut more often. It is also easier to salvage mortality, if the smaller trees are marketable. On the other hand, there is usually a minimum operable harvest volume. Longer cycles allow increasing the volume per unit of area harvested because more growth is available to cut. This, in turn, can lower per unit of volume logging costs because there is more volume per acre to absorb fixed costs. In addition, the longer the cycle, the more growth taken, and the more even-aged the stand will become. There is a tendency to shorten cutting cycles because too long a cycle results in an even-aged stand and because shorter cycles provide better timing of cash flows and better biological control.

Obtaining Regulation

The preceding discussion presented the uneven-aged regulation model once accomplished: a picture of the regulated forest. Those questions that must be answered to determine what the picture will look like were discussed. However, as discussed in Chapter 11 on even-aged management, few forests are regulated initially, if ever, and the forest manager is faced with determining the best series of cuts and other management actions to obtain the regulated forest.

This is the question that the proportionate acre analysis in Chapter 11 sought to answer. Determining the number of proportionate acres to cut each year determines, at least in conjunction with a cutting rule such as "cut the oldest stand first," the cut between the present time and that time when the forest becomes regulated. Indeed, as discussed, some forest managers are perpetually trying to obtain a regulated forest rather than managing a forest that has already been regulated.

Adams and Ek (1974, 1975), whose work is discussed further below, offer a theoretical solution to this question, which they call the *transition problem*. They define the starting stand diameter distribution as a vector of the number of trees in each diameter class, $N(0)^s$. The desired distribution, at the end of a transition period of length T, is a similar vector, $N(T)^\star$. They state the transition from $N(0)^s$ to $N(T)^\star$ as a maximization problem, subject to constraints, and suggest the problem might be solved using optimal control theory, network analysis, or nonlinear programming. Each of these approaches presents problems in obtaining a solution for actual, large-scale forest management plans. However, Adams and Ek do provide a conceptual starting point for future work.

AN OPTIMIZATION MODEL

Adams and Ek (1974, 1975) have presented an uneven-aged management model that answers most of the preceding major questions in a quantitative manner for individual stands in an uneven-aged forest. The model is based on individual tree stand growth and yield models. Individual tree growth and yield models start with a known stand structure, often a map of trees in a stand, and "grow" the trees from one diameter class to another until the individual trees are cut or removed by mortality. Yield is estimated by "stopping" the model at the desired time period and adding up the volume in the trees still present. Growth is the difference between yield in two time periods.

The Adams–Ek model uses an individual tree model, developed by Ek, to formulate a nonlinear program. The solution of the program produces a starting diameter distribution, stated as the number of trees in each diameter class, which maximizes harvestable growth. Harvestable growth may defined as either timber volume or timber value. Thus, the major question of optimal diameter distribution is answered.

One of the program constraints is the stocking level. Adams and Ek suggest that the program be iteratively solved for several different stocking levels. The amount of the harvestable growth can then be noted for each of these different stocking levels and the highest value chosen. This maximum harvestable growth, calculated as a function of different stocking levels, defines the optimal stocking level. That is, the optimal stocking level is the one with the largest harvestable growth. Thus, the major question of optimal stocking level is answered.

The determination of an optimal cutting cycle length is slightly more complex but follows the same basic scheme. Recall that the growth model can "grow" the stand year by year until the desired growth period, which is equal to the cutting cycles, is reached. However, the model can be stopped at any one of the intermediate years, for example years 1, 2, 3, and 4 for a 5-year growth period, and the growth and yield estimated in that year. Adams and Ek suggest this be done for all the years equal to and less than the number of years in the cutting cycle. In addition, the calculations are iterated for the different stocking levels, as explained in the preceding paragraph, in each of these years. This results in a set of growths for different length cutting cycles and, within each of these cutting cycle lengths, a growth figure for each of the different stocking levels. It is then suggested that the maximum growth within any cycle length be chosen, thus defining optimal stocking for that cycle length. Then, the maximum growth between each cycle length is selected, thus defining both the optimal stocking level and cycle length.

This model is also used, in the manner described above, to solve the transition problem between unregulated and regulated stands. However, the major question of species composition is still left unanswered, although some authors believe continued work with individual tree growth models can provide useful guidelines. In addition, the authors cite several problems with their model. First, because the models are nonlinear, computation times can be very long and sometimes the problem never converges on a solution. In fact, the possibility of an infeasible solution exists. Further, as discussed in Chapter 15, nonlinear program algorithm capacity, and the capacity of the computers using them, can easily be exceeded by applied problems.

Hann and Bare (1979) in reviewing the Adams–Ek model, suggest that five "problem areas" exist that keep such models from being fully operational. These problem areas are: (1) better computer and algorithm capacities; (2) interfacing stand simulators and nonlinear programs; (3) better uneven-aged growth and yield simulators; (4) determining optimal species mix; and (5) scheduling cuts forestwide rather than in just a single stand.

Perhaps the main point to be drawn is that uneven-aged management guidelines can be developed quantitatively and need not be based only on intuition and judgment. Uneven-aged management does not need to be viewed as an art rather than a science. However, it should also be evident that quantitative techniques here are much less well developed than those for even-aged management and that a great deal more work is required before parity can be reached.

ROTATION DETERMINATION

13

ROTATION AGE IS the focal point of traditional even-aged management. The rotation age determines the tree's age, hence, it largely determines the size, quantity, and quality of the timber. The number of acres cut per year, in a fixed size forest, are also a function of the rotation age and, therefore, so are the site preparation and planting requirements for the forest. Rotation age also affects the regulation possibilities, as demonstrated in Chapter 11, and thereby the age distribution of the forest. Thus, rotation age is thought by many to be the single most important decision affecting timber management.

Recall that both regulatory and cutting rotation ages were defined. The cutting rotation age may be less than, equal to, or greater than the regulatory rotation age. In general, the cutting rotation age is determined by productivity as reflected in the yield functions. For example, the criterion used to determine cutting rotation age when wood yield maximization is the objective is the mean of the yield function with respect to age. Other rotation criteria take into account both costs and revenues. Revenues are a direct function of yield although costs are largely unaffected by yield function differences. Stated differently, the cutting rotation age is determined largely by the physical production possibilities of the forest.

The regulatory rotation age is often determined by the management regime adopted. The management regime modifies the cutting rotation age. For example, mean annual increment may culminate in cubic feet for Shortleaf pine at 28 years, and this becomes the cutting rotation age. However, the chosen management regime may be clearcutting with site preparation 1 year after cutting and machine planting 1 year after site preparation. Therefore, the regulatory rotation age is 30 years—28 years to grow the trees, 1 year to site prepare, and 1 year to plant. In this case, the cutting rotation age is less than the regulatory rotation age.

The regulatory rotation age has great significance because it determines the acres of land needed for a specified harvest. For example, suppose a pulpmill used

500,000 cords of wood a year, planned to provide 0.4 of this from company-managed land, and had an average yield of 40 cords per acre on a 28-year cutting age rotation. Then,

$$\text{Cords from company land} = 500{,}000 \times 0.4 = 200{,}000 \text{ cords}$$

and

$$\text{Annual harvest} = \frac{200{,}000 \text{ cords}}{40 \text{ cords/acre}} = 4000 \text{ acres}$$

Now if the company wanted a 200,000-cord sustained yield and was on a 30-year regulatory rotation it would have to own or control 120,000 acres (4000 × 30). The required acreage could be reduced to 112,000 acres (4000 × 28) if the regulatory rotation could be reduced to the cutting rotation, say by better equipment scheduling or improved site preparation or planting techniques.

The shorter regulatory rotation age requires 8000 fewer acres for the 200,000-cord sustained yield. This, in turn, frees capital funds that can be invested elsewhere within the company to earn a profit. For example, suppose land cost $500 per acre. Then $4,000,000 (8000 × $500) could be reinvested at the ARR of, say, 15 percent and an additional $600,000 ($4,000,000 × 0.15) earned for the company each year.

Note that this assumes there is no return on timberlands to offset the ARR. Timberlands usually have a positive IRR but, for several reasons, it usually is less than the ARR. The difference between ARR and IRR is the opportunity cost of the extra 8000 acres and can be substituted for the ARR in the preceding calculations to derive the savings to the firm by reducing the rotation age. The regulatory and cutting rotation ages are assumed to be equal in the following discussions. This is done to simplify the presentations.

A single rotation age is usually quoted in response to questions about rotation age length. However, there are usually several rotation ages, as is the case with "the interest rate." Ideally, the rotation age should be recalculated as the physical site conditions and/or costs and revenues change. For example, the rotation age increases as the site quality decreases. Any large differences should be reflected by managing stands for individual rotation ages. Sometimes these differences are not great enough to warrant individual rotation ages. This can be due to the flatness of the growth curves and the practical considerations that cause early or late cutting.

More advanced harvest scheduling techniques, discussed in Chapter 16, calculate a unique rotation age for individual stands in the forest. These mathematical programming techniques are widely accepted but not universally applied because a great deal of technical knowledge and data are needed. Nonetheless, there is still a central tendency toward a single rotation age due to biological similarities.

Strictly speaking, the landowner chooses an objective and the rotation criterion is determined by that objective once it is chosen. Shorter rotations tend to be favored because stands are entered more often, wood and cash flows occur sooner, and the number of age classes to be regulated are reduced, thereby simplifying regulation. However, the more often a stand is entered, the greater the potential impact on environmental factors, such as soil stability. Also, the value of the standing volume is less and this may not be desired by some owners.

Rotation criterion implicitly assume that thinnings have already been included in calculating the criterion values and thus the rotation age. The wood and cash flows generated by thinnings should have been used in calculating the criterion in those instances where they are feasible or desirable. Thus, theoretically, thinning regimes are not determined *after* rotation age but are part of determining rotation age. Actual practice, however, may not follow the theory.

The remaining sections of this chapter contain discussions of different criteria used to determine rotation age. The basic procedure is to calculate the value of a criterion for many different stand ages. Then, the age at which the criterion value is maximum is chosen as the rotation age. Each criterion maximizes something. The correct criterion to use depends on the management objectives. The landowner must first choose the management objective and then the criterion that maximizes it.

MEAN ANNUAL INCREMENT

The *mean annual increment* (MAI) is the total volume per acre divided by the age of the stand at that time, or

$$\mathrm{MAI}_A = \frac{Y_A}{A} \tag{13.1}$$

where

MAI = mean annual increment
A = the stand age
Y = yield, or volume of wood that will be harvested at age A

The MAI is, simply, the average annual growth in any particular year. It is the same as the average physical product (APP) found in production economics literature.

The *periodic annual increment* (PAI) is the change in volume between two ages divided by the number of years between these observations, or

$$\mathrm{PAI}_{A'} = \frac{Y_{A+n} - Y_A}{n} \tag{13.2}$$

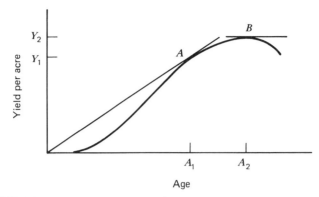

FIGURE 13.1 *Hypothetical yield function.*

where

> PAI = the periodic annual increment
> $A' = a + 0.5n$
> A = the stand age
> n = the number of years between observations
> Y = yield or volume of wood that will be harvested at age A

The PAI is the growth rate or increment of the stand. It is the average annual change in stand volume between time periods. PAI is the first derivative of the yield function and is the same as the marginal physical product (MPP) found in production economics literature.*

The maximum MAI can be demonstrated graphically with the typical sigmoid yield function. It is point A where a straight line through the origin is just tangent to the curve (Figure 13.1). This produces a yield of Y_1 as opposed to a yield at point B of Y_2 at age A_2. B is the point of maximum total yield.

Wood yield is maximized over perpetual rotations if the stands are cut at the age where MAI reaches a maximum, often called the culmination of MAI, rather than at the age where wood yield is maximum. This can be demonstrated by assuming that maximum MAI (point A) is 100 cubic feet per acre a year and occurs at age 30 and that the MAI at maximum total growth (point B) is very close to this, say 99 cubic feet per acre per year, and occurs at age 31. Then, total wood yield can be estimated for a very long time period to approximate infinity, say 30 million years.

---

*These relationships can be succinctly expressed as:

> Yield = $Y = f(A)$
> MAI = $Y/A = f(A)/A$
> Growth = PAI = $dY/dA = f'(A)$, where A is stand age

The total yields at 30- and 31-year rotations are

$$Y_{30} = 100 \text{ cubic feet} \times 30 \text{ years} = 3,000 \text{ cubic feet per acre}$$
$$Y_{31} = 99 \text{ cubic feet} \times 31 \text{ years} = 3,069 \text{ cubic feet per acre}$$

The total number of rotations in the time period is

$$R_{30} = 3 \times 10^7/30 = 1 \times 10^6 = 1,000,000$$
$$R_{31} = 3 \times 10^7/31 = 9.66742 \times 10^5 = 966,742$$

Yield during the entire 30-million-year period then equals

$$TY_{30} = (1 \times 10^6)(3,000) = 3 \times 10^9$$
$$TY_{31} = (0.66742 \times 10^5)(3,069) = 2.9669 \times 10^9$$

or a difference of about 3.3×10^7 (33 million) cubic feet of wood less by continuing production to the point of maximum total yield.

Rotation determination using maximum MAI can be demonstrated using Schumacher's (1939) yield function for longleaf pine for site index 50. The function predicts yield (V) in thousands of cubic feet and is

$$\log V = 0.8521 - 20.88371(1.0/t)$$

where

V = the stand yield in thousands of cubic feet per acre
t = the stand age in years

The main reason for choosing this function as an example is that stand age (time) is the only independent variable. This allows a clearer development of the principles because the examples become less obscured by several independent variables.

Yields and MAIs have been calculated in columns 2 and 3, respectively, of Table 13.1. Volumes were converted to cubic feet per acre for clarity. The rotation age for this stand would be set at 50 years, which is the maximum MAI when calculated in 5-year increments. Notice the relative flatness of the MAI curve around the maximum. The stand could be cut 5 years earlier at the cost of 1 cubic foot in MAI or 5 years later at the cost of 4 cubic feet MAI.

The MAI rotation age also depends on the site quality. Generally the poorer the site, the longer it takes to grow the trees and the longer the rotation age. The unit of volumetric measurement also affects the rotation age for any particular stand. The maximum MAI rotation in cubic feet is shorter than that for cords,

TABLE 13.1 Sample Rotation Age Calculations.

Age (years)	Yield[a] (cubic feet)	MAI (cubic feet)	Money yield table[b] ($)	Cost per acre[c] ($)	Forest rent ($)	Land expectation value[d] ($)	PNW[e] ($)	IRR (%)
10	58	5.8	8.70	20.00	−1.13	−32.07	−22.03	—
15	288	19.2	43.20	25.00	1.21	0.82	−12.55	2.4986
20	642	32.1	96.30	30.00	3.32	22.24	−1.71	4.7974
25	1,039	41.6	155.85	35.00	4.83	31.14	4.33	5.4470*
30	1,432	47.7	214.80	40.00	5.83	31.45*	.96*	5.3970
35	1,801	51.5	270.15	45.00	6.43	7.59	2.13	5.1472
40	2,138	53.4	320.70	50.00	6.77	21.44	−3.05	4.8473
45	2,444	54.3	366.60	55.00	6.92	14.65	−9.20	4.4975
50	2,719	54.4*	407.85	60.00	6.96*	8.01	−15.51	4.1977
55	2,968	54.0	445.20	65.00	6.91	1.91	−21.51	3.8979
60	3,192	5.32	478.80	70.00	6.81	−3.48	−26.96	3.6480

[a]From Schumacher (1939).
[b]Calculated at $150 per MCF.
[c]Calculated at $10 / acre establishment cost plus $1 / acre / year management cost.
[d]Calculated at 5% interest rate.
[e]Calculated at $25 / acre land value.
*Indicates using rotation age this criterion.

which is shorter than that for board feet. It takes longer to grow a board foot than a cord and longer to grow a cord than a cubic foot.

MAI Characteristics

The MAI criterion does not directly consider the value of the products produced. Sawtimber price may be five times pulpwood price but the criterion is insensitive to the difference. The decision to grow a particular product is made independent of the criterion.

The MAI criterion does not take into account direct production costs. Land costs, annual management and tax costs, and cultural practice costs are all omitted from the analysis. The time value of money is also not considered; the reason for mentioning this separately is because some criteria do consider other costs but not the time value of money.

The MAI criterion is generally popular with public agencies. Many state and federal forests are managed with their rotation determined by MAI. A "conventional wisdom" rotation age is often found in practice. This is the rotation age quoted by practicing foresters in response to the question, "What is the rotation on the forest?" The conventional wisdom rotation age has meaning because it is based on the current practice observed on the practicing forester's and surrounding lands. It is usually very near the MAI rotation age for the average site of the species.

The MAI criterion is a good first approximation for rotation determination because it reflects the forest's physical production possibilities. These physical possibilities form the constraints within which most forest managers must operate.

MONEY YIELD TABLE

The money yield table is the first step in considering dollars. An average stumpage price is applied to the yields and the maximum is chosen for the rotation age. The money yield table criterion will result in a rotation age at point B, age A_2 in Figure 13.1, if a *constant* stumpage price is assumed for all ages. This is because the money yield table will be a linear transformation of the yield function; hence, the maximum will occur at the same age.

Stated differently, the money yield table multiplies the values on the y axis of Figure 13.1 by a constant amount. The yield curve is therefore shifted upward everywhere, but it is *not* shifted to the right or left along the x axis. Therefore, the maximum occurs at the same age. Note that these results mean that neither dollar nor wood yield will be maximized over time when a constant price and a money yield table are used. Maximum yield over time required rotation age at A_1 rather than A_2 (Figure 13.1).

Different prices over time are often assumed for the money yield table. This is done to reflect the changing products produced by the forest. For example, a pulpwood price may be assumed for the first 30 years, a mixed pulpwood–sawlog price for years 31–50, and a mixed pulpwood–sawlog–veneer log price over 50 years of age. This causes a rotation age different from that calculated using a constant price.

A money yield table has been calculated in column 4 of Table 13.1, (we assume that there is a constant price). The maximum value occurs in year 60 and that would be the rotation age chosen, given the information present. However, the information is incomplete because it is not known whether the value at year 65 will be greater than the value at year 60 and thus establish a new maximum. In general, the values must be calculated until the downturn (point B, Figure 13.1) is found. A problem arises because some yield functions do not have a downturn or the downturn occurs far beyond the data observations and so is suspect.

Money Yield Table Characteristics

The implied management objective of the money yield table criterion is to maximize total revenue in a single rotation, but not over time. Also implied, if a constant price is used for calculating the criterion, is maximization of the total yield in a single rotation. Neither production costs nor the time value of money are considered.

Few organizations are interested in maximizing only their total revenue because the costs of producing that revenue should always be taken into account. Most organizations would want to maximize net revenue (revenue minus costs); hence, this criterion is seldom used. However, the money yield table is a necessary step for calculating other criteria that have more merit and are more widely used.

FOREST RENT

Forest rent is the average net income per year and is calculated by subtracting the cost per acre from the revenue per acre and dividing by age. In formula form

$$FR_A = \frac{TR_A - TC_A}{A} \tag{13.3}$$

where

A = the age of the stand
FR = the forest rent in year A
TR = the total revenue from harvesting the stand at age A, the money yield table
TC = the total costs of growing the stand to age A

Assume, for example, establishment costs of $10 per acre and annual taxes and management costs of $1 per acre. Then, using the data from Table 13.1, we obtain

$$TC_{10} = \$10.00 + (10 \text{ years} \times \$1.00)$$
$$= \$20.00$$

and

$$FR_{10} = \frac{\$8.70 - \$20.00}{10}$$

$$= -\$1.13/\text{acre/year}$$

or

$$TC_{25} = \$10.00 + (25 \text{ years} \times \$1.00)$$

$$= \$35.00$$

and

$$FR_{25} = \frac{\$155.85 - \$35.00}{25}$$

$$= \$31.14/\text{acre/year}$$

Note that these costs are lower than those found in practice. They are used for consistency in this example.

The total costs per acre have been calculated and are shown in column 5 of Table 13.1. The calculated forest rents, using these costs and the money yield table in column 4, are shown in column 6. The forest rent is greatest in year 50 and so this would be the rotation age chosen using the forest rent criterion. Note that a maximum is observable in this case, whereas it was not observable in the money yield table.

Forest Rent Characteristics

The implied management objective is maximization of *average* net revenue. However, only the operating costs are included in the calculations. Neither the cost of land nor the time value of money is included; thus, some costs that should be considered, if financial maximization is the goal, are omitted.

Forest rent maximization is equivalent to "profit" maximization in perpetuity. This can be demonstrated in the same manner as MAI maximization was demonstrated. However, the exclusion of the time value of money and land cost precludes serious consideration of forest rent as a rotation criterion. Exclusion of land cost omits one of the major investment costs in forestry. The reasons for its inclusion have already been discussed in Chapter 5. Exclusion of the time value of money eliminates the interest payments on the invested funds. Chapter 14 of Gregory (1972, p. 293) contains an excellent discussion on this important point.

Bentley and Fight (1966) have shown that forest rent and land expectation value (L_e) will provide the same rotation age if zero interest is used for L_e. This result is logical because, it will be recalled, L_e assumes zero land value and the zero interest rate, in effect, charges no interest. These are the two characteristics lacking in forest rent that were mentioned above.

LAND EXPECTATION VALUE

Land expectation value was one of the decision criteria studied in Chapter 5. It is discussed again here as a rotation age criterion. Land expectation value as defined in Eq. 5.6 as

$$L_e = V_0 \times \frac{(1.0 + i)^n}{(1.0 + i)^n - 1.0}$$

Recall also that it is a special case of the PNW criterion due to four assumptions: (1) the land value is zero; (2) the land has no residual stand; (3) the land will be forested in perpetuity; and (4) the cash flows from the forest will be the same in perpetuity.

L_e is calculated and shown in column 7 of Table 13.1, assuming the same cash flows as for forest rent and a 5 percent interest rate. Then, for the 10-year-old stand,

$$V_0^{10} = -\$10.00 - \left(\frac{(1.0 + i)^n - 1.0}{i(1.0 + i)^n}\right)^* \times (\$1.00)$$

$$+ \left(\frac{1}{(1.0 + i)^n}\right)^{**} \times (\$8.70)$$

$$= -\$10.00 - (7.7217) \times (\$1.00) + (0.6139) \times (\$8.70)$$

$$= -\$12.379$$

and

$$L_e^{10} = V_0(1.0 + i)^n \times \left(\frac{1.0}{(1.0 + i)^n - 1.0}\right)^\dagger$$

$$L_e^{10} = -\$12.379 \times (1.6289) \times (1.5901)$$

$$L_e^{10} = -\$32.07 \text{ per acre}$$

The superscripts have been added to the dependent variables to indicate the rotation age for which the variable is being calculated.

The maximum L_e in the example is found at year 30 in column 7 and is the indicated rotation age (Table 13.1). Again, the maximum is observable.

Land Expectation Value Characteristics

The implied management objective for this criterion is the maximization of the investment's residual value when land cost is excluded. Stated differently, the criterion maximizes the capitalized land value. The criterion considers all costs and revenues except land cost, which is specifically excluded. However, the time

---

*Eq. 4.13.

**Eq. 4.8.

†Eq. 4.15.

value of money is considered and this is an important inclusion. Including the time value of money usually shortens the rotation; thus, L_e has shorter rotations than MAI and the other criteria previously discussed.

Bentley and Fight (1966) have shown that L_e will provide the same rotation age as forest rent if zero interest rate is used. The L_e rotation age in our example is about 20 years less than the forest rent rotation age because a positive interest rate is used. Generally, the higher the interest rate, the shorter the rotation. This is also true for all criteria using discounting.

L_e maximization is an incomplete financial criterion for rotation age determination because land value is excluded from the costs. There is always the alternative of investing the funds used to purchase land elsewhere; hence, an opportunity cost is incurred if the current investment returns less to the land value than if that money were invested at the next best alternative. The exclusion of land cost for a land purchase decision is proper because, as shown earlier, the residual value then becomes a guideline for the purchase price of the land. However, land cost should be included in rotation age calculations that seek to maximize financial returns.

PRESENT NET WORTH

The difference between the PNW and the L_e criterion is that land cost, and its subsequent sale, is included in the PNW criterion and that the analysis is made for a single rotation. The criterion could be placed on a perpetual basis by using the L_e formula and substituting PNW for V_0 in the equation.

PNW is calculated in Table 13.1 in the same way as V_0 in the L_e section above except land costs are taken into account. For example, if we assume a $25 per acre land cost,

$$PNW^{10} = V_0^{10} - \$25.00 + (\$25.00) \times \left(\frac{1}{(1.0 + i)^n} \right)^*$$

$$PNW^{10} = -\$12.379 - \$25.00 + \$25.00(0.6139)$$

$$PNW^{10} = -\$22.03$$

The superscripts again indicate the stand age at which PNW is calculated. A land purchase price of $25 was assumed. This is unrealistically low however this price was chosen to maintain continuity in the example.

PNW is maximum at stand age 30, hence, 30 years is the indicated rotation age (Table 13.1). The L_e and PNW criterion indicate the same rotation age but this is not always the case and is due, in part, to the small change in costs in the example. Inclusion of land costs, or other costs, in the early years of an investment usually shortens the rotation, as compared to excluding these costs.

---

*Eq. 4.8.

Present Net Worth Characteristics

The implied objective of the PNW criterion is the maximization of the present value of future cash flows. It considers all future costs and revenues as well as the time value of money. PNW is perhaps the most widely accepted single criterion for management, and hence PNW is the most widely recommended single criterion for rotation determination. Recall, however, that there are often several management objectives and that they sometimes conflict. Therefore, although PNW is often the chosen criterion, it is also often maximized under constraints, such as maximum and minimum wood flows. PNW also usually indicates a shorter rotation than MAI, and the higher the interest rate, the shorter the rotation.

INTERNAL RATE OF RETURN

The internal rate of return (IRR) criterion is calculated for a single rotation and based on the same cash flows as the PNW. Recall that the IRR *is* the interest rate when the PNW equals zero. The actual calculation of IRR is done by iteration; hence, no formula is presented. The interested reader should refer to Chapter 5 where calculations are discussed more fully.

Results of the IRR calculations are shown in column 9 of Table 13.1. The maximum IRR occurs at 25 years and represents the indicated rotation age.

Internal Rate of Return Characteristics

The implied management objective for this criterion is the maximization of the return on investment. This criterion also has the same characteristics as the PNW criterion; inclusion of all costs and revenues, consideration of the time value of money, and a shorter rotation than that of MAI or other criteria.

The maximization of return on investment is a widely accepted criterion; however, the maximization of IRR is not widely used for rotation determination or in computer programs. One reason is the multiple root problem discussed in Chapter 5. Another problem is the iterative calculations needed for IRR. These calculations are both lengthy and difficult to state as an objective function in mathematical programming techniques.

Gregory's (1972) analysis indicates that L_e, PNW, and IRR will all indicate the same rotation age if the maximum L_e is included in the PNW and IRR cash flows as land cost. The differences in rotation age indicated by the L_e, PNW, and IRR criteria may be more academic than real. The ready availability of electronic computers allows calculating all three criteria, which can then be compared. Furthermore, the flatness of the criteria curves near the maxima and the modifying influences of "logging the mill" emphasize again that these are guidelines or targets for management.

FINANCIAL MATURITY

The concept of financial maturity was developed and first published by Duerr, Fedkew, and Gutenberg in 1956. A timber stand, or individual tree, is "financially mature" when the increase in selling value in the period between cuts is equal to the alternative rate of return. As an example, the increase in selling value between 25 and 30 years (money yield table, Table 13.1) is

$$g = \sqrt[5]{\frac{\$214.15}{\$155.90}} - 1.0 = .0656$$

and between 45 and 50 years is

$$g = \sqrt[5]{\frac{\$407.87}{\$366.53}} - 1.0 = .0216$$

These calculations are made prior to each time a stand or tree might be cut and cover the period until the next time a cut might occur. The stands in the above example would be 25 and 45 years old and it would be possible to cut them again in another 5 years. The increases in selling value are then compared to the owners' alternative rate of return (ARR). The tree or stand is cut if the ARR is more than the increase in selling value. For example, suppose the ARR were 6 percent. A cut would not be made at year 25 but would be made at year 45. These calculations indicate the *unadjusted* financial maturity (Duerr 1960).

Financial maturity is represented graphically as

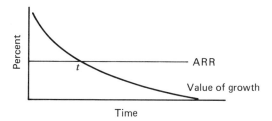

The stand or tree is financially mature at time t, when the ARR equals the rate of value growth. The rate of the value growth is obviously determined by the stand characteristics, changes in product value, and so on. The curve will generally slope downward and to the right but it may sometimes have upward movement—for example, when a stand grows from pulpwood to sawtimber and the value per unit of volume increases.

Financial Maturity Characteristics

Financial maturity was offered by the authors as a field guide. They recognized that certain costs were omitted in the formulation, hence the name "unadjusted" financial maturity. However, they felt the lack in accuracy was compensated for by the gain in simplicity.

Duerr (1960) states that two costs were omitted: Type-b and Type-c. A Type-b cost is the cost of delaying the yield from the stand (tree) in question by not cutting it until the next entry in the stand. A Type-c cost is the cost of lengthening the rotation age on all stands (trees) in the forest. Gregory (1972) states that including these costs will result in the same rotation age as indicated by the L_e criterion. He also states that "...present net worth will be maximized when total revenue is increasing at the preselected rate of interest," and when, at the same time, all costs are incurred at the beginning of the rotation. Otherwise, "...the percent change in revenue must equal the percent change in costs." Thus, financial maturity would not yield the equivalent of PNW maximization if there are costs whose rates change with stand (tree) age.

SUMMARY AND CONCLUSIONS

The use of the criteria discussed above is simple and straightforward. The criterion is chosen to match the landowner's management objectives. The criterion is then calculated for several possible rotation ages based on projected yields, revenues, and costs. The stand age when the criterion is largest is chosen as the rotation age. This procedure can be applied to each even-aged stand in the forest and the wood flow for the forest is determined by these rotation ages.

The rotations are as realistic as the assumptions and data used to calculate them. However, there are several modifying influences causing divergence from a strict rotation age. First, the yield functions are relatively flat near their maxima; hence, cutting a stand a few years before or after the maximum may have a relatively small effect on total yield.

Second, the objective that the criterion reflects is usually not the only objective; therefore, the rotation may be modified accordingly. One example may be a firm in the sawmill business. This firm may want to grow sawtimber regardless of the PNW; therefore, it will choose a rotation that maximizes board foot PNW even if a pulpwood rotation has a greater PNW. Constant wood flow may be another objective. A stand may be cut before rotation in order to maintain it or held longer than rotation as insurance if, for example, it is on a dry site.

Third, all the biological factors are not usually shown in the data. For example, susceptibility to insect attack increases as age increases and may not be shown in the yield tables. Or stand location in an insect outbreak area may not be conveniently included in the analysis. Similar disease and fire protection considerations may also apply. These biological considerations may cause the forest manager to choose a rotation age different from that indicated by the criterion.

Finally, there are external forces that can delay or accelerate the cut. Examples of these are weather, labor supply, and market conditions. These and other external forces are discussed further in Chapter 14.

It is concluded once again that rotation determination is a useful tool for forest management, but it remains a guideline rather than an indelible rule that must be slavishly followed. Forest management decisions must remain flexible so that they can meet the changing conditions in the forest and the world outside the forest.

CALCULATING ALLOWABLE CUT

14

$\mathbf{T}$HE ALLOWABLE CUT is the amount of timber considered available for cutting during a specified time period, usually 1 year. It is the amount of timber the forest manager would like to have cut and thus is a target or guideline that the manager attempts to reach. However, there are many external reasons why the allowable cut is not reached in a particular year, or even in a particular decade.

One of the more important reasons is fluctuations in the forest products market. There may be an overall decrease in economic activity and hence a decrease in demand for corrugated shipping containers, which is ultimately reflected in decreased pulpwood demand. Similarly, decreased housing starts can cause decreased sawtimber demand. There may also be local shifts in demand, such as the opening or closing of a mill. Stumpage cannot be sold nor the allowable cut met if there is no demand for the forest products. Conversely, landowners may increase their cut if stumpage prices rise because of an increased demand for forest products.

Cyclical weather conditions can affect annual cuts for several consecutive years. Extremely wet cycles can make it impossible to go into the woods to perform scheduled harvesting and extremely dry cycles can make harvesting of usually inaccessable timber possible. Woods labor availability can have similar effects. For example, the demand for agricultural or factory labor can shift the labor force out of the woods and reduce harvesting. These and other forces external to the forest can cause an under- or overcut of the previously determined allowable cut.

There are other forces within the "forest system" that can cause under- or overcuts and the periodic adjustment of allowable cut. The most obvious are additions to or subtractions from the managed land base. New land acquisitions must enter the regulatory stream, or land sales and trades can cause adjustment in their districts' allowable cut.

The under- or overcuts caused by the external forces discussed above must often be compensated for by adjusting the allowable cut in subsequent time periods. Also merchantability standards change constantly over time. Smaller trees that were unmerchantable 20 years ago are merchantable today. For example, "chip-n-saw" headrigs have allowed the sale of smaller diameter sawtimber.

In addition, changes in logging technology have made previously inaccessible areas accessible. Also less accessible areas are now accessible during more days in a year. These areas can then be added to the allowable cut. Finally, the forest landowner may desire to increase his cash flow during a particular period, perhaps to take advantage of a new investment opportunity. Increasing the cut generates cash by not only the revenues it brings but also by reducing income tax liability through the depletion accounts.

Allowable cuts are usually developed for large geographical areas and for long time periods. Forests may be divided into districts and districts subdivided into working circles. Allowable cuts are sometimes calculated for working circles and often calculated for districts. These are then aggregated for the forest or total ownership. Allowable cut, then, is a large area concept and infrequently applied to individual stands.

Allowable cuts are often calculated for long time periods. The length of the time period depends on the organization's planning horizon and can cover variable-length time periods. For example, an allowable cut may be calculated annually or biannually for the first 5 years, in 5-year increments for the next 20 years, and in 10-year increments for the next 50 years.

Orientation toward large areas and long time periods is purposeful because it facilitates averaging the cut over time and space. Few forest managers expect the annual allowable cut to be precisely met. Rather, they hope to average the cut over, say, a 5-year period to meet fluctuations in the external and internal forces discussed above. This planned cutting flexibility is usually needed in an operating forest business to meet unpredictable events and is one method of handling uncertainty.

The concept of an allowable cut has fallen into disrepute in some circles because of misuse in certain applications. Long-term timber inventory projections have been made and the annual allowable cut has been used as the estimated actual cut. This allowable cut was often based on biological criteria rather than a combination of biological and economic criteria. Market forces have caused under- or overcuts during these periods, resulting in imprecise projections. Allowable cut has been criticized as being at least partially at fault for the imprecision. The real error was considering allowable cut as a *prediction* of what would happen rather than as a forest management objective.

Another difficulty has arisen when allowable cuts have been published for large areas, such as several counties or whole states. Wood buyers have then tried to buy the wood shown in the allowable cut but have been unsuccessful in finding it for sale. Allowable cut has again been criticized as indicating "nonexistent" wood sources. Part of this problem occurs because allowable cut is calculated on a volume control basis (discussed below) and the actual timber source is unidentified. Furthermore, allowable cut has sometimes been calculated using those formulas discussed in Chapter 10, or others like them. As mentioned, the age distribution must approach normal for the calculations to be precise. This may not always be true and so the published allowable cuts can be misleading. Another part of the discrepancy may be due to ignoring the market. Timber might be available if the price offered were a bit higher.

The following discussion is divided into area and volume control techniques for calculating allowable cut. This is done to clarify the presentation. The student should realize that in most cases allowable cut is calculated by combining the two techniques. An outline of one such system is also presented.

The techniques discussed are useful primarily on those forests that lack data, are extensively managed, or cover several different ownerships, or when the manager wants to spend money for only a rough estimate or reasonableness check. Intensively managed forests often have very specific information on individual stands. There may be stand-specific rotation ages and these, combined with other inventory information, allow the forest manager to use yield tables to estimate the harvest year and yield from each stand. These stand-by-stand estimates are then aggregated to estimate the allowable cut for the whole forest.

CALCULATING ALLOWABLE CUT
WITH AREA CONTROL

Recall that area control requires cutting equal areas or areas of equal productivity annually or periodically. This requires cutting the same number of acres each year in the simplest case of the normal forest with equal productivity on each acre. For example, a 6000-acre forest on a 60-year rotation would have a 100-acre annual cut, as follows:

$$\text{Annual allowable acres cut} = \frac{6,000}{60} = 100 \text{ acres per year}$$

The volume of the annual allowable cut is estimated by looking up the yield in the appropriate table and multiplying by the number of acres. Suppose, for example, the yield at 60 years were 45 cords. Then, the volume of the annual allowable cut is estimated as

$$\text{Annual allowable volume cut} = 100 \text{ acres} \times 45 \text{ cords/acre} = 4,500 \text{ cords}$$

The 5- or 10-year estimate is then simply the annual estimate multiplied by the appropriate number of years. For example, a 5-year estimate would be:

Allowable acres cut$_5$ = 100 acres × 5 years = 500 acres

Allowable volume cut$_5$ = 4,500 cords × 5 years = 22,500 cords

Allowable cut estimation becomes more complex if the acres in the forest have different productivity levels. This requires cutting areas of equal productivity rather than equal area. Suppose, for example, that the forest was a pure, natural, unthinned Loblolly pine stand with 110 feet of basal area and on a 30-year rotation. Assume further that the site indices (SI) were unequal and distributed as shown in Table 14.1.

Unmodified area control requires cutting 34.17 (1025/30) acres each year. However, this would result in unequal volumes each year. For example, cutting in SI_{50} results in about a 680-cord annual cut (34.17 × 19.9), whereas cutting in SI_{90} results in about a 1350-cord annual cut (34.17 × 39.5). There is almost a 100 percent fluctuation between the cuts. These great fluctuations would be very difficult to accommodate if one were attempting to maintain an even wood flow for a manufacturing plant or an even cash flow as a management objective.

The allowable cut can be modified for equal productivity by using the mean yield as the numerator and calculating *equivalent acres* such that cutting an equivalent acre in any site class results in a yield equal to the mean yield per acre. The mean yield per acre is simply the mean weighted by the number of acres in each site class or

$$\overline{Y} = \frac{\sum_i (Y_i \times A_i)}{\sum_i A_i}$$

TABLE 14.1   Example of Equivalent Acre Calculation

SI^a	Acres	Cords[b]	Total yield	Equivalent acres
50	100	19.9	1,990	1.389
60	250	23.4	5,850	1.182
70	375	27.4	10,275	1.009
80	225	32.3	7,267	0.856
90	75	39.5	2,963	0.700
Total	1,025		28,345	

$\overline{Y} = \dfrac{28{,}245}{1{,}025} = 27.65$ cords / acre $EA_{Si=50} = \dfrac{27.65}{19.90} = 1.389$

[a]Base age 50.

[b]*Source*: Burkhart, Parker, and Oderwald (1972). Volume to 4-inch top, OB.

where

$\overline{Y}$ = the mean yield per acre for the forest
i = the ith site class
Y_i = the yield per acre in the ith site class
A_i = the number of acres in the ith site class

For example, column 2 of Table 14.1 contains the number of acres in each site class and column 3 the yield per acre. Column 4 is the product of columns 2 and 3 and is the expression in parentheses above. The sum of column 4 is the numerator and the sum of column 2 the denominator. The mean volume per acre is

$$\overline{Y} = \frac{28{,}345 \text{ cords}}{1{,}025 \text{ acres}} = 27.65 \text{ cords/acre}$$

Note that this implies a mean site index of 70.05 feet.

Equivalent acres are calculated by answering the question: "What must the yield in the ith site class be multiplied by to make it the same as the mean yield?" The equivalent acre is the multiplier. In formula form

$$EA_i \times Y_i = \overline{Y}$$

and solving for EA_i, we obtain

$$EA_i = \frac{\overline{Y}}{Y_i} \tag{14.1}$$

where

EA_i = the equivalent acres for the ith site class and all other variables are as defined above

For example, the EA for the first site class, SI_{50}, is

$$EA_i = \frac{27.65}{19.90} = 1.389$$

and for the last site class

$$EA_5 = \frac{27.65}{39.50} = 0.700$$

This implies that the number of acres that must be cut to equal the mean yield is 1.389 for the first site class and 0.700 for SI_{90}.

The year a particular acre is cut is determined by its age and position in the age distribution. The site index is known for the stand. Then, the number of acres cut is the product of the unmodified area control acreage and the EA_i. For example, the unmodified annual acres cut is 34.17; however, the annual acres cut modified for productivity will be

$$SI_{50} = 34.17 \times 1.389 = 47.46 \text{ acres}$$
$$SI_{90} = 34.17 \times 0.700 = 23.93 \text{ acres}$$

The result is the same mean annual volume cut, except for rounding errors, namely,

$$SI_{50} = 47.46 \text{ acres} \times 19.9 \text{ cords/acre} = 944.45 \text{ cords}$$
$$SI_{90} = 23.93 \text{ acres} \times 39.5 \text{ cords/acre} = 945.24 \text{ cords}$$
$$\text{Mean} = 34.17 \times 27.65 \text{ cords/acre} = 944.80 \text{ cords}$$

Advantages and Disadvantages

There are several advantages that make area control a highly popular technique. First, it is uncomplicated. The concept of harvesting the prescribed number of acres each year is easy to understand and the mathematics used to calculate those acres is simple. Second, the area on the ground to be harvested is readily identified when area control is used with a harvesting rule, such as "harvest the oldest stand first." The combination of a specified number of acres and the harvesting rule identifies those acres on the ground that will be harvested, if we assume, of course, that the forest has been inventoried so that the manager knows which stands are the oldest.

Another advantage is that area control will readily produce a regulated forest. The discussion in Chapter 11 showed how cutting 1 proportionate acre a year will produce a regulated forest in the shortest possible time. Finally, area control seems particularly well suited to even-aged management, which is the most prevalent form of management in the United States today. Thus, area control is widely applicable.

There are several disadvantages. One of the most serious from a commercial viewpoint is that unmodified area control can cause large fluctuations in the volume harvested. This can be caused by different quality sites with different yields, as was demonstrated earlier in this chapter, or by different levels of stocking. Fluctuations in volume harvested caused by different stocking levels will theoretically be eliminated when the forest is fully regulated. However, adjustment must always be made for differences in yield due to differences in site.

A second disadvantage is that area control must be combined with some type of volume control when applied to uneven-aged stands. That is, area control can indicate the number of uneven-aged acres to harvest each year, but the amount harvested from each acre must be determined independently because the acres are not clearcut. Similarly, some type of harvesting rule, such as "oldest stand first," must be specified to identify the specific acres on the ground that will be cut under even-aged management.

The student should also recognize that the simplifying assumption of a single rotation age was made in the preceding analysis of equivalent acres. One rotation age was assumed to apply to all sites classes. This assumption is not strictly true because, as was seen, poorer sites usually require longer rotations to reach the theoretical maximum. The seriousness of this erroneous assumption will depend on the shape of the growth function and how much is lost by cutting too soon on the poorer sites and too late on the better sites.

CALCULATING ALLOWABLE CUT WITH VOLUME CONTROL

Volume control requires cutting equal volumes annually or periodically. The allowable cut is determined by one of several formulas, and this volume is then cut each year. However, many of these formulas are quite different, so it is important to be familiar with each before using it. As in any other model, the user should be certain that it reasonably fits the actual facts of the particular situation on the ground.

Hundeshagen's Formula

Hundeshagen's Formula has already been discussed (Chapter 10). The allowable cut calculation is simply another of its applications. Recall the formula is

$$Y_a = \frac{Y_r}{G_r} G_a$$

where

Y_a = actual yield, or in this case, allowable cut
G_a = actual growing stock
Y_r = yield in a fully stocked forest
G_r = growing stock in a fully stocked forest

Hundeshagen's Formula is used to estimate allowable cut in the same manner in which it was used to estimate yield. The ratio Y_r/G_r is formed from a yield table or yield function that is applicable to the forest in question. The value for Y_r is read directly from the yield table and the value for G_r may be estimated by the Summation Formula. The values of these two variables in the Chapter 10 Douglas-fir example were 13,500 and 390,500 cubic feet, respectively, and the value of the ratio is 0.0346. The procedure for determining annual allowable cut is to estimate the total growing stock on the forest or stand in question and then to simply multiply that estimate by the ratio. For example, the allowable cut is 3460 cubic feet if the growing stock estimate is 100,0000 cubic feet and the allowable cut is 50,994 cubic feet if the estimate is 1,473,823 cubic feet.

Recall also the special assumptions or conditions necessary to apply Hundeshagen's Formula. The first is that the yield table or function from which Y_r and G_r are obtained is applicable to the stand or forest for which allowable cut is being estimated. Second, a straight line must be a good representation of the relationship between a fully and under- or overstocked stands. Finally, the forest must be regulated or have a normal age distribution.

Von Mantel's Formula

Recall also from Chapter 10 that Von Mantel's Formula, as modified by the triangle formula, is

$$Y_a = \frac{2(G_a)}{R}$$

where

Y_a = actual yield, or in this case, allowable cut
G_a = actual growing stock
R = rotation age

This formulation is the ultimate simplification, because not even a yield table is needed to estimate allowable cut. All that is needed is an estimate of the actual growing stock and the rotation age of the timber. The allowable cut for 100,000 cubic feet of growing stock is 2857 cubic feet and that for 1,473,823 cubic feet growing stock is 42,109 cubic feet, if we assume that there is a 70-year rotation. Recall also Von Mantel's Formula could be modified for the age at which volume was first measurable. The allowable cut estimates would change to 3636 and 53,594 cubic feet, respectively, if volume were first measurable at age 15. Von Mantel's Formula, as with Hundeshagen's Formula, requires a forest that is regulated or has a normal age distribution and that yield has a straight line relationship with growing stock. The existence of rotation age as a variable implies that the formula be used only on even-aged stands.

Neither Hundeshagen's nor Von Mantel's formula specifically considers growth. Hundeshagen's Formula depends on an existing yield table and Von Mantel's Formula on the triangle relationship that substitutes into Hundeshagen's Formula. There are other formulas that do consider growth. Some of these are discussed in the following sections.

Meyer's Amortization Formula

Meyer's Amortization Formula specifically includes stand growth and is

$$V_n = V_0(1 + i_t)^n - a\frac{(1 + i_m)^n - 1}{i_m}$$ (14.2)

where

V_n = growing stock volume at future time n
V_0 = growing stock volume today (time zero)
i_t = compound growth percent on entire stand, including ingrowth
i_m = compound growth percent on the cut portion of the stand
a = annual cut
n = number of years in the estimate period

This is another formula that looks formidable but that is really only common sense. Basically, it says future volume (V_n) is equal to current volume (V_0) less the cut (a). Then, quite logically, it recognizes that the forest is growing and adjusts for this growth. The formula compounds present volume up to the end of the period by the expression

$$V_0(1 + i_t)^n$$

the future value of a single payment.

Equal annual cuts of a are assumed. However, growth has already been added for the entire period so it must now be subtracted from the volume harvested before the end of the period. Therefore, the cut is multiplied by the future value of a terminating annual annuity, or

$$a\frac{(1 + i_m)^n - 1}{i_m}$$

Note that differential growth rates, i_t and i_m, accommodate differences in growing stock and cut. Trees cut may be older and therefore slower growing. Further, the stand, in addition to growing faster, may also have ingrowth, which is included in i_t.

Allowable annual cut can be estimated by solving (Eq. 14.2) for a, as follows

$$a = \left(V_0(1.0 + i_t)^n - V_n\right) \times \frac{i_m}{(1.0 + i_m)^n - 1.0}$$ (14.3)

where all variables are as defined above. The expression $V_0 \times (1.0 + i_t)^n$ is the amount the stand would have grown if no timber were cut. V_n is subtracted from this expression so that the result is the amount available for cutting expressed in the "future value" at year n. The far right-hand expression is the Sinking Fund Formula. Multiplying by it tells you how much timber you can cut at the specified growth rate, i_m, in order to obtain equal cut each year.

For example, suppose you had an uneven-aged sawtimber forest on a 5-year cutting cycle, that $V_0 = 30$ mbf, $V_n = 32$ mbf, $i_t = 0.06$, and that $i_m = 0.04$. Then, the amount available for cutting throughout the 5-year cutting cycle, in terms of the end of the cutting cycle, is

$$\left(30(1.06)^5 - 32\right) = (40.146 - 32) = 8.146 \text{ mbf/acre}$$

The Sinking Fund Multiplier for 4 percent at 5 years is 0.1846; therefore, the allowable annual cut is

$$a = 8.146 \times 0.1846 = 1.504 \text{ mbf/acre}$$

A forest-wide estimate is made by multiplying the allowable cut per acre times the number of acres in the forest. Alternatively, total forest growing stock estimates could be used in the formula.

The special assumptions or requirements for using the formula are that all parts of forest have the same growth percent if the formula is applied forest-wide and that growth percents remain the same before and after cutting regardless of stocking. The latter assumption implies the cut must be equally distributed over all age classes and that the relative age distribution is unchanged by the cut. Another assumption is that the cut is equal each year. Difficulties in meeting this condition were discussed at the beginning of this chapter.

Meyer's Formula is particularly well suited to uneven-aged management because it directly considers growing stock levels and growth percent. For example, changes in reserve growing stock are accomplished by making V_n equal to the new desired level. However, a lot of growth data are needed to determine the two growth percents and these may not always be available.

Austrian Formula

The Austrian Formula is a simplified version of Meyer's formula and is

$$\text{Annual cut} = I + \frac{G_a - G_r}{a} \tag{14.4}$$

where

I = annual increment
G_a = present growing stock (V_0 in Meyer's)
G_r = desired growing stock (V_n in Meyer's)
a = adjustment period chosen

Assume, for example, the same figures as in the Meyer's Formula example and that $I = 1.8$ mbf. Then,

$$\text{Annual cut} = 1.8 + \frac{30 - 32}{5} = 1.4 \text{ mbf/acre}$$

The Austrian Formula is quite simple, requiring only that the annual increment (I) be cut, plus or minus the average of any change desired in the growing stock $(G_a - G_r)/a$. The formula must thus have good increment data to be effective. But note that this is a simplification, because I should change each year, rather than remain constant, if the then current growing stock changes and if the growth percent is constant.

Hanzlik Formula

The Hanzlik Formula was developed for old growth in the Douglas-fir region as a glance at it will indicate. The formula is

$$\text{Annual cut} = \frac{V_m}{R} + I \tag{14.5}$$

where

V_m = volume of overmature timber
R = rotation age
I = annual growth averaged over the rotation

Both this and the Austrian Formula cut annual increment. However, Hanzlik's formula assumes the growing stock needs no adjustment and that only the overmature timber need be changed. This is seen in the first expression, which distributes the overmature cut over the entire rotation. The decision to cut overmature timber throughout the entire rotation is completely arbitrary and ignores any of the financial or age class considerations previously discussed. R can be varied to reflect these considerations, but there is no guide for deciding on its value. If there is little or no V_m, you are left with cutting I. Further, there is no allowance for increasing or decreasing the level of growing stock. These characteristics of the formula should be kept in mind by anyone seeking to apply it. The formula was developed for a special application and future users should question, as with any of these formulas, how well the application fits their situation.

Advantages and Disadvantages

One of the main advantages of volume control is that some estimates can be made with very little data. For example, Von Mantel's Formula needs only an estimate of total growing stock, which may be made by an extensive timber cruise, and rotation age. Thus, these allowable cut estimation techniques can be applied as rough first estimates or when better data simply are unavailable, as in developing nations. They can also be a useful overall guide and first step toward regulation because the actual cut, currently made on the forest, can be easily compared to the target calculated cut. Finally, those formulas specifically including growth and growing stock level manipulation are particularly well suited to uneven-aged management.

A disadvantage for those formulas requiring little data is that the estimates may be imprecise and inaccurate. Poor or nonexistent data carry their price and estimates based on insufficient information will usually be poor. Several of the formulas required growth or increment estimates. These can be expensive and difficult to make if they are not already available. Finally, there is the previously discussed disadvantage of knowing the volume to cut but not where it is located. For example, the Austrian Formula indicated a 1.4 mbf/acre annual cut, but did not indicate the size trees to cut or the stands from which to cut them.

COMBINATION AREA AND VOLUME CONTROL

A combination of area and volume control, with perhaps a bit more emphasis on area control, is often found in practice. This section contains a discussion of a combined procedure cast in the light of even-aged management, although it is equally applicable to uneven-aged management.

The first step is obtaining inventory data. A series of cover-type maps is probably most common. They are often developed from an overlay on aerial photos that have been field typed by the district forester. The information recorded about each stand varies by organizational needs but certainly would include species or species association, age class, and level of stocking. Regeneration method is often used as a surrogate for level of stocking. Also, approximate estimates of volume or yield might be included if they cannot be inferred from the preceding data. Estimated site quality and silvicultural condition and treatment needs, if these also cannot be inferred from the preceding data, might be included.

In the second step individual stands would probably be arrayed in descending order with those to be cut first at the top. A preliminary rotation age has probably already been estimated, if only to help define the age classes for data collection.

First in the array may be overmature stands, and those with an overmature overstory needing release. These may be followed by understocked mature stands, which should be regenerated soon to avoid the opportunity costs of understocking. The fully stocked mature stands may then follow and, finally, the immature stands may be simply aggregated because they will not be cut for many years.

The array may then be rearranged in an age class distribution, stand by stand, such as was discussed in even-aged regulation. Several variables for each stand, including a way to identify it, its size in acres or hectares, and the volume or probable yield, are kept readily accessible when making the array.

Some preliminary cut estimates might be made as the third step. Unmodified area control might be used as a first approximation because it will always lead to a fully regulated forest. The first array in step 2 might be used to determined sequence of cut. A proportionate acre analysis, discussed in Chapter 11, might be made, and wood flow would certainly be estimated for many years in the future. Concurrently, some type of volume control estimate, using one of the formulas discussed, would probably be made. This might be modified by the financial cash flow needs of the firm; by the mill's wood needs, and by procurement's assessment of what it can buy on the open market.

An iterative adjustment process might be the next step. For example, assume that the forest contains 120,000 acres on a 60-year sawtimber and pulpwood rotation. Unmodified area control indicates 2000 acres annual cut. It may also have been determined that the annual allowable cut should be 40 million bf and 10 thousand cords, the equivalent of 20 mbf/acre and 5 cords/acre. These figures may be the direct result of the volume control calculations discussed earlier in this chapter or they may already have been modified in light of the procurement department's assessment of open market wood availability.

Next, the cut from the first 2000 acres of stands arrayed in step 2 would be added to see how close it comes to 40 million bf and 10,000 cords. It would probably be less than the desired volume because of the overstory and under-stocked stands.

Therefore, some of the mature, well-stocked stand might be harvested to increase the cut. The procurement department might also be asked to reassess their estimates or if they could open a new procurement area to help alleviate the undercut. PNWs may also be calculated for each of the alternatives to examine the effects on the financial aspects of management.

An acceptable solution may be found on the first iteration. Conversely, several additional iterations may be required to find an acceptable compromise between the biological needs of the stand, the wood flow needs of the mill, and the financial requirements of the corporation.

The end result of this process will be a *cutting budget*, which is a plan, or budget, specifying which stands will be cut, when they will be cut, and how they will be cut. The cutting budget ties down the planned action to specific acres on the ground. It identifies just which of the many stands will be cut and approximately when they will be cut. It may specify the exact year or it may list the stands in order of precedence during a 5-year planning cycle. The cutting budget is a guideline and is followed flexibly. No one expects all stands to be cut exactly when specified.

The cutting budget will also explicitly or implicitly indicate how the stand is to be cut. Standard practice may be a clear-cut and anything not specified differently may be considered a clear-cut. The overstory cut, on the other hand, would be a selection cut.

The time period covered by the cutting budget is arbitrary, but is usually in 3- to 5-year increments in, for example, the southern United States. Detailed stand-by-stand analysis may not be needed for more than one or possibly two periods in the future because changing internal and external conditions will probably change some of the specifics by the time the stands are cut.

All the detailed information on the inventory is needed to array the stands in the correct order. However, the cutting budget assignment of specific stands need only be done for one or two periods because the cutting budget will not be entirely met, therefore, the second budget will have to be adjusted anyhow. Furthermore, changing technology and merchantability standards will change the yields from the lands. Thus, there is no need to go to the trouble and expense of unneeded detailed plans unless computer techniques, such as those discussed in Chapter 16, provide them at very low additional cost.

PRESENT AND FUTURE MANAGEMENT TECHNIQUES

PART

MATHEMATICAL PROGRAMMING AND FOREST MANAGEMENT

15

COMPUTER USE IN forestry has increased steadily since the early application of automatic data processing in the 1950s and early 1960s. Many early applications manipulated continuous forest inventory data for private lands or for statewide inventories made by the USDA Forest Service. Use continually increased over a wide range of applications. These included: production scheduling in forest products plants; designing balanced logging systems using different types of equipment; analyses for low cost wood procurement; inventory control in woodyards; industrial location analyses; and many others. Three bibliographies contain citations of many applications and the interested reader should refer to these (Bare, 1971; Martin and Sendak, 1973; Field, various dates).

Computer use should not be confused with mathematical programming. Today's electronic computers are useful for many data manipulations. They are well suited for these manipulations because they can perform arithmetic operations at great speed and do not make computational errors once the programs are "debugged." These uses are particularly helpful in forestry, where often a great number of individual observations must be manipulated to obtain the desired answers—for example, individual tree observations to obtain volume estimates on timber cruises. These applications are not considered mathematical programming. Mathematical programs are usually techniques or specific algorithms that allocate resources to optimize a particular objective. Optimization means either minimizing or maximizing the objective, which is often stated as an objective function. For example, some mathematical programs may be used to minimize the cost of producing 1000 board feet of timber, while others might be used to maximize the lumber recovery from a log in a sawmill.

There are many types of mathematical programs. These types are often categorized by the different mathematics used to obtain the optimum. The next section contains brief summaries of the most prevalent types of mathematical programs. The section's coverage is neither exhaustive nor are its definitions stated mathematically. Rather, it is intended to give the undergraduate forester a brief, general knowledge of the programs and how they work. It is hoped this will make the student a more knowledgeable listener, and perhaps a more competent commentator, during on-the-job discussions of forest management applications.

SUMMARY OF MATHEMATICAL PROGRAMMING TECHNIQUES

Many of these categories are not mutually exclusive. Sometimes programs exist that may not precisely fit into a category or are ambiguously defined. A new category becomes defined when enough of these programs exist. However, sometimes the student must contend with the program before the new category is formed, and this can be confusing.

Linear Programming

Linear programming (LP) is the most widely used technique in forestry and probably in mathematical programming. There are several reasons for this. First, the technique was developed and implemented during World War II and thus has had many years to be perfected. Further, LP can handle large data sets with many alternative solutions in a very efficient way using the revised simplex solution technique. This is because the technique does not need to examine every possible solution to find the optimum one. LP is also very flexible and can be applied to a wide variety of problems. Thus, it has broad application once the methodology is learned. In addition, LP computer algorithms are well documented and generally available on most computer systems so there is little difficulty in running an LP. Finally, sensitivity analyses are performed easily so the characteristics of the optimal solution can easily be examined.

The general linear program either maximizes or minimizes a linear function, called the objective function, subject to a set of linear equalities and/or inequalities. The general linear program has several requirements, or assumptions which must be made, of the system being analyzed. First, the relationships in the system must be linear or well represented over the range of analysis by linear functions. This requirement is perhaps one of the most serious limitations for using LP. Nonlinear programs have been developed to overcome this difficulty. Another requirement is that the variables in the equations are divisible. For example, an LP may be solving for the number of acres to cut in different timber types. The solution may indicate that a fraction of an acre should be cut or that a fraction of a man-day of labor should be used to cut it. Some systems do not allow this divisibility but require that integer values of the variables be used. For example, one cannot build a fraction of a dam for irrigation and flood control, nor can one use a fraction of a tractor to build it. Integer programming has been developed to help solve this problem. Finally, LP requires that all relationships are stated deterministically. The equations must be stated as mathematical equalities or inequalities. They cannot be stated as probabilities. Stochastic linear programming has been developed for those instances in which this requirement is too restricting.

Linear programming is discussed at length at the end of this chapter. A broader knowledge of LP is necessary because of its wide application in forestry and because many other programming techniques are modified LPs.

Integer Programming

An integer program is a linear program that has been modified so the variables in the objective function take only integer values. A pure integer program has all the objective function variables restricted to integers, whereas a mixed integer program has only some of the objective function variables restricted to integers. Sometimes, one can simply change an LP solution to all integer values and not bother with an integer program. However, this can result in a solution that violates some of the constraints and thus is impossible to implement or that is not as close to the optimal solution as the analyst might believe. Integer programs are useful to be sure this does not happen.

Nonlinear Programming

A nonlinear program (NLP) is a program in which nonlinear equations are optimized. Nonlinear equations include those with geometric terms, such as sine, cosine, and tangent; those with logarithmic and other exponential functions; and those with interactions between two variables, such as $X_1 X_2$ or $X_1^{X_2}$. Quadratic programming is a special case of NLP in which the objective function is a quadratic form but the constraints are linear. Thus, it is similar to LP.

However, one big dissimilarity between LP and NLP is that NLP has no single-solution techniques, such as the revised simplex technique in LP. Rather, a great number of techniques and programming algorithms are used. A Taylor's series approximation or first and second derivatives are two that are commonly used. Numerical search techniques are also used, particularly when analytical techniques are inapplicable. Another dissimilarity is that only in certain cases is it known whether the NLP solution is a local or a global optima. In general, NLP has inefficient solution techniques and is used on small problems that are easily defined.

Dynamic Programming

Dynamic programming is used to solve problems that can be divided into different, sequential stages. A decision is made at each stage based on the input from the preceding stage, or the initial conditions if the program is just beginning. The decision determines the output from that stage. This output becomes the input for the next stage. Thus, a recursive process is defined where there is a sequence of outputs and inputs from one stage to the next.

A dynamic program starts at either the first or last stage of the sequence and determines the optimal solution at that stage. The program then moves to the next stage in line and determines the optimum based on the preceding stage solution. This procedure continues until the first, or last, stage is reached.

Dynamic programming can be used with either linear or nonlinear functions and with discrete or continuous variables. However, like NLP, there is no standard solution technique and each dynamic program must be individually programmed. Furthermore, the number of calculations needed for a solution explodes as additional stages are added so the technique is most useful for small problems. This is a particularly serious drawback in forest management planning where, for example, cutting schedules must be derived for many different time periods and cover types.

Network Analysis

Network analysis is another mathematical programming technique that has many solution methodologies. Network analysis seeks to find the optimal or most efficient route through a system of lines or channels that have connecting nodes or points. The relationships are usually deterministic, although stochastic elements may be included.

Transportation problems and standard assignment problems, two standard LP methodologies, are network analyses. The transportation problem is generally concerned with delivering a product or commodity located at several different points (sometimes called "supply" points) to a set of other locations (sometimes called "demand" points) at minimum cost. The classic transportation problem involves minimum cost delivery of merchandise from a set of warehouses to a set of retail outlets. Planning a minimum cost procurement system for a pulp or sawmill is an obvious forestry application. The assignment problem, which is often concerned with assigning different jobs to different machines, can have applications in wood processing plants, such as furniture factories. Assignment problems often use the transportation solution algorithm for their calculations.

Two other network analysis techniques are widely known: the Program Evaluation and Review Technique (PERT) and the Critical Path Method (CPM). These are management techniques that allow the planning, scheduling, and controlling of large projects. They require documenting each step in the process beforehand; thus, potential barriers and delays may be predicted and, it is hoped, avoided. They also allow scheduling each step in order to minimize the delay in subsequent steps that depend on it. Finally, this knowledge allows coordinating and controlling operations to maintain the production schedule. PERT, which was developed by the U.S. Navy in the 1950s to help build the Polaris submarine, incorporates stochastic elements. It can calculate the probability of meeting product deadlines at various points throughout the process and also the expected value of completion time. CPM is similar to PERT but uses deterministic functions.

Markov Processes

Markov processes are a subset of the more general category of problems called "random processes." These are processes that develop over time and are difficult to predict. Thus, the processes are not deterministic and a great many stochastic elements are used to model them. Markov processes are widely used because the large number of simplifying assumptions make them easier to apply than other, non-Markovian processes. Markov processes may be either discrete or continuous.

In the simplest case, a Markov process looks at the state, or condition, of a system at different points in time. For example, one might want to predict the volume of a forest stand at the end of every 5 years. The volume each 5 years is the "state" of the process and the movement from one state to another is described by a "transition probability." The probability of moving from one state to another in the next time period is calculated with the assumption that the current state depends only on the preceding state and that the future state depends only on the current state. In our example, the stand condition today depends only on the condition 5 years ago. And, the condition 5 years from now depends only on the condition today. Thus, a matrix of probabilities, p_{ij}, can be defined where i is the state in the current time period and j is the state in the next future time period. This "transition matrix" is needed for each time period in which the next state is predicted. Sometimes it is assumed that the probabilities do not change from one transition to another. The process is then called stationary and only one transition matrix is needed. Markovian processes can be used to predict the probability of a system occupying any particular state in any future time period and can be used to calculate an expected value when a point estimate is desired.

Queueing Models

Queueing models examine a type of problem but are not a solution technique. In fact, many queueing models use a Markov process for their solution. The models examine the arrival of items at a server to discover the reasons for congestion and delay. Solutions may be possible once the reasons are known. These models can provide estimates of the number of items waiting to enter a system, the number of items in a system, and the expected time spent waiting and in the system. One forestry application would be analysis of turnaround time for trucks in a woodyard.

Inventory Models

Inventory models are another class of problem-oriented models. They examine the flow of items into and out of an inventory. The flow into the inventory is sometimes called the replenishment process and the flow out the demand process. Many solution techniques are used and they may be either deterministic or stochastic. A classic, early model is the Economic Order Quantity (EOQ) model. This model examines the costs of ordering and holding an inventory, in its simplest form, and uses calculus to determine the order size that minimizes costs. Other inventory models may use LP for their solution. Managing pulpwood inventories is an obvious forestry application.

Simulation Models

The term "simulation," like the term "model," is very general and can have different meanings to different people. The term even has a general meaning within mathematical programming. The usual meaning is that a computer model is built of a real-world system using mathematical or logical relationships. This model is then used to perform experiments. Next, data generated by the experiments are analyzed, often using statistical techniques as in any other data analysis, and conclusions drawn about the real-world system. Thus, there are four main elements in simulation: modeling the real-world system, performing experiments to obtain data, analyzing the data, and drawing conclusions.

Each of these main elements can have many substeps and be described in great detail. Model building requires much knowledge of the real-world system and a great deal of imagination and ingenuity in combining what is known about the real-world system with the programming and analytical techniques that are available. Thus, it can be both art and science. Simulation models may use any of the programming techniques already discussed, either alone or imbedded in a computer program containing several techniques and/or mathematical relationships. Models should be verified to see that they behave the way they were designed to behave and should be validated to see that a reasonable abstraction of the real-world system was created.

The experimental element requires considering such things as the experimental design (e.g., latin squares), which variables in the model will be experimented on, the number of interactions or simulation runs, and the initial, ending, and incremental values of the variables during the simulation. The statistical analysis may use standard techniques such as correlation or regression analyses.

Simulation can be used when direct analytical techniques can not be used or when the real-world system cannot be experimented on directly. For example, too little may be known about a system to estimate coefficients in an equation or the system may be too complex for an analytical solution. Simulation could then be used to generate data to estimate coefficients or to estimate the end result of complex interactions. Also, one may not want to experiment directly on a system such as a production process or a functioning organization for fear of disrupting the process during experimentation and incurring high costs. Simulation may be used here. There are many forestry examples in which experimentation is not possible. Perhaps growth and yield prediction is one of the best. Here, the time required to experiment with different plantation spacings or thinning regimes makes experimentation on the real-world system impossible. Computer models simulating the growth of forest stands, such as PTAEDA, developed by Daniels and Burkhart (1975), allow analysis of different spacing and thinning regimes in a matter of minutes rather than decades.

Two types of information can be obtained from simulations. One is a better understanding of how the real-world system behaves and the other is an estimate of variable values, which will optimize the real-world system. Both types of information are often obtained simultaneously from simulation. For example, growth and yield simulations not only tell the analyst how a forest stand will behave through time but can also indicate the spacing necessary to optimize yield.

Simulation models can be written in any general computer language, such as FORTRAN or COBOL, or can be written in a special simulation language. The names of these special languages are familiar to many students and include GASP, GPSS, SIMSCRIPT, and DYNAMO. Some advantages of simulation languages are as follows: building and debugging the model is simplified thus saving time and trouble; the model is more easily changed during the experimentation element; and the simulation language usually contains random and stochastic variable generators and some kind of time flow process, thereby relieving the analyst of the task of building these into his program. The major disadvantage is the time required to learn the simulation language. This investment may not be worthwhile if a general language is already known and only one or two models will be written.

LINEAR PROGRAMMING — A GRAPHICAL SOLUTION

As stated, the general linear program either maximizes or minimizes a linear function, called the *objective function*, subject to a set of linear equalities and/or inequalities called the *constraints*. All large computer systems have a prewritten program to solve LPs. These programs use the *revised simplex method* of calculation, which is based on the *simplex method* developed by G. B. Dantzig. The simplex method uses simple arithmetic in a predetermined sequence to solve the LP. Students are often required to solve LPs using the simplex method and hand calculators. However, the method is not presented here because the calculations are lengthy and not particularly insightful and because the method is not used for computer programs. Rather, a graphical solution to a linear program is discussed because this method provides intuitive understanding of the function of LPs and defines several LP terms. Almost any operations research book will explain the simplex method for those students interested in it.

The General Mathematical Model

The general mathematical model is presented before the graphical solution because it is often seen and because it also helps define some common LP terms.

The general form for a maximization problem is:

Maximize $\quad Z = c_1 x_1 + c_2 x_2 + \cdots + c_n x_n$ $\qquad$ (15.1)

Subject to $\quad a_{11} x_1 + a_{12} x_2 + \cdots + a_{1n} x_n \leq r_1$ $\qquad$ (15.2)

$\qquad\qquad a_{21} x_1 + a_{22} x_2 + \cdots + a_{2n} x_n \leq r_2$

$$\vdots$$

$\qquad\qquad a_{m1} x_1 + a_{m2} x_2 + \cdots a_{mn} x_n \leq r_m$

and

$$x_j \geq 0 \qquad\qquad\qquad (15.3)$$

$$j = 1, 2, \ldots, n$$

$$i = 1, 2, \ldots, m$$

where

Z = the objective to be maximized
x_j = choice variables for which the problem is solved
c_j = coefficients of the choice variables and are already known. They are the contribution of each choice variable to the objective which is being maximized
r_i = constraints or restrictions imposed on solving the problem and are already known
a_{ij} = coefficients which quantify the effect of the ith constraint on the jth choice variable and are already known

The general form shows the three major parts of an LP, the objective function (Eq. 15.1), the set of inequality constraints (Eq. 15.2), and the nonnegativity constraints (Eq. 15.3). The *choice variables*, x_j, are those for which the problem is solved in order to obtain the maximum value for the objective, Z. For example, Z may be profit and the choice variables may be the thousands of board feet of different lumber dimensions that a sawmill could cut. The coefficients, c_j, are the profit per thousand board feet for each of the n dimensions that can be cut.

The constraints on the objective function are contained in Eqs. 15.2 and 15.3. The *nonnegativity* constraints (Eq. 15.3) simply state that the choice variables cannot have a negative value. In our example, the sawmill could not cut a negative number of board feet of pine two-by-fours.

This means that the graphical solution, presented below, is restricted to the northeast quadrant. The *inequality constraints*, r_i, contain other constraints (sometimes called restraints or restrictions) on the solution. They may be constraints placed by the maximum number amount of two-by-fours, two-by-sixes, and two-by-eights that a particular machine can manufacture or they may be the maximum volume of different-sized logs (say, $r_1 = 10$-in. logs, $r_2 = 12$-in. logs, and so on) that are expected during the production period. The constraint is related to the choice variable by the a_{ij} coefficient. This coefficient quantifies the effect of the ith constraint on the jth choice variable. For example, a_{11} may be the number of board feet required from 10-in. logs to make two-by-fours, a_{12} the number required to make two-by-sixes, and a_{21} the number required from 12-in. logs to make two-by-fours. The value of any a_{ij} may be zero.

The nonnegativity constraints are usually unstated in practice and simply understood to exist. Most prewritten LPs automatically enter the nonnegativity constraints; thus, the user does not have to specify them. Therefore, people are almost always talking about the r_i's when they talk about constraints. The prewritten programs also contain computational techniques that allow the constraints to be stated as any inequality ($\leq$, $<$, $\geq$, $>$) or as an equality ($=$).

The preceding general form may also be stated in summation notation as

$$\text{Maximize} \quad Z = \sum_{j}^{n} c_j x_j \tag{15.4}$$

$$\text{Subject to} \quad \sum_{j}^{n} a_{ij} x_j \leq r_i \tag{15.5}$$

$$\text{and} \quad x_j \geq 0 \tag{15.6}$$

where all variables are as previously defined or may be further reduced by using matrix notation to

$$\text{Maximize} \quad Z = cx \tag{15.7}$$

$$\text{Subject to} \quad Ax \leq r \tag{15.8}$$

$$\text{and} \quad x \geq 0 \tag{15.9}$$

The matrix of a_{ij} coefficients represented by A in Eq. 15.8 is called the A matrix.

The minimization problem may be stated in summation and matrix notation as

$$\text{Minimize} \quad Z = \sum_{j}^{n} c_j x_j \tag{15.10}$$

$$\text{Subject to} \quad \sum_{j}^{n} a_{ij} x_j \geq r_i \tag{15.11}$$

and $\qquad x_j \geq 0$ $\hspace{4cm}$ (15.12)

and

Minimize $\qquad Z = cx$ $\hspace{4cm}$ (15.13)

Subject to $\qquad Ax \geq r$ $\hspace{4cm}$ (15.14)

and $\qquad x \geq 0$ $\hspace{4cm}$ (15.15)

The objective function (Eqs. 15.10 and 15.13), inequality constraints (Eqs. 15.11 and 15.14), and nonnegativity constraints (Eqs. 15.12 and 15.15) are all present as before. The only difference is that the objective, Z, is now being minimized instead of maximized and the sign in the inequality constraints now goes in the opposite direction.

A Maximization Problem

An example will help clarify the ideas presented so far. Suppose there are two tracts of land. Tract 1 has 44 acres and an allowable cut of 1200 cubic feet per acre. Tract 2 has 88 acres and 1600 cubic feet per acre allowable cut. It costs $1 per acre to prepare and administer a timber sale on either tract. The total appropriation for preparation and administration is $100. At least 10,000 visitor days of recreation must be provided. Tract 1 can provide 200 visitor days per acre while Tract 2 can provide 500 visitor days per acre. Of course, recreation is lost when an acre is cut. The problem is to determine how many acres to cut in each tract to maximize timber cut.

The first step is to restate the problem in the general form. Often, this is the most difficult step. The preceding problem statement tells us timber production is to be maximized, and we must find the number of acres in each tract to cut. We also know that Tract 1 yields 1200 cubic feet for each acre cut and Tract 2 yields 1,600 cubic feet. Thus, the objective function is

Maximize $\qquad Z = 1{,}200x_1 + 1{,}600x_2$ $\hspace{3cm}$ (15.16)

where

Z = the cubic feet of timber cut
x_j = the number of acres to cut in the jth tract, $j = 1, 2$

Formulating the inequality constraints is more difficult. First, the LP must be instructed that only 44 acres in Tract 1 and 88 acres in Tract 2 are available for cutting. Thus,

$1.0x_1 \leq 44$ Tract 1 acres
$1.0x_2 \leq 88$ Tract 2 acres

The a_{ij} coefficient for both these constraints is 1.0 because each acre cut (x_1 or x_2) contributes 1 acre to the constraint.

Next, there are only $100 available to administer the sale and it costs $1 for each acre cut. So, the budget constraint is

$$\$1.00x_1 + \$1.00x_2 \leq \$100.00$$

The a_{ij} coefficient is $1 because each acre cut uses $1 in the budget constraint.

The recreation constraint is perhaps the most difficult to formulate. The two tracts combined will provide 52,800 visitor days (VD) recreation if no cutting occurs (44 acres × 200 VD/acre + 88 acres × 500 VD/acre). However, 200 or 500 visitor days per acre are lost for each acre cut and at least 10,000 visitor days must be provided. These figures are combined into a recreation constraint as

$$52{,}800 - 200x_1 - 500x_2 \geq 10{,}000 \text{ visitor days}$$

which may be put into the standard maximization form by subtracting 52,800 from both sides and multiplying by -1 to obtain

$$200x_1 + 500x_2 \leq 42{,}800 \text{ visitor days}$$

The constraints are summarized below. Zero coefficients have been added to illustrate that the A matrix is the same as in Eq. 15.2.

$$1.0x_1 + 0.0x_2 \leq 44$$
$$0.0x_1 + 1.0x_2 \leq 88$$
$$\$1.00x_1 + \$1.00x_2 \leq 100$$
$$200x_1 + 500x_2 \leq 42{,}800 \tag{15.17}$$

Finally, there are the nonnegativity constraints:

$$x_j \geq 0.0, \quad j = 1, 2 \tag{15.18}$$

The problem is solved graphically by working only in the northeast quadrant. This was required by both the nonnegativity constraint (Eq. 15.18) and logic. Some acres of land can be cut and no acres of land can be cut but a negative amount of acres of land cannot be cut. This is shown in Figure 15.1, where the number of acres to be cut in Tract 1 is shown on the y axis and the number of acres to be cut in Tract 2 is shown on the x axis. Also shown are the first two inequality constraints. There are only 44 acres in Tract 1 and 88 in Tract 2, thus, these are upper boundaries for the number of acres cut. Any solution must lie on or below the number of acres in Tract 1 and on or to the left of the number of acres in Tract 2.

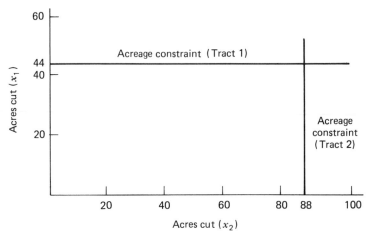

FIGURE 15.1 *Acreage constraints.*

The area in which a solution may occur is further reduced by adding the budget and recreation constraints. The constraint may be plotted by first calculating the intercept with one of the axes and then calculating the slope. For example, if zero acres of x_1 are cut the budget allows 100 acres of x_2 to be cut, or

$$1.00(0.0) + 1.00x_2 = 100$$
$$x_2 = 100$$

The slope may be calculated by setting the constraint equal to zero and solving for x_2, or

$$1.00x_1 + 1.00x_2 = 0$$
$$x_2 = -1.00x_1$$

The slope tells us that for each additional acre of x_2 that is cut, one less acre of x_1 may be cut. The budget constraint is then plotted on the graph. Similarly, the slope and intercept are calculated for the recreation constraint, which is also then plotted (Figure 15.2). Again, the solution may occur either on or to the left of these two new constraints.

Part of the budget constraint falls to the right of the recreation constraint. This part of the budget constraint is *redundant* because it is superseded by part of the recreation constraint. The entire Tract 2 acreage constraint becomes redundant with the addition of the recreation constraint. The double line and the axes within it define the *feasible region*. A solution occurring in or on the boundary of this region is a feasible solution given the constraints placed on problem. Any solution outside the region is an infeasible solution because one of the constraints will be violated. The intersection of two constraints, or a constraint and an axis,

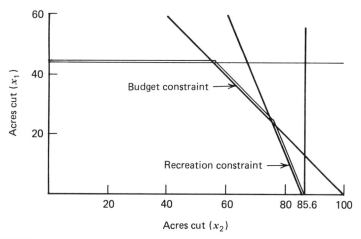

FIGURE 15.2 *Budget and recreation constraints.*

defines an *extreme point*. These are important because one of the LP theorems states the solution will occur at an extreme point or, in a special case, on the line between two extreme points.

The value of the objective function could be calculated at each extreme point and compared to other extreme point values until the maximum is found. This is essentially what the computer programs do. However, the solution may also be found by plotting the objective function on the graph and moving it to the right until it is tangent with the farthest point in the feasible region. This is done by solving the objective function for x_2, considering Z as a variable, and plotting a family of curves with the same slope. Thus,

$$Z = 1,200x_1 + 1,600x_2$$

$$x_2 = Z - \frac{1,200}{1,600}x_1$$

Several parallel lines in the family are plotted (Figure 15.3). The farther right the curve, the higher the value of Z. Thus, the value of Z is maximized at the last place on the feasible region that the objective function can touch, where $x_1 = 24$ and $x_2 = 76$ in our example. No greater value can be obtained for Z because the solution will be outside the feasible region and thus infeasible. The value of the objective function at this point is

$$Z = 1,200(24) + 1,600(76) = 150,400 \text{ cubic feet}$$

The solution can occur anywhere on the boundary between two extreme points in the special case where the objective function's slope is the same as the boundary's. Then, the objective function is tangent to the boundary both at and

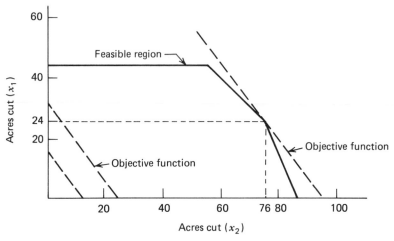

FIGURE 15.3 *Objective function and solution.*

between the two extreme points. Any combination of choice variables along this line is an optimum solution.

The amounts of the other constraints that were used can be found by substituting the solution values into the equations. The entire budget was used [$1(24) + $1(76) = $100] and exactly the required number of visitor days provided [52,800 − 200(24) − 500(76) = 10,000].

The solution can be checked by trying to increase the cut. Suppose 1 more acre in Tract 2 were cut because that tract has the largest allowable cut. However, we must decrease the Tract 1 cut so that the budget constraint, which was exactly met, is not violated. The total cut does increase to 150,800 cubic feet [1200(23) + 1600(77) = 150,800] but the visitor days drop to 9700 [52,800 − 200(23) − 500(77) = 9,700] and the recreation constraint is not met. The interested student may try other combinations of the choice variables to see whether the cut can be increased while still meeting all constraints.

HARVEST SCHEDULING WITH MATHEMATICAL PROGRAMMING

16

HARVEST SCHEDULING, AS discussed earlier, is one of the most critical sets of forest management decisions. It determines the age distribution, forest structure, and the flow of forest products and hence forest revenues and costs. It is also one of the more complex decisions because the entire forest should be scheduled to obtain optimal productivity. Yet, the large number of timber stands and other variables that must be considered for forest-wide optimization cause inumerable alternative schedules. Choosing the optimal schedule, or even getting close to it, easily boggles the mind if manual techniques are used. Thus, harvest scheduling is a natural application for mathematical programming.

One of the first published applications was that of Kidd, Thompson, and Hoepner (1966), followed by Ware and Clutter (1971) and Navon (1971). Since then, many models have been developed—for example, Chappelle (1966); Clutter, Fortson, and Pienaar (1978); Sassaman, Holt, and Bergsvick (1972); Tedder, Schmidt, and Gourley (1980a); and Walker (1971). Many of these use linear programming techniques to optimize an objective function. Space limitations and teaching objectives preclude lengthy discussions of all programs. Rather, an early, published application that demonstrates the basic LP solution procedure is discussed first, followed by other applications building on this base.

A GENERAL LINEAR PROGRAMMING PROCEDURE

Most LP harvest scheduling models follow the procedure in Ware and Clutter (1971). It is a good introductory procedure because even-aged management with a single clear-cut harvest, artificial regeneration, and a single product are all scheduled. Multiple products, intermediate and partial cuts, and other complexities are thus abstracted. The general procedure may be discussed in five parts: (1) select time period lengths; (2) identify cutting units; (3) identify cutting regimes for each unit; (4) calculate objective function values for each cutting unit and for each cutting regime; and (5) maximize the objective function, under constraint, to determine the harvest schedule.

Select Time Period Lengths

Two time period lengths must be selected. The first is the length of the planning horizon. The planning horizon is the total number of years in the future for which you would like to plan. It is the time period over which optimization will occur and the harvest will be scheduled.

The planning horizon is often set by administrative policy in the forest organization. You may simply be told that the vice-president would like either a 25- or a 50-year projection. On the other hand, it is desirable to make the planning horizon long enough so that the effects of the harvest schedule on the forest and its regulation become evident. Ware and Clutter (1971) suggest, as a rule of thumb, a planning horizon $1\frac{1}{2}$ or 2 rotations long.

The second selection is the cutting period length. The cutting period is a subdivision of the planning horizon and corresponds roughly to the frequency of more traditional forest management plans. It is the time period during which one set of management plans would have been executed. It is the smallest time period for which a harvest scheduling program will schedule the harvest. For example, a 5-year cutting period means harvests will be scheduled in 5-year increments. The forest manager must then allocate the harvest over those 5 years by some other method. Cutting period length is arbitrary but is generally shorter when rotation ages are shorter and longer when rotation ages are longer. Thus, cutting periods in the southern United States may be 3 or 5 years and those in the West 10 or more years. Sometimes the cutting period is the same length as the continuous forest inventory cycle.

For example, assume that MAI is a maximum at 25 years for the average site index on your forest. Then, a planning horizon of 50 years ($2 \times 25 = 50$) might be chosen. The cutting period length might be arbitrarily set at 5 years so that there are 10 cutting periods ($50/5 = 10$) for which harvests will be scheduled. The cutting periods must be identified to formulate the LP. Following Ware and Clutter, the cutting period length equals t years; therefore, in our example $t = 5$. There are n cutting periods, each with a unique number $1,\ldots,n$, where

$$n = \frac{\text{years in planning horizon}}{t} \tag{16.1}$$

In our example, $n = 50/5 = 10$. This can be shown graphically using a time line (Figure 16.1).

The planning horizon and the cutting period length are always chosen so that n is an integer and almost always chosen so that n is a multiple of 5 or 10.

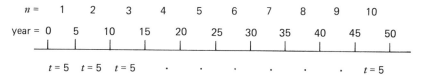

FIGURE 16.1 *Time line of cutting period length and number.*

Management activities, costs, and revenues are assumed to occur in the middle of the cutting period. For example, any harvest or regeneration in the first cutting period is assumed to occur at year $2\frac{1}{2}$. Timing the activity is necessary so that costs and revenues can be discounted.

Identify Cutting Units

The cutting unit is the area, on the ground, that will be scheduled for harvesting. In the most general situation, this need not actually be an area that is uniquely identifiable, for example, with marked boundaries. It can also be the area in a particular cover type or age class. This approach is more common in the western United States. Ware and Clutter assume that individual stands or unique blocks of timber have been identified. These areas maintain their identity throughout the planning horizon and are continually managed as separate stands.

Cutting units are seldom formed just for mathematical harvest scheduling. Indeed, the forest organization, whether public or private, has usually progressed through several stages of increasingly sophisticated management before the relatively sophisticated stage of mathematical programming is reached. This usually means that a detailed inventory system has been established and that cover type maps or other inventory data exist for the entire forest. The forest is likely to have been divided into cutting units already and these are often adopted, sometimes with slight modification, for mathematical programming.

Identify Management Regimes

A management regime is the sequence of harvests that may take place on a particular cutting unit within the planning horizon. Other forest management activities are usually associated with the harvest sequence, such as thinning, pruning, or regeneration. Costs and revenues are also associated with these.

Thus, a management regime defines one alternative for managing the cutting unit and the costs and revenues for that alternative. A management regime may be associated with an age class in those programs using age classes instead of cutting units. *All* possible management regimes on *every* cutting unit must be identified by the cutting period number in which they occur. This is usually accomplished by specifying the minimum and maximum ages at which a cutting unit may be cut, expressed in cutting periods. Current stand age must also be known.

| Management | Cutting period | | | | | | | | | |
regime	1	2	3	4	5	6	7	8	9	10
1					C				C	
2					C					C
3						C				C
4							C			
5								C		

FIGURE 16.2 *Alternative management regimes for newly planted cutting unit.*

Suppose, for example, a cutting unit was just planted and must be between 20 and 40 years old to harvest. Suppose also that a 5-year cutting period and a 10-period planning horizon were established. Then, the unit can be harvested for the first time in cutting period 5, when the stand is $22\frac{1}{2}$ years old, and for the last time is period 8 when it is $37\frac{1}{2}$ years old. (Figure 16.2). If the unit is cut at the first possible period, period 5, it can be replanted and cut again in either the ninth or tenth periods (Figure 16.2, management regimes 1 and 2). Delaying cutting until the sixth period allows a second cut only in the tenth period (management regime 3). Only one cut is possible if the unit is not cut until the seventh or eight periods (management regimes 4 and 5).

It appears that management regime 2 or 3 is the best because two cuts are obtained and hardly any inventory is left standing. However, this is not patently true. Something must be known about yield functions, changes in products and product prices as the stand gets older, and most importantly, how the harvest of this stand coincides with the harvest of other stands in the forest. This latter point is when mathematical programming becomes worth the great effort it requires because numerous alternative management regimes must be reviewed to find the optimal combination.

For example, the number of management regimes for a cutting unit depends on when the stand must be cut. Ware and Clutter (1971) in their example assume that all existing stands must be cut before period 8 and that harvest age must lie between 15 and 40 years. In these circumstances they find 54 alternative management regimes for *each* cutting unit and that their will be 54^s different management regimes if a forest consists of s different cutting units. Fifty different cutting units ($s = 50$) results in 4.2×10^{86} management regimes.

Calculate Objective Function Values

Objective function values must then be calculated for each management regime for all of the cutting units. This step assumes that the management objective has already been identified. Any objective function whose values are calculable may be used—for example, those discussed in Chapter 4. The two most common objectives are PNW and harvest volume maximization. PNW becomes an undiscounted cash flow when the discount rate is set to zero.

Calculating objective function values for each management regime is time-consuming and tedious. Most harvest scheduling models, as discussed below, contain ancillary programs that make these calculations and automatically enter them into the optimization program. However, the basic information about timber yields, costs, and revenues must still be provided to the program by the analyst.

Optimize Objective Function

The final step is to optimize the objective function. This is the step when the harvest is actually scheduled. In the simplest case, where there are no constraints, one would simply search the lists of objective function values for each management regime in each cutting unit. The management regime in the first cutting unit with the highest objective function value, say the highest PNW, is chosen, thus defining the management regime. That management regime, in turn, defines the cutting periods (and incidently, the rotation age) in which the cutting unit is harvested and hence, the harvest is scheduled. The maximum PNW for the second cutting unit is chosen, which, as above, schedules the harvest. This procedure continues over all cutting units, each having its rotation determined and harvest scheduled by the particular management regime that has the optimal PNW (or other objective function value) for the cutting unit.

This search could be performed occularly or by using a computer program that chooses the maximum number in a list. Then why is mathematical programming needed for optimization? The reason is that objective functions are seldom simply optimized but rather, they are optimized under some kind of constraint. These constraints usually cannot be met if the maximum PNW is chosen. The set of submaximum PNWs, which satisfy the constraints while providing the maximum PNW of all sets that satisfy the constraints, must be chosen.

Two common constraints and those used by Ware and Clutter in their example are harvest volume and acreage cut or regenerated. Mills lose a great deal of money if they close for even a day or two, and this, of course, would happen if they ran out of wood to pulp, peel, or saw. A sustained, nonfluctuating, wood yield is also a public forest management objective. Thus, harvests are usually scheduled so that the total cut lies between an upper and lower limit. A fluctuating acreage cut is administratively undesirable because it complicates timber sale administration and artificial regeneration; thus, it is also constrained. Constraining wood flow, acreage cut, or other variables usually means cutting some units either before or after the objective function is at a maximum. Nonmaximum harvesting is done to shift the timber volume or acreage cut from one cutting period to another to meet the constraints. The number of these alternative shifts is extremely large in an operational forest and simply selecting the maximum objective function value for each cutting unit will not meet the constraints. Thus, mathematical programming is needed.

Linear programs were chosen as the programming technique for the many reasons discussed in the preceding chapter. Following Eq. 15.4, the coefficient c is the PNW for one of the management regimes for one of the cutting units. The choice variable x is the proportion of the cutting unit that is cut using the management regime indicated by the coefficient, c. Formally, the objective function is

$$\text{Maximize} \quad Z = \sum_{i=1}^{m} \sum_{j=1}^{n} C_{ij} X_{ij} \tag{16.2}$$

where*

$Z =$ the present net worth
$C_{ij} =$ the present net worth for cutting unit i when managed by regime j
$X_{ij} =$ the proportion of cutting unit i managed by regime j
$\quad i = 1,\ldots,m$, the number of cutting units
$\quad j = 1,\ldots,n$, the number of management regimes

The student may think of the objective function as a series of CX's, one for each management regime in each cutting unit. The objective function, in effect, shows the choice procedure described above. Within the first cutting unit, $i = 1$, the objective is maximized over all regimes, $j = 1,\ldots,n$; then, $i = 2$ and the procedures are repeated until all m cutting units have been maximized. This maximization of course may be subject to constraints.

The constraint equation, Eq. 15.5, is expanded to ease variable identification. The choice variable is still represented by X, but the A matrix is now represented by two variables: Y, the yield from the acres that are cut, and Z, the number of acres that are cut.

The constraint on the wood flow from the harvesting is

$$\sum_{i=1}^{m} \sum_{j=1}^{n} Y_{ijk} X_{ij} \leq b_k \tag{16.3}$$

$$\sum_{i=1}^{m} \sum_{j=1}^{n} Y_{ijk} X_{ij} \geq c_k \tag{16.4}$$

---

*The coefficients and choice variables are shown in Eq. 15.4 as lowercase letters. This is because matrix algebra convention uses lowercase letters for vectors and uppercase letters for matrices. These variables in (16.2) have become matrices with the addition of two dimensions, cutting units and management regimes, and so upper case letters are used. This is also true for variables appearing in the constraints.

and the acreage constraint is

$$\sum_{i=1}^{m} \sum_{j=1}^{n} Z_{ijk} X_{ij} \leq d_k \tag{16.5}$$

$$\sum_{i=1}^{m} \sum_{j=1}^{n} Z_{ijk} X_{ij} \geq e_k \tag{16.6}$$

where

> Y_{ijk} = yield from cutting unit i when managed by regime j during period k
> Z_{ijk} = acres available for regeneration in cutting unit i when managed by regime j during period k
> b_k = the maximum harvest desired during period k
> c_k = the minimum harvest desired during period k
> d_k = the maximum acreage that may be regenerated during period k
> e_k = the minimum acreage that may be regenerated during period k

and other variables are as defined above.

The total planned wood flow from the forest is simply the product of the yield for the cutting unit during the cutting period (Y_{ijk}) multiplied by the proportion of the cutting unit harvested during the cutting period. The constraints state that during cutting period k this wood flow must be equal to or less than some maximum amount, b_k, and equal to or greater than some minimum amount, c_k (Eqs. 16.3 and 16.4). A parallel interpretation is made for the acreage constraints (Eqs. 16.5 and 16.6). Thus, upper and lower bounds are specified as absolute amounts. Other variables can be constrained, depending on management needs, or the same variables can be constrained differently. For example, wood flow can be expressed as a function of the volume harvested in the preceding cutting period and constrained to a stated percentage increase or decrease.

The solution of the above LP model should provide a different harvest schedule rather than simply choosing maximum management regimes. The reason is that this model is constrained, whereas the earlier model was not. A greater PNW is expected for the unconstrained (sometimes called "unrestricted") solution than is expected for the constrained solution because the constraints prevent the management regime with the highest PNW from being chosen. Most analysts always calculate an unrestricted solution. The difference between the objective function value in the unrestricted and constrained solutions (and differences in other variables also) show the opportunity cost of placing the constraints on the problem. Ware and Clutter (1971) found an opportunity cost of only about $20,000 PNW on an unrestricted PNW value of $3.16 million.

The harvest schedule for a solved LP is developed by knowing the management regime used for each cutting unit. Knowing the management regime defines the cutting period in which harvest occurs, and the cutting schedule is developed from that information. The LP only provides the management regime. Translation into cutting unit identification number, wood and cash flow tabulations by cutting period, cost estimates, and other management reports must usually be accomplished by ancillary programs. These programs are written to take data coming from the LP, perhaps combine it with data that were input earlier, and translate them into reports containing information in the format that managers desire. Programs that do this will now be discussed.

GENERAL LP SCHEDULING MODELS

Large computer models take many years to develop, and those that remain in use usually undergo continual modification. One or two men usually provide leadership and continuity during development and modification, and a number of individuals, who change with time, contribute varying amounts to the revisions. Thus, the older models are often written by many persons, each contributing different amounts to the current version.

The general LP scheduling program usually has three major parts: a matrix generator, an LP, and a report writer. The matrix generator takes much of the voluminous and detailed input data and manipulates it to "generate" the LP matrix and other LP input data. The manipulations possibly change from program to program but can include calculating PNWs at specified interest and inflation rates, projecting cutting unit yields for calculating PNW and wood flow, and calculating and assigning A matrix values. In terms of the simplified model presented above, this would include the harvest yield for each cutting unit under each management regime for every cutting period. The acreage harvested or needing regeneration is also calculated for each management regime. Furthermore, these variables are all placed in the correct sequence to be received by the LP. Preparing input data in the LP format can be a huge task for operational harvest schedules. A matrix generator saves an enormous amount of keypunching and data input time, particularly when repetitive runs are made using similar data.

The second major part, the linear program, may be designed especially for the harvest scheduling program or it may be a canned LP that is called from the system library. The LP takes the data from the matrix generator and calculates the optimal mix of choice variables. However, the LP usually does not present results in a format easily interpreted by an untrained analyst. Further, the LP may not directly output all the data desired, such as ending timber inventories or expenditures in each cutting period. Therefore, the report writer part of the scheduling program is needed.

The report writer takes the LP results, input variables, and data calculated in the matrix generator and transforms them into the desired reports. These can include positive and negative cash flows, discounted and undiscounted cash flows, wood flows by product class and in total, lists of the cutting units to be harvested, lists of input variables, acreage harvested and regenerated, ending inventories, and so on. This detail is available, usually, by cutting period, cutting unit, and in total for the planning horizon. Indeed, the combinations of data that are potentially available are dangerously copious because the amount printed can be so great that the analyst becomes confused. The report writer often performs the calculations and also contains the format and printing statements to produce the desired report format. Several general scheduling programs are discussed in the remainder of the chapter but some of them are not LPs.

MAX MILLION II

MAX MILLION II, called MAX2 by its authors (Clutter, Fortson, and Pienaar, 1978), is the current version of the theoretical model presented by Ware and Clutter (1971). Early work on the predecessor models was performed in the 1960s and supported in part by the southern forest industry, predominantly pulp and paper corporations. Thus, the model is oriented toward, but not conceptually restricted to, pine management in the southern United States. Further, proprietary rights were reserved at the time of writing so that much of the model detail is not public information. Many different versions of the system are reputed to exist because, over the years, the corporate supporters were provided with models that they then modified to fit their own unique needs. Thus, many different versions resulted from a common base.

MAX2 has the three major parts discussed above: a matrix generator, an LP that was written for it using mathematical programming system language, and a report writer. One of the program features, which reflects the authors' interest in growth and yield prediction, is that MAX2 takes stand data records from tape inputs and will project growth and yield based on these data for use in calculating PNWs and wood flows. Either a yield table or a stand table projection system is used. Yields for Loblolly and Slash pine in natural stands and plantations can be estimated. Provision is also made for including yields from perpetual rotations beyond the planning horizon.

Financial analyses are emphasized and several admirable calculating features are included. For example, cash flows may be calculated on both a before- and after-tax basis. The ordinary and capital gains tax rates are specified by the users, as are the depletion rates for different forest products (up to three are allowed). In addition, separate inflation rates can be specified for costs and revenues and the cash flows can be calculated in either constant or current dollars.

Another special feature is different analyses for fee simple and leased land. Any cash flows occurring after the planning horizon are ignored for leased lands, whereas the present value of land and standing timber at the planning horizon is included for fee land. Another feature allows the analysis of a cost differential, which may be incurred if wood must be purchased on the open market because of insufficient cut on controlled land.

Many different reports may be printed. Data or reports from each of the three major program parts may be obtained. The matrix generator provides reports or summaries of data put into it and values calculated by it. These include, but are not limited to: input data including inflation, discount and depletion rates; linear programming constraints; yield, acreage, and PNW for each cutting unit and management regime; and the harvesting schedule, yield, acreage, and PNW for the unrestricted solution. The linear programming part has complex reports that require special training to interpret. In fact, the authors refer readers to the IBM user's manual for further information about MAX2 output.

The report writer produces financial data by cutting period including income, volume dependent costs, total costs, and net income and cash flow. IRR and PNW for the whole forest are also reported, both before and after tax, and inflated and not inflated. Harvest volumes by cutting unit, product class, logability class, and cutting period are available, as well as projected open market wood purchases by product class, cutting period, and price level. Finally, harvest and regeneration acreages are reported by logability class, product class, cutting unit, and cutting period.

Timber RAM

Timber RAM was developed by Navon (1971) and others at the Pacific Southwest Forest and Range Experiment Station, USDA Forest Service. The original concept was to develop a resource allocation method (RAM) that could be used for multiple-use planning. Timber RAM was the harvest scheduling part of the system. To my knowledge, it was also the only part ever transferred to a wide variety of users.

Timber RAM was also developed during the 1960s, but it was developed in the western United States by the public sector. Hence, it is oriented toward, but not restricted to, timber management of western forests on public lands. Timber RAM is widely known and has been used on many industrial and public forests in both the eastern and western United States. It is public information and the USDA Forest Service has been extremely cooperative and generous in assisting new users to adapt the system to their forests.

Many similarities exist between MAX2 and Timber RAM, although sometimes the nomenclature changes. For example, in Timber RAM, management regimes are present but referred to as activities, cutting periods are called planning periods, and the term timber classes is used instead of cutting units. Timber classes are more compatible with the timber cover-type strata used in western inventories but present no problem in southern application because individual cutting units are simply identified as different timber classes.

There are also three parts in Timber RAM: a matrix generator called Timbram-Matrix, a linear program, and a report writer called Timbram-Report. Timbram-Matrix and Timbram-Report are integral parts of the program; however, the linear program must be supplied from the user's computer system. This has been done on many systems, including CDC, IBM, and UNIVAC. However, actually adapting Timber RAM to one's system is very complex and can take many months depending on the system, the available manpower, and the user's level of knowledge.

The program accommodates up to 35 variable-length cutting periods. The user specifies both the cutting period length and the planning horizon. The program is divided into conversion and postconversion periods and the user must also specify the length of the conversion period. The basic idea is that the forest is being regulated during the conversion period and that it will follow a standard management regime during the postconversion period. Management regimes are manipulated to maximize the objective function only during the conversion period.

Note that Timber RAM thus incorporates the concept of the regulated forest. The idea exists of a fixed or constant rotation age and a management regime that is in some sense optimal for each timber stand or cutting unit. There is also a period during which the forest is manipulated until this desired stage is reached. And the objective function is optimized only during this conversion period. Some readers may object to this procedure, preferring to optimize over the entire planning horizon. This is easily done by setting the conversion period equal to the planning horizon.

Any one of five objective functions may be chosen: volume harvested, gross revenue 1, gross revenue 2, cost, and net revenue. Net revenue is always the difference between gross revenue 2 and cost. Furthermore, up to seven discount rates may be used for either costs or revenues. Of course, a great deal of data must be entered into the matrix generator to calculate values for these objective functions. All of these inputs are too numerous to discuss here, but the major categories can be mentioned.

Timber classes that are mutually exclusive and that contain all cutting possibilities must be identified and entered. That is, all the timber that can be cut must be placed in a timber class and timber may not appear in more than one class. Each class must be named; have its area and age in cutting periods specified; be categorized by whether it is understocked, one, or two storied; and have the proportion of the class accessible during each of the first five cutting periods specified. Timber RAM, like MAX2, maintains the identity of the timber classes throughout the planning horizon. This allows the forest manager to know exactly which stand has been indicated for cutting, if the timber classes are synonomous with stands on the ground. Some harvest scheduling programs, like ECHO and Model II, do not maintain the identity of timber classes or cutting units during the planning horizon.

A separate set of timber activities (management regimes) must be specified for each timber class (cutting unit), although one set of activities can be used for any number of timber classes. These too must be entered. The timber classes to which the timber activities apply must be identified and assigned codes that show where the yields, revenues, and costs applying to the management regimes will be found. Further, five different harvesting regimes may be specified, including clearcutting and partial cutting with thinnings. Timbram-Matrix will use these data to generate all possible management regimes for the timber classes.

Yields, revenues, and costs are entered on separate sets of cards. There is no way to calculate yields from stand data, as in MAX2. The yield and corresponding costs and revenues for each management regime must be entered separately. They, combined with the timber activities, provide the data to calculate the objective function values.

Finally, the linear programming constraints are entered. These can constrain area, volume harvested, and positive or negative cash flows. The constraints can be stated in any one of three ways. First, they can be absolute constraints; for example, harvest must be less than 150,000 cords and more than 100,000 cords. Second, a range around the preceding period's value may be specified—for example, last period's harvest plus 20 percent or minus 10 percent. Third, a range around an average period level may be specified—for example, the average periodic harvest plus or minus 10 percent. All constraints may be changed in each planning period; thus, for example, a gradually increasing or gradually decreasing harvest could be planned.

Timbram-Report gives the option of writing any one, or any combination, of five reports. These are: the Timber Harvest Schedule, the Problem Schedule or Objective Report, the Harvest Report, the Economic Report, and/or the Harvest Graph. The Timber Harvest Schedule presents the total volume and the volume per acre cut by planning period and management regime. In addition, the cut for each period is summarized by volume in overstory, intermediate, and harvest cuts and also the total of these three.

The Problem Schedule provides the value for all five objective functions for each management regime by cutting period. The summary contains the sum over all regimes for each cutting period by overstory, intermediate, harvest, and total cuts. This report defaults to the Objective Report, which contains the total value and the value per acre contributed to the objective function by each regime.

The Harvest Report shows, by planning period and type of cut, the acres and volume harvested in that period and the volume harvested in that type of cut to date. The Harvest Graph simply plots the total harvest in each planning period and shows the planning period in which the postconversion period starts. The Economic Report displays the gross revenues, costs, and net revenues for each discount rate for each period and accumulated to that period.

ECHO

One of the early criticisms of linear programming formulations like MAX2 and Timber RAM was that the timber price was assumed to remain constant regardless of how much timber was cut from the forest. Critics felt that in many cases, such as USDA Forest Service timber sales in the western United States, the cut from one owner was so great a proportion of the market that the market price of timber became a function of the volume that particular owner had harvested. The forest owner faced a downward sloping demand curve and thus had to allow for decreasing timber prices as harvest from the forest was increased. This could have profound effects on harvest scheduling, where the objective is PNW maximization. Sloping demand curves were not compatible with linear programming, which requires a linear objective function, and hence other techniques were applied. One was quadratic programming.

A downward sloping demand curve might be included in the preceding models by specifying the objective function as a second-degree equation. The objective function would change from Eq. 16.2 to

$$\text{Maximize } Z - \sum_{i=1}^{m} \sum_{j=1}^{n} \left(C_{ij} X_{ij} - C_{ij} X_{ij}^2 \right) \tag{16.7}$$

Quadratic programming, a kind of NLP, could solve this program, however, existing quadratic algorithms are inefficient and limited to smaller problems (see Chapter 15 for further discussion). Thus, quadratic programming was not operationally useful.

Walker (1971) therefore developed a solution technique based on a first difference equation and a binary search procedure to find the harvest schedule that maximizes present net worth over time. This is a numerical search technique discussed in Chapter 15. The program containing the technique is called the Economic Harvest Optimization Model (ECHO) and its heart is the first difference equation:

$$V_t(MR_t - MC_t)(1 + i) = V_{t+1}(MR_{t+1} - MC_{t+1}) \tag{16.8}*$$

where

V_t = the volume per acre of the last (youngest) age class harvested at time t

V_{t+1} = the volume per acre of the first (oldest) age class harvested at time $t+1$

MR_t = the marginal revenue of the last unit of wood harvested at time t

MR_{t+1} = the change in total revenue at the time $t+1$ if a unit of wood of the first (oldest) age class is not harvested in $t+1$

MC_t = the marginal cost of the last unit of wood harvested in time t

MC_{t+1} = the change in total cost at time $t+1$ if a unit of wood of the first (oldest) age class is not harvested in $t+1$

i = the rate of interest for equating net cash flows at times t and $t+1$

*Source: Walker (1975).

As a first approximation, it is easiest to think of Eq. 16.8 as applying to a single age class of timber that has a constant site and stocking level. Volume (V) is solely a function of age and increases at a decreasing rate. A downward sloping demand curve is specified; thus, marginal revenue (MR) decreases as the amount harvested (V) increases. Increasing marginal costs (MC) are also allowed. They will increase as the volume harvested increases. A harvesting rule is specified that states that the oldest stands are cut first.

The MR and MC terms are carefully defined so that they calculate the marginal net revenue to the system for the last unit volume of wood cut in period t and the first in period $t + 1$. These are the terms within parentheses in Eq. 16.8. They are then multiplied by the volume per acre in each time period (remember, volume changes as a function of time) to obtain the marginal net revenue per acre in t and $t + 1$. The compound interest factor $(1 + i)$ in effect charges interest to the cutting in time t. That is, the equation states the marginal net revenue per acre in t plus the interest $(1 + i)$ must equal the marginal net revenue in $t + 1$.

Timber age is known, thus, both V_t and V_{t+1} are known because volume is a function of age. In the simplest case, MR and MC are a function of the volume harvested. Now, if we start from an arbitrary user-specified harvest level, the variable values and both sides of the equation are calculated. Suppose the right-hand side of the equation is the largest. The volume harvested in t is decreased and the volume in $t + 1$ increased. This causes an increase in MR_t and a decrease in MC_t, both of which cause the left-hand side to increase. Furthermore, the shift of volume to $t + 1$ causes a simultaneous decrease in MR_{t+1} and an increase in MC_{t+1}, which causes the right-hand side to get smaller. V_t and V_{t+1} are changed continuously until values are found that balance the equation. Thus, a harvest for the first cutting period is calculated.

Walker (1975) states that selection of the first cutting period harvest determines the harvest in all future periods given the demand, cost, growth, and other program conditions. The program structure allows solving an equation for harvest (h) in the next time period (h_{t+1}) if harvest in the current time period (h_t) and other independent variables are known. The harvest in the first time period, h_1 (that is, where $t = 1$), is known from solving Eq. 16.8. Therefore, the harvest h_2 can be calculated. The harvest h_3 can be calculated once h_2 is known because the harvest in t equals the $t + 1$ harvest from the previous iteration. The harvest for the next time period, $t + 1$, is repeatedly calculated until a solution is found for the entire planning horizon that satisfies all conditions. The initial harvest (h_1) is then increased or decreased by a specified amount and the whole procedure repeated until the change in PNW falls within a specified limit.

The actual program can accommodate many age classes and multiple site, species, and density classes. The program finds the conditions for all these that satisfy Eq. 16.8 for any cutting period t and then iterates in the next cutting period until the planning horizon is reached, as described above. The age classes, sites, species, and so forth specified for cutting in each period represent the harvest schedule.

ECHO has been criticized on several counts. One is that acreage and volume constraints cannot be specified. On the other hand, some authors feel this is a strength because it allows finding monetary optima. Another criticism is that cutting unit identity is not maintained throughout the planning cycle. The parts of a stand that are cut in any one time period, t, are merged with other stands cut in that same time period, and can only be identified as belonging to that age class in future years. Future harvests are essentially identified by volume of cut and age class.

Others question the analysts' abilities to accurately identify and estimate an organization's current demand functions no less the one that will apply throughout the planning horizon. Similar questions are raised about estimating the cost function. The position is taken that estimating single prices and costs is difficult enough, but that estimating price–quantity relationships over decades is almost impossible. Finally, ECHO only allows one objective function, present net worth maximization. Some analysts prefer a choice of objective functions so that they can explicitly optimize other variables such as volume or cost.

It is easy to criticize large models of complex relationships projecting variables for decades. Many assumptions and estimates must be made to make the models operational. ECHO has had a very great impact on harvest schedule modeling and is used by several organizations.

TREES*

The Timber Resource Economic Estimation System (TREES) was developed and is being maintained by the School of Forestry at Oregon State University. The model was originally constructed by N. L. Johnson, H. L. Scheurman, and J. H. Bueter to analyze Oregon's timber supply (Beuter, Johnson, and Scheurman 1976). TREES has been expanded, documented, and presented for public use since then.

TREES is an inclusive harvest scheduling program. It allows both even-aged (age distribution) and uneven-aged (diameter distribution) stands. Further, there are up to seven different criteria available to determine the harvest schedule. These criteria cover the current range of management objectives, from outright harvest specification to PNW maximization. Up to 33 age classes, 5 site classes, 30 species types, and 7 management intensities can be specified for even-aged management. There are several different methods to project stand growth and yield, all internal to the program. Acres may be shifted between management intensity types during execution. Harvest, regeneration/cultural treatment, inventory, and total harvest/economic reports are available. The first three of these four reports have both detailed and summary formats. Space limits do not allow great detailed coverage of so large a program; hence, only the basic structure and the harvest scheduling criteria are discussed.

---

*This section is based on Tedder, Schmidt, and Gourley (1980, a and b); Schmidt and Tedder (1980); and Gourley, Tedder, and Schmidt (1980).

TABLE 16.1   TREES Harvest Scheduling Methods

Method	Even-aged	Uneven-aged
Fixed		
Absolute amount	X	X
Percent inventory	X	X
Area control	X	
Variable		
Even flow	X	X
Even flow as a function	X	X
Present net benefits	X	
Present net worth	X	

Either even- or uneven-aged forest inventory data are entered for a Basic Resource Unit (BRU), which is identified by a unique number but which is not manipulated by the program. One or more BRUs are aggregated to make a Grouped Resource Unit (GRU). The GRU is manipulated, records are maintained, and reports made available; however, apparently all GRUs within an Allowable Cutting Unit (ACU) must be manipulated in the same way. For example, the growth and yield relationships and harvest scheduling methods remain the same within the ACU.

There are seven different criteria used to determine the harvest schedule. All may be used for even-aged stands but only four can be used for uneven-aged stands (Table 16.1). These methods are divided into fixed and variable categories. The fixed methods specify the harvest volume before the program starts and the specified harvest is unaffected by the program, unless volumes requested were not available for harvest. The variable methods require some type of search or optimization routine to occur within the program, and the harvest is specified by the program and not the analyst.

Absolute Amount

The analyst specifies the absolute amount of the harvest desired for each cutting period. A different amount can be specified in each period. The analyst specifies the harvest level however he sees fit. Either oldest age class first, minimum growth, or maximum value must be specified as a harvesting priority. This criterion might help analysts simulate the effects of different scenarios proposed by management.

Percent of Inventory

A constant proportion of the inventory existing in any cutting period may be specified for harvest. Alternatively, a linear equation may be specified when the proportion of inventory harvested is a function of the cutting period. These percents may be constrained within maxima and/or minima. This criterion could be used to approximate some of the volume control criteria studied earlier. For example, a growth percent could be estimated and that percent, plus or minus a bit to decrease or increase inventory, could be specified for harvest. Minimum diameter or age class cut must be specified.

Area Control

TREES will apply the classic area control formula to the total acres available for harvest during the first cutting period. The analyst need only specify the rotation in cutting periods. However, as in the actual forest, the process must begin again when acres are added or deleted if the even age distribution is desired. Harvest volumes can also fluctuate widely if acreage is unevenly stocked because the same number of acres are harvested each year.

Even Flow of Volume

The even flow of volume (EFV) criteria are patterned after harvest scheduling techniques developed by the federal government in the western United States. Both simple and sequential criteria are possible, and both depend only on the biological properties of the forest, including growth. Prices, discounting, or economic criteria are not used. The volume harvested is optimized in both cases.

Both criteria require the analyst to specify a harvest for the first cutting period and an "inner cycle." The inner cycle is the number of cutting periods over which the harvest is optimized and may be equal to or less than the planning horizon. An ending condition, either that harvest is equal to growth or that harvest be taken from specified age or diameter classes, must be supplied.

The simple EFV is similar to the Bureau of Land Management's SIMAC program (Sassaman, Holt, and Bergsvik, 1972). It takes the specified first period harvest volume as a start and searches for the maximum harvest volume that is sustainable for the entire inner cycle while still fulfilling the ending conditions. Suppose an inner cycle of five 10-year cutting periods were specified, an initial harvest of 100,000 cubic feet, and the ending condition that harvest equal growth. The program searches for the highest single harvest that is sustainable over the 50 years (5 periods × 10 years) and still has growth equal to cut. This volume is the harvest scheduled for each of the cutting periods. That is, the harvest in the ith cutting period, h_i, is equal for all periods, or, $h_i = h_1$ for all i.

The sequential EFV, similar to SORAC (Chappelle, 1966), calculates cut in the first period and then checks to see if it is sustainable for the inner cycle, sometimes called the "look-ahead period." However, the harvest volume is not held the same for each cutting period because the program treats each period as if it were the first and recalculates the maximum volume for that period. An outer cycle can also be specified. The outer cycle is the total number of periods for which harvests and inventories will be calculated. It is the planning horizon. For example, suppose the inner cycle were 5 periods, the outer cycle 10, and the length of the cutting period 10 years. Then, volume harvested is calculated by searching for the maximum sustainable volume for the next 5 periods, for each and every period, for the next 10 periods. Harvest sustainability in period 1 is checked for periods 1 through 5; in period 2 for periods 2 through 6, and in period 10 for periods 10–15. The volumes are almost always unequal in each period so that $h_i \neq h_j$ for all $i \neq i$.

These criteria can be stated as linear programs (Johnson and Schuerman, 1977), but the original SORAC, SIMAC, and TREES algorithms use search routines. Schmidt and Tedder (1980) believe that the EFV search algorithm can accommodate many more combinations of species site and stocking than an LP and is likely to have lower running costs. They point out that the search routine is not strictly optimal; however, they believe it is generally unlikely to differ significantly from the optimal, particularly when changes in the harvest to meet operational necessities are considered.

Even Flow Function of Volume

Even flow of a function of volume (EFFV) simply substitutes another variable for volume and an even flow of this variable is then sought. For example, suppose

$$E_t = a + bH_i$$

where E and H are employment in wood using industry and harvest in the ith cutting period and a and b are coefficients. Then, the maximum sustainable flow of employment would be found instead of the maximum sustainable flow of harvest. A search routine is also used for this criterion and both a simple and sequential version are available.

EFFV allows variation in the harvest and acres cut over time because the dependent variable is the one stabilized, not the independent. However, both EFV and EFFV can use a harvest constraint in which the $t + 1$ harvest is plus or minus a proportion of the period t harvest. Ending conditions may also be specified for EFFV.

Present Net Worth

The present net worth (PNW) criterion optimizes PNW using "...an advanced version of the original ECHO algorithm..." (Schmidt and Tedder, 1980). A "unique quadratic interpolation" has been added to the growth part of the TREES algorithm that apparently allows it to accommodate more complicated inventories and growth projections than the 1971 version of ECHO. However, Eq. 16.8 is still the heart of the model and the same basic search procedure is used to find the optimum.

Present Net Benefit

The present net benefits (PNB) algorithm attempts to optimize consumer-plus-producer surplus, which many believe is a better measure of contribution to social welfare than PNW. Other than this, the PNB algorithm is the same as the PNW algorithm. The PNB algorithm "... will generally produce higher harvest level in early periods and lower levels later on..." (Schmidt and Tedder, 1980) if static linear demand functions and constant cost functions are assumed.

General Comments on TREES

The TREES manuals discuss a variable that constrains harvest volume to a proportion of a preceding period's volume; however, no mention was found of constraining volume by any other method or of constraining area cut. Thus, it appears these options are not available in TREES. This can be a serious disadvantage for industrial and perhaps governmental users.

The general question of solution stability has been raised about ECHO in the past, and so by extension, about TREES. The first question is whether the algorithm will find a solution, or perhaps more precisely, whether there are particular cases in which the solution will not be found. The second question is about the configuration of wood flow over the planning horizon. An even flow, or one that increases or decreases slowly and smoothly, is usually desired. However, some solutions could fluctuate with a fairly large amplitude or even explode. Schmidt and Tedder (1980) observe that their PNW algorithm, with a stable demand function, will tend to give stable harvests but that "where demand curves change over time, stable harvest levels and harvests equaling growth are not compatible."

A related question is whether a regulated forest will be obtained. There is nothing inherent in TREES or the LP models discussed earlier in this chapter requiring that a "regulated forest" be the end result of the calculation. The analyst must constrain the LP to obtain it or use the Area Control option in TREES. However, recall that a regulated forest "... yields an annual or periodic crop of about equal volume, size, and quality" (Chapter 9). That is, regulation is defined by volume flow and the size and quality of that volume. The concept of a normal forest, with equal area in all age classes, or a forest with optimal J-shaped diameter distributions, is only used to gain this even flow. Thus, in one sense, forest regulation is irrelevant as long as the optimal flow continues. The forest is regulated when the equal flow is achieved (presumably in perpetuity). The presence of age and diameter classes is just the means to that end.

In another sense, regulation is still relevant. One would like the assurance of continued even flow beyond the planning horizon. One would also like this assurance by looking at the age and/or diameter distributions of the remaining stands. A regulated forest can provide this assurance and so remain an objective. As observed, this may occur, especially when a well-regulated forest already exists at the start of the planning period.

Model I and Model II

No discussion of harvest scheduling would be complete without mentioning K. N. Johnson and the seminal monograph, "Techniques for Prescribing Optimal

Timber Harvest and Investment Under Different Objectives—Discussion and Synthesis" (Johnson and Scheurman, 1977). Johnson has been a steady contributor to harvest scheduling and, as already noted, did much of the early work on TREES.

The monograph does indeed discuss and synthesize many of the traditional harvest criteria as well as some of the new ones. It is written within a linear and quadratic programming framework. The criteria discussed include simple financial maturity, soil rent, financial maturity with land-holding costs, Timber RAM, SIMAC, SORAC, and ECHO. These models are analyzed and reconciled to a linear or quadratic programming format, thereby allowing more ready comparison and examination of differences.

The authors distinguish between Model I and Model II in their analysis. Indeed, these categories are two sets into which the other criteria are placed. The several criteria are then discussed as different elements, or "forms," in these two

TABLE 16.2   Additional Differences Between Model I and Model II

Model I	Model II
1. Activities are actions on the *management units* during the planning horizon.	1. Activities are actions on an *age class* that exists during the planning horizon.
2. Thus, an activity is needed for each possible harvest sequence, for each management unit.	2. Thus, a sequence of activities are needed for four kinds of stands: those existing at $t = 0$ and being cut, $t \le N$ (where N equals the planning horizon); those existing at $t = 0$ and being cut at $t > N$; those regenerated during the analysis $(t > 0)$ and being cut during it $(t \le N)$; and those being regenerated during the analysis $(t > 0)$ and not being cut until after the planning horizon $(t > N)$.
3. Choice variable is the number of acres cut in management unit i using management regime j.	3. Choice variables are: (1) the number of acres of existing age classes harvested, and (2) acres of regenerated age classes left as ending inventory.
4. Acreage is constrained so that the total cut in each management unit does not exceed the total acreage in that unit.	4. Acreage is constrained so that the total cut in the cutting period does not exceed the total acreage on the forest.

sets. Form I of both Models I and II is a general statement of the model. Other criteria are specific forms, for example, simple financial maturity is Model II, Form III. Some criteria can fit into either Model I or Model II.

The major difference between Models I and II, from an applied viewpoint, is that Model I allows specific identification of the area harvested on the ground and in the forest, whereas Model II combines harvested volume into age classes, thus making it difficult or impossible to identify specific harvest acreage throughout the planning horizon. Other differences are outlined in Table 16.2.

Johnson has constructed operational forms of the models discussed in Johnson and Scheurman (1977) and has used them extensively for research and policy analyses. However, published documentation was unavailable at time of writing; thus, further discussion is limited.

MULTIPLE-USE MANAGEMENT

17

MULTIPLE-USE PLANNING and management are needed because the forest is a joint production process. Joint production occurs when producing one product automatically produces another. For example, producing lumber produces sawdust. Joint production can be in either fixed or variable proportions. There is always one hide produced per head of deer harvested, but the volume of sawdust per thousand board feet of lumber will depend on the size of trees and lumber being sawed. Rival products are those in which producing one product causes less of another to be produced. For example, harvesting an acre of timber may cause an increase in deer because of increased food, but a decrease in camping because cutover land is undesirable for camping. And, of course, society must desire the joint products in order to make planning and managing multiple uses worthwhile.

Multiple-use planning and management are planning and managing for the several joint products that the forest can produce. Multiple-use is really the forestry counterpart of land use planning and management and may be considered a subset of land use. The two terms are sometimes used interchangeably in forestry literature.

Multiple-use planning and management also imply multiple management objectives. The forester wants to produce timber, recreation, hunting, and grazing all from the same forest. This means that many mathematical programming techniques discussed in Chapter 15 that have *single* objective functions are not directly applicable to multiple-use planning. For example, some way must be found to accommodate linear programming (LP) to multiple-use planning because LP can only maximize a single variable, such as timber production or present net worth. Techniques are available to do this, as well as other techniques that accommodate multiple objectives.

Actual management for multiple uses can follow one of two extremes, or perhaps a modified middle ground. One extreme is that each and every acre on a forest is managed to produce each and every product that it can produce. This view can be modified somewhat by introducing the economic criterion that management should maximize the present net worth of all the products an acre can produce. This criterion at least allows zero production of a good that is of no value to society.

The other extreme is that a particular acre is managed for a *dominant* or primary use and that other uses are permitted as long as they do not interfere with maximizing the dominant use. For example, timber production may be maximized on one multiacre tract and hunting permitted to the extent that it does not interfere with timber production. The forest is then divided into multiacre areas, each having a different dominant use, until all the desired multiple products are obtained from the forest. The dominant use view can be modified to encourage production of one or more secondary uses so that the dominant use is near, but not at, its maximum.

AN ECONOMIC MODEL OF MULTIPLE USE

An economic model that rationalizes these two views and that indicates the theoretically desirable production level of two products has been presented by Gregory (1955, 1972) and Duerr (1960). This model is useful because it provides a theoretical framework for determining the most desirable mix of multiple-use products and because it indicates those cases in which a dominant use approach to multiple-use management makes economic and practical sense.

The model examines the output for two products, timber and forage.* Timber and forage are produced simultaneously because this is, by definition, a joint production process. For any level of inputs, expressed in dollars as cost, a combination of timber and forage will be produced. Usually, the more timber produced, the less forage, and vice versa. More timber and forage are produced as more inputs are added, but the same proportion of timber and forage production may not be maintained at different input levels.

These ideas can be shown on an *isocost* curve. An isocost curve shows the various combinations of production that are possible for one cost level. For example, $100 worth of inputs can produce a combination of 500 lbs of forage and 110 cubic feet timber, or 2,250 lbs of forage and 50 cubic feet timber, or some other combination shown on the $100 curve (Figure 17.1a). Theoretically, isocost curves can be calculated for every dollar or even every penny of cost. Thus, the production space is filled everywhere with a family of isocost curves.

It is also possible to calculate an *isorevenue* line, if we assume that there are fixed product prices. This line shows the combination of products that will

---

*This is an abbreviated presentation of the model. The reader interested in the full development should see either Gregory (1955, 1972) or Duerr (1960).

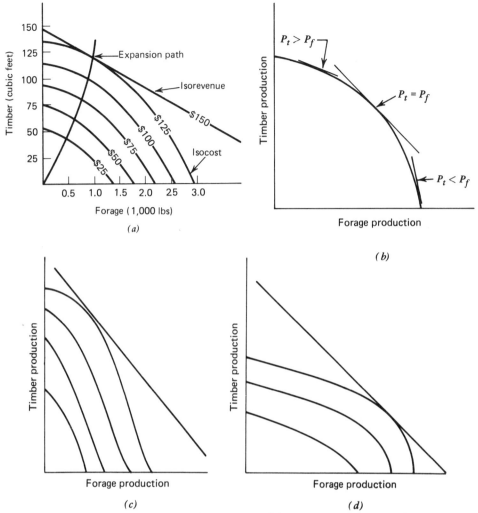

FIGURE 17.1 *An economic multiple-use model: (a) isocost curves and expansion path; (b) effect of relative price on production; and isocost curves favoring (c) timber production and (d) forage production.*

generate the level of revenue shown by the line. For example, 130 cubic feet of timber and 750 lbs of forage would generate $150 in revenue, and so would 90 cubic feet of timber and 2000 lbs of forage (Figure 17.1*a*). Isorevenue curves can also be calculated for every dollar or every penny of revenue; thus, the production space is also filled everywhere with a family of isorevenue curves.

Now, it can be demonstrated that net revenue is maximized at the production combination where an isorevenue curve is tangent to an isocost curve. Thus, the combination of products produced for a cost or revenue level is defined by the combination that causes total variable cost to equal total revenue. Connecting these points on the production surface defines the *expansion path*.

The expansion path shows the combinations of timber and forage that will maximize net revenue at each level of production. But, it does not show the combination that will provide the overall maximum net revenue. This point is found by calculating the total cost and total revenue for each product combination along the expansion path and then calculating the marginal cost and marginal revenue. The combination in which marginal cost and revenue are equal is the most desirable multiple-use product combination for the area being analyzed.

Production Determinants

The expansion path and ultimately the optimal combination are determined by the tangencies of the isocost and isorevenue curves. That is, the path is defined by the place where the slope of these two curves are equal for a given dollar level. Now, it can be shown that the slope of the isorevenue curve, sometimes called the price line, equals the price of the product on the x axis (P_x) divided by the price of the product on the y axis (P_y), or in Figure 17.1 the price of forage divided by the price of timber. Algebraically,

$$\text{Isorevenue slope} = \frac{P_x}{P_y}$$

Thus, the *relative* prices of the multiple-use products partly determine the economically optimal production level. The price line slope is 1 (45°) where the prices are equal, tilts toward timber when the price of timber is greater than the price of forage, and tilts toward forage when the forage price exceeds that of timber (Figure 17.1b).

The shape (slope) of the isocost curve is the other determinant of the expansion path. Isocost curve shape is determined by the production function that, in turn, is determined by the relative efficiency of the process in producing one product or another. Land that is relatively more efficient for producing timber will have isocost curves that favor producing more timber than forage (Figure 17.1c). Land better suited to forage will be the opposite (Figure 17.1d).

Thus, the model allows for sensitivity to both societal needs and physical possibilities. Societal needs are reflected in the price system, if it is functioning properly. When more timber is desired, its relative price will increase; the price line will shift; and the model will indicate that more timber should be produced. Similarly, for any given price line, production is indicated on the relatively more efficient land. This provides a sound rationale for the dominant use view and indicates it can be supported by an economic efficiency argument.

The model, however, does not provide complete multiple-use guidelines. There are several deficiencies, as the authors readily admit. First, the model uses static analysis, which is restricted to one time period. This is particularly serious in forest management, where decisions must be made today about processes that continue decades into the future. Today's prices and production possibilities may not be a good guide for the next 20 or 30 years.

Second, the production functions and joint production relationships of the many multiple-use products are often unknown. For example, timber harvest and wildlife are related, but the increased head of deer per acre harvested is seldom quantified. Finally, many of the products are nonmarket and their prices are unknown. For example, the price of scenic driving, wilderness camping, or a hunter day are all unknown. Thus, the isocost and isorevenue curves are incalculable.

CURRENT APPROACHES

One approach, often found in practice, is the *ad hoc* approach or what Gregory (1972) called the *squeaking wheel* approach. Here, the forest managers recognize multiple-use production but decide on product mixes and management actions depending on the pressures they are receiving at the moment. Wildlife management may dominate, or least be increased, if there is a particularly strong and vocal hunters group present. Similarly, each potential product may have its set of advocates. Those products with no or weak advocates tend to be deemphasized.

This process can be detrimental because forest production takes long time periods and, often, heavy early investment. Changing objectives throughout the production process can increase costs and reduce yields, making the process less efficient. Furthermore, some organizations are more sensitive to public opinion than others. Appropriately, the public sector seems more sensitive than the private sector, but this can be bad if changes are made that should not have been made in the public sector or if changes are not made that should have been made in the private sector. Furthermore, there is usually little guidance about the size of the change even if the direction is indicated.

Several different approaches to multiple-use planning have been suggested. These usually rely on mathematical programming techniques to accommodate the many variables involved in multiple-use planning. A sampling, but by no means all, of these techniques is discussed below.

A Linear Programming Model

One linear programming (LP) approach to multiple-use planning was developed and applied on the Jefferson National Forest in Virginia (Leuschner *et al.*, 1975). This approach treated multiple-use planning as the process of matching a set of production objectives with a set of management activities that could be used to obtain those objectives. The sets of objectives and activities are usually constrained by administrative policies and budgets and by the resource's production potential.

Multiple-use objectives included timber, camping, picnicking, swimming, horseback riding, several kinds of hunting, bicycling, and several other objectives. The longstanding problem of different units of measurement precludes stating all these objectives in the objectives function. That is, LP requires that all choice variables in the objective function be measured in the same units (commensurability). The varied and diverse objectives obviously are incommensurable and thus cannot be included in the objective function. Instead, the objective function was stated as timber production maximization and the other objectives were stated as constraints on timber production. Note that this means timber is maximized *only after* all other multiple-use goals are met.

Recall that the general LP model had three major parts: the objective function, the inequality constraints, and the nonnegativity constraints. The authors subdivided the inequality constraints into those constraining multiple-use production, budget constraints, and cutting constraints (Table 17.1).

The objective function maximizes the volume of timber cut by choosing how many acres to cut in area X_j. X_j was a cell in a grid system superimposed on the study area. The multiple-use production constraints (Eq. 2, Table 17.1) follow an inventory model. They begin with the current level of production (H_i), subtract ($a_{ij}X_j$) what will be lost due to cutting the chosen number of acres, and add back ($b_{ijk}Y_{ijk}$) what can be gained from management activities Y_{ijk}. All of this must be equal to or greater than the desired level of multiple-use production (R_i). These levels were generally measured as visitor or hunter days, but other units of measurement could have been used. The a_{ij} values were the estimated number of days lost per acre cut, and the b_{ij} were the estimated number of days gained per unit of management activity.

The budget constraints (Eq. 3, Table 17.1) are less complicated than they appear. Basically, the constraint multiplies the cost per unit of a management activity (d_{ajk} and e_{ajk}) times the number of units of that management activity (Y_{ijk} and X_j). The two left-hand terms are needed because timber management had to be separated from other management activities. Otherwise, one term would have sufficed. The sum of the expenditures must then be equal to or less than the budget constraint (E_q).

The clear-cutting constraint (Eq. 4, Table 17.1) was required because area control was used to regulate clear-cutting and these objectives had to be met. The last constraint (Eq. 5, Table 17.1) simply assures that the acres designated for cutting by the LP in any particular area do not exceed the acres available for cutting in the area.

An unconstrained solution (Eqs. 2 and 3 omitted) showed that the maximum timber harvest was 29 million board feet of timber over the 10-year planning period. The addition of budget and multiple-use production constraints reduced this to 24.3 million, an average reduction of not quite half a million board feet a year or about 66 board feet per acre per year when averaged over the entire

TABLE 17.1   Summary of a Linear Programming Multiple-Use Planning Model

Maximize $\quad T = \sum_{j=1}^{n} C_j X_j$ $\qquad\qquad\qquad\qquad\qquad\qquad$ (1)

Subject to

$$H_i - \left(\sum_{j=1}^{n} a_{ij} X_j \right) + \left(\sum_{j=1}^{n} \sum_{k=1}^{p} b_{ijk} Y_{ijk} \right) \geq R_i \qquad\qquad (2)$$

$$\sum_{j=1}^{n} \sum_{k=1}^{p} d_{qjk} Y_{ijk} + \sum_{j=1}^{n} \sum_{k=1}^{p} e_{qjk} X_j \geq E_q \qquad\qquad (3)$$

$$\sum_{j=1}^{n} x_j \geq F \qquad\qquad\qquad\qquad\qquad\qquad\qquad (4)$$

$$X_j \geq G_j \qquad\qquad\qquad\qquad\qquad\qquad\qquad\qquad (5)$$

where

T = the total timber volume cut for the 10-year period

C_j = the estimated average yield per unit of area cut in the jth cell

X_j = the area cut in the jth cell — the choice variable

n = the number of cells

H_i = the existing capacity on the unit to provide the ith multiple-use product

a_{ij} = the loss per unit of area cut of the ith multiple-use product in the jth cell

b_{ijk} = the average contribution to the ith multiple-use product in the jth cell of the kth management activity

Y_{ijk} = the number of units of the kth management activity contributing to the ith multiple-use product in the jth cell

R_i = the production objective for the ith multiple-use product

p = the number of management activities

d_{qjk} = the cost per unit of management activity of the kth management activity in the jth cell chargeable to the qth budget spent on the ith nontimber multiple-use product

e_{qjk} = the cost per unit of area cut for the kth timber management activity in the jth cell chargeable to the qth budget

E_q = the budget constraint for the qth budget for the planning period

F = the area clearcutting objective for the unit during the planning period

G_j = the total number of acres that may be cut in the jth cell

71,000 acres in the planning unit. Of course, all multiple-use production goals were met or exceeded.

Goal Programming Models

Many analysts prefer not to use LP for multiple-use planning because the objective function only allows the statement of one management objective. They prefer a different programming technique that allows specification of the multiple objectives themselves. Goal programming (GP) has become popular for this purpose.

Goal programming, a variation of LP, was first documented by Charnes and Cooper (1961). An early discussion of forestry applications was presented by Field (1973), and Bell (1976) presented the conceptual application to multiple-use planning, complete with hypothetical example. Concurrently, Bartlett, Bottoms, and Pope (1976) published a GP program listing and user manual.

The General Model
Recall that the general LP model was stated in Eqs. 15.4 through 15.6 as

Maximize $\quad Z = \sum_{j}^{n} c_j x_j$

Subject to $\quad \sum_{j}^{n} a_{ij} x_j \leq r_i$

and

$\quad x_j \geq 0$

where

Z = the objective to be maximized
x_j = choice variables for which the problem is solved
c_j = the contribution of each choice variable to the objective
r_i = constraints or restrictions place on the problem
a_{ij} = coefficients that quantify the effect of the ith constraint on the jth choice variable

The general goal programming model parallels this model except that the objective function is changed to deal with deviations from the stated goals, the multiple objectives are added as a set of equality constraints with deviations, and some changes are made in the nonnegativity constraints.

More specifically, the general GP model is

Minimize $\quad Z = \sum_{k} w_k d_k^- + w_k d_k^+$ $\qquad\qquad$ (17.1)

Subject to $\quad \sum_{i} a_{ij} x_j \leq r_i$ $\qquad\qquad\qquad$ (17.2)

$\quad \sum_{k} b_{kj} x_j + d_k^- - d_k^+ = g_k$ $\qquad\qquad$ (17.3) and

$$x_j, d_k^-, d_k^+ \geq 0 \tag{17.4}$$

where

d_k^- = the negative deviation or underachievement of the kth goal
d_k^+ = the positive deviation or overachievement of the kth goal
w_k = either ordinal or cardinal weights for the deviational variables
r_i = constraints or restrictions placed on the problem
x_j = the choice variable for which the problem is solved
a_{ij} = coefficients that quantify the amount of constraint i needed for each unit of the choice variable
g_k = the multiple objectives or goals the manager seeks to attain
b_{kj} = coefficients that quantify the contribution of the jth choice variable to the kth goal

The multiple-use management objectives are stated in vector g_k. These may be in any combination of units that is convenient—for example, cubic feet of timber, visitor days of recreation, animal unit months (AUMs) of grazing, and so on. Commensurability of objectives is no problem because each is stated as a separate equality in the constraints (Eq. 17.3), with the amount of under- or overachievement of the equality (d_k^- and d_k^+) included in the left-hand side of the equation. The amount of under- or overachievement is added to the actual achievement ($b_{kj}x_j$) to always maintain the equality.

The objective function (Eq. 17.1) now minimizes the deviations (d_k^- and d_k^+) from the objective (g_k). Thus, GP really does not have multiple objectives but rather has a single objective of minimized deviation from a set of goals that are contained within the constraints. There is a difference between this and the LP model just presented. The LP model will, if a solution is feasible, continue to satisfy the constraints at the expense of the objective function. That is, the program will decrease (increase) the objective function in order to satisfy the constraints. A GP, on the other hand, tries to reach each goal as closely as possible, subject to the assigned weights (w_k).

The weights (w_k) may be used either to rank the objectives in an preemptive ordinal manner or to assign them cardinal weights. Most authors currently favor cardinal weights, and Dress and Field (1979) state that they result in solutions that are from "non-inferior alternatives." Cardinal weights will minimize the weighted sum of absolute deviations from the objectives, whereas the preemptive weights first minimize deviations for the first ranked objective, then for the second, and so on.

Finally, the under- and overachievement vectors are constrained, therefore, they are nonnegative (Eq. 17.4). This explains why, in Eq. 17.3, the underachievements (d_k^-) are added to, and the overachievements subtracted from, the actual achievements.

A GP Application

Schuler and Meadows (1975) made an early application of GP to multiple-use planning on about 11,000 acres of the Mark Twain National Forest in Missouri. They identified eight production objectives (g_k, Eq. 17.3), which included four timber objectives stated in cubic feet, three hunting and recreation objectives stated in visitor days, and one grazing objective stated in animal unit months (Table 17.2). The choice variables (x_j, Eq. 17.2) were the number of acres to be managed by each of eight different management regimes (Table 17.2). Each of these regimes contained a set of specific management activities and the associated stand age at which the activities would be performed. For example, one regime specified a precommercial thinning, three intermediate cuts, and a harvest cut. Thus, these management regimes parallel those management regimes used in the harvest scheduling models discussed in Chapter 16. Additional variations of these eight management regimes were also specified so that there were over 30 choice variables in the program.

Several different constraints (r_i, Eq. 17.2) were used. First, the number of acres that could be allocated to any one management regime were constrained. The authors felt this necessary "...in the spirit of multiple-use...." The coefficient value (a_{ij}, Eq. 17.2) is one in this case because each acre contributes the value of 1.0 to the acreage constraint. Different budget levels were also used as

TABLE 17.2   Goals and Choice Variables Used in Mark Twain National Forest Goal Program

Goal	Goals (g_k) Unit of measurements	1974 Goal level
Dispersed recreation	Visitor day	20,000
Hunting—forest species	Visitor day	30,000
Hunting—open land species	Visitor day	4,000
Softwood timber	Cubic feet	360
Hardwood timber	Cubic feet	10,000
Softwood pulpwood	Cubic feet	180
Hardwood pulpwood	Cubic feet	20,000
Grazing	Animal unit months	2,000

Choice variables (x_j)

Even-aged management	Cedar – hardwood management
All-aged management	Old-growth management
Pine type management	Open glades management
Savannah management	Old field management

Source: Schuler and Meadows (1975).

constraints. In this case, the coefficient value is the dollars per acre required for implementing each of the management regimes.

One of Schuler and Meadows' study objectives was to examine the effects of different weighting schemes (w_k, Eq. 17.1) on the indicated management guidelines. Thus, the GP was run using several different weighting schemes. A different, single-budget constraint was used in each GP run to examine the effects on production of the different budget levels. Finally, the GP models were run for both 1974 and 1979 goal levels. Thus, many different guidelines were suggested and results were reported for items other than management guidelines. The following comments report only the general results pertaining to multiple-use management guidelines.

The authors found that there was generally no problem meeting dispersed recreation goals, but that hunting goals were difficult to achieve even with an unconstrained budget. Also, the hardwood and softwood sawtimber objectives were generally exceeded, but some difficulty existed in meeting the pulpwood objectives. Schuler and Meadows felt that GP had promise for multiple-use management planning, but problems did arise in determining objective weights (w_k's) and input-output coefficients (b_{kj}'s). They also believed that interactive GP might be a more promising technique than GP with preemptive ordering.

Another GP Application

Bartlett, Bottoms, and Pope (1976) used GP on the Pawnee National Grasslands in Colorado as an example in their user's manual. The Grasslands is administered by the Rooseveldt National Forest and is located northeast of Fort Collins. There were then 43 ranches with grazing permits and their interests had to be reconciled with other interests that the Forest Service was obligated to represent.

Initially, eight different goals (g_k) were identified. These included grazing measured in AUMs, several types of recreation measured in user days, and cultivation and mineral and energy development measured in acres. The grazing goal was further subdivided by type and size (class) of operation (Table 17.3). Hunting was also divided into small and big game.

Three different types of range were identified and specific management regimes developed for each. The number of acres each management regime is applied to was the choice variable (x_j).

Weights (w_k) for each goal were set by having a livestock association panel, the USDA Forest Service, and a combined panel of both these groups rank the original eight objectives. A GP was run for each of these three rankings. There was a great deal of agreement among the groups—the first and second ranks and last and next to last ranks were the same. And the priorities in between were close.

Each GP run indicated the same achievement levels for each goal, except for the small game hunting and mineral and energy development (Table 17.3). The grazing goals, ranked first by all groups, were precisely met with neither under-

TABLE 17.3 Goals and Achievement Levels for Pawnee National Grasslands

Goal	Unit of measurement	Goal level (g_k)	Achievement level
Grazing			
Cow–calf, Class 1	Animal unit months	10,800	10,800
Cow–calf, Class 2	Animal unit months	14,264	14,264
Cow–calf, Class 3	Animal unit months	13,451	13,451
Cow–calf, Class 4	Animal unit months	16,119	16,119
Cow–calf, Class 5	Animal unit months	13,419	13,419
Cow–calf, Class 6	Animal unit months	7,990	7,990
Steer, Class 1	Animal unit months	4,050	4,050
Steer, Class 2	Animal unit months	1,566	1,566
Steer, Class 3	Animal unit months	1,701	1,701
Steer, Class 4	Animal unit months	594	594
Bird watching	User days	1,150	5,282
Small game hunting	User days	1,000	333[a]
Big game hunting	User days	50	61,592
Rock hunting	User days	500	500
Camping	User days	28,200	5,630
Mineral and energy development	Acres	150	100[a]
Cultivation	Acres	6,440	6,440
Motorcycling	User days	750	0

Source: Bartlett, Bottoms, and Pope (1976).
[a] Average of three models.

nor overachievement. Underachievement occurred only for small game hunting, mineral and energy development, and motorcycling.

Comments on GP

Goal programming is indeed a promising and useful tool for multiple-use planning. It has an advantage in that multiple goals may be stated in the constraints for incommensurable objectives. Further, GP will advance to completion if one or more of the goals cannot be achieved simply by assigning an underachievement (d_k^-) value. LP, on the other hand, would terminate because of an infeasible solution. GP, however, is not a panacea.

First, many of the conveniences of GP can be approximated by judicious use of LP. For example, goal levels can be stated as LP constraints (see the LP model above) and the infeasibility problem can be solved by a second LP run with a "looser" constraint.

Perhaps the greatest problem in GP is setting the weights. There is no unambiguous, nonarbitrary method for doing so. Research, experimentation, and published alternatives continue in this area. Also, the desired goal levels must be chosen. Many analysts set these equal to the results of an unconstrained LP run that maximizes that particular goal.

Finally, GP and LP share the common problem of quantifying the coefficients (a_{ij}, b_{kj}). This quantification often depends on relationships that are presently unknown or about which only very limited information is available. In many cases the coefficient value is really only a "best guess," regardless of whether it is for LP and GP. Thus, as in many other instances, it is the knowledge, skill, and care of the analyst that determine the quality of the analysis rather than the technique used for the analysis.

Other Models

Many authors have been working on other methods to aid in multiple-use planning and management. These methods are not all necessarily mathematical programming methods.

An Integrated System

Betters (1978) reports an integrated system that identifies issues, develops alternatives, analyzes trade-offs, and formulates a plan. This system combines several existing computer programs, used by the USDA Forest Service in some of their planning, to obtain the end result. The programs are usually executed separately, and their output is used to develop input for the next program in the sequence.

The first program, called PUBLIC, helps to define the objectives desired by public participation groups and to rank those objectives from most to least preferred. The program depends on data generated in public workshops where the participants ordinally rank their preferences for multiple-use production objectives. These rankings are then used to divide participants into groups, by factor analysis, and an ordinal ranking of objectives is provided for each group and the entire workshop. The rankings can then be used to set management goals and write management strategies. Note that this procedure substitutes public opinion as the criterion for setting management goals rather than some other criterion such as cost minimization, production, or net revenue maximization.

A matrix generator, named MAGE5, is used to adjust inputs and outputs from the production process for the passage of time. The program also allows adjustments to this flow for the implementation of management programs in different time periods. Thus, the results of implementing a program in, say, the first, second, and third time periods can all be projected and used in further analysis.

MAGE5 can be used to estimate inputs and outputs for each management strategy identified by PUBLIC. An LP is used to define the optimal levels of inputs and outputs needed by the production process for each management strategy. These results are then passed to the EA (economic analysis) program. EA is based on an input–output analysis (I–O). I–O is a well-documented and recognized form of economic analysis used to study regional or national economies.

Briefly, an I–O analysis divides an economy into a number of different sectors or industries. The demands of each sector for inputs into its production process are related to the sectors that supply these demands as their output. For example, in a simple two-sector model, say that involving coal and steel, the requirements of the coal industry from both itself (coal) and the steel industry to produce a ton of coal are shown. Similarly, steel's requirements from coal and steel to produce a ton of steel are also shown.

The EA program, as any I–O analysis, may be used to project the impact of a particular set of economic activities on income and employment in the region, as well as on other industries in the region. These projections may then be used to judge the relative merits of the different management strategies based on their differential impacts on income, employment, and other industries. Note that I–O analysis does not provide an optimizing routine. In this case, the optimization is obtained in the LP part of the system. Note also that regional economies differ, so the analyst should be sure the I–O model fits the regional economy being analyzed. Otherwise, misleading results can occur.

In summary, this system uses PUBLIC to help define public desires for forest management. These results are used to order priorities and to define a set of management strategies. MAGE5 is used to project inputs and outputs for these strategies over time and to adjust for implementing different parts of a strategy in a different time period. An LP is then used to define the optimal level of activities for each strategy, and EA is used to examine the regional economic impact of each. The desired strategy, or course of action, is chosen on the basis of this analysis.

An Interactive Model

Steuer and Schuler (1981) extended Schuler and Meadows' earlier work to a different 2000 acres on the Mark Twain National Forest. This model used an interactive multiple objective linear program (MOLP). The interactive MOLP allows multiple objectives and uses an LP to perform a series of interactions. A number of possible solutions (achievement levels) are presented within each iteration. All are feasible and Pareto-efficient.* The analyst chooses the solution he thinks most desirable, and the LP then performs another iteration with another set of solutions, which are close to the most desired solution. The iterations continue, and the analyst chooses the most desirable solution at each iteration,

---

*A Pareto-efficient solution is one in which no one can be made better off without someone else becoming worse off.

until a predetermined number of iterations are completed. The analyst then makes a final choice of the most desired solutions.

Seven goals were specified: four hunting goals and a dispersed recreation goal measured in visitor days, a pasturage goal measured in AUM, and a timber goal measured in board feet. The choice variables were six management regimes, each containing a subset of management activities as before. There was also a budget constraint and a series of acreage constraints that assured the allocation of the management regimes over the 2000 acres within predetermined maximum and minimum levels. Each solution tells the analyst the achievement level that can be reached for each of the seven objectives by managing the specified number of acres by each of the six management regimes.

One of the program's advantages is that it provides Pareto-efficient solutions. That is, all achievement levels are such that no one level can be increased without decreasing some other level. However, the major advantage of this procedure is that it allows the analyst the advantages of a GP without having to specify the weights (w_k, Eq. 17.1). The weights implied by the choice made at each iteration are calculated and used to determine sets of weights for the next iteration. Thus, the analyst chooses the most desired achievement levels from sets of levels that are all feasible. The implied weights of the chosen set of levels are calculated and, in the next iteration, several more sets of feasible achievement levels are calculated with similar weights. In this manner, the analyst examines the production surface around the area found to be most desirable. The judgment of desirability is made based on production levels rather than on abstract weights used in GP. Note, however, that the solution ultimately chosen reflects the *analyst's* value system rather than some type of overall maximizing function. On the other hand, all solutions are optimal in the sense that they are Pareto-efficient.

An Input–Output Model

Flick (1974) made an imaginative application of the input–output model for multiple-use planning on the Bureau of Land Management's (BLM) Eugene District in western Oregon. BLM's activities on the district were divided into seven timber sectors: three fish and wildlife sectors, three recreation sectors, four road sectors, and one sector each for air and water pollution. Budget and labor sectors showed the dollars and man-months needed for the preceding activities.

The basic I–O model indicates the amount of output needed from the other sectors for a sector to produce a certain amount of its own output. For example, water pollution, in the form of sedimentation, is a "required" input for constructing roads. These data are manipulated to produce *technical coefficients* and *interdependency coefficients*. The technical coefficients show the number of units of input needed from one sector for one unit of output from another—for example, the number of tons of sediment "required" (produced) per mile of road constructed. The interdependency coefficients consider the dependencies between all the sectors and account for what is sometimes called the multiplier effect. For example, the water pollution required for road production may in its turn "require" an input from the fish sector. The interdependency coefficients will show this chain relationship. That is, they will show that building a road requires some water pollution and that water pollution in its turn requires a reduction in fish. Finally, dollar and man-month labor "values" can be placed on production by using the budget and labor sectors.

Flick believes this model can be used for decision evaluation, allocating primary inputs, planning, research, and training. Perhaps the most appealing application is using the dollar and labor sectors to calculate shadow prices for the outputs, particularly the nonmarket outputs such as deer, fish, and recreation. Indeed, shadow prices can be calculated using this technique. However, the analyst must remember that these prices are based on BLM policy and decisions concerning budget allocation and the relative desirability of certain programs. Thus, the prices reflect the BLM's collective value system rather than that of the public at large, a particular user group, or the market value.

THE MANAGEMENT PLAN

18

A MANAGEMENT PLAN is usually a written statement of how the landowner hopes to manipulate the forest to obtain objectives. It may also contain large sections detailing forest data and information and the logic used in formulating the plan. A forest management plan can cover all phases of multiple-use management. A timber management plan is an integral part because the trees must be manipulated to reach management objectives.

Many of the techniques in this book can be used in writing the management plan. These techniques can be combined to provide the overall management guidelines. There can be a very complete and detailed analysis followed by detailed steps, sometimes including estimates of the machines, manpower, and materials needed to accomplish the plan. This type of plan is most often found among the larger landowners.

Conversely, management actions may be only a vague concept in the minds of some landowners. Many landowners may be thinking: "I'll save the timber to cut in case of a financial emergency and then, maybe, I'll replant if a subsidy is available." Lack of a formal, written plan, however, does not mean that a landowner will not follow sound management practices. Many mental or informal plans are soundly based, thanks to the work of extension and industrial foresters.

The point is that management plans may take many forms, ranging from the precisely detailed to the almost nonexistent. Plans take time and money to formulate. Not all landowners need the kind of detail contained in larger plans or can afford their cost. Thus, we are left again with the prescription that landowners should make plans suitable for *their* needs. However, a landowner should at least consider all possible management objectives and have some idea on how they will be pursued.

Plans are also made at many different levels. Plans may include the general plans for the overall management of a forest. These are necessarily long-term, extending one or more rotations into the future. Often the length of time covered is determined by the expiration of long-term timber leases. These plans are usually the least detailed of any made.

Intermediate plans are sometimes made that cover the next 3 to 5 years. These plans are sometimes keyed to the continuous forestry inventory cycle and are written after completing the inventory, based on the new data. These intermediate plans are more detailed and often quite specific. They may, for example, include lists of stands to be harvested, in order of priority, during the planning period. The long-term plans, on the other hand, may simply contain a statement of allowable cut and estimates of total growing stock existing at the end of the period.

The intermediate plans may also contain estimates of machines, manpower, regeneration, and other costs that are expected in the period. They can also include land acquisition and sale plans and, in the case of industrial forests, the wood flow from company land, the open market, and plans to cope with under- or overachievement of mill needs. This information is often needed by upper echelon administrators to prepare budgets and/or determine project corporate cash flow needs. The data, which might seem superfluous to the person in the field, allows the administrators to assure resource availability in future years when needed. Forest management plans usually, but not always, refer to plans made for long or intermediate time periods.

Even more detailed annual plans may be requested. These are usually due several months or a half-year before the end of the fiscal year. They are also used for budgeting and planning the coming year's activities but with greater precision compared to the multiyear plans. Annual plans are more binding as targets for performance than are multiyear plans. Finally, quarterly, monthly, or even weekly plans may be required, depending on the organization. These short-term plans are needed to help the man in the field take the necessary steps at the proper time to accomplish organizational objectives.

Planning is a continuous process. Each month plans are made for the next month, each year for the next year, and each five years or decade for the next five years or decade. This provides the continuity in planning needed for smooth operations over time. It also allows increasing precision. As a general rule and as a matter of common sense, one is able to predict the nearer time periods with greater accuracy than the farther time periods. Thus, the projection for the 10th year into the future can be improved at the end of the next 5-year cycle and improved once again when its turn comes in the annual cycle.

The field forester may sometimes lose patience with repeated requests for detailed planning data. These are time-consuming and burdensome to prepare and, in the field person's opinion, may be so imprecise as to be practically worthless. However, there are several good reasons for planning. The first has already been mentioned. Plans allow marshalling of the men and materials needed to implement the plans so that the men and materials arrive in sufficient quantity at the right place and at the right time. It is imperative that the seedlings for this year's plantations be sowed several years before. Likewise, funds for land acquisition must also be arranged in advance. Industrial forestry operations, as compared to nonforestry operations, often have a large impact on cash flow due to the depletion generated and the requirement that regeneration costs be capitalized. Thus, corporate financial managers need estimates of these many years in the future in order to do their job properly.

A second reason is that plans provide continuity in management. Forestry is a particularly long-term enterprise and personnel are certain to change over the time period between planting and harvesting a stand. A written plan is a reference for the new manager and helps continue programs begun by the predecessor.

In addition, planning can result in the critical analysis of forest management problems. It provides a time when managers can concentrate their efforts on deciding which alternatives will best enable them to reach their objectives. This kind of analysis is sometimes difficult to accomplish in the daily press of operations. A recurrent planning cycle makes certain there is time to do this. The written plan then provides the reference during the daily operations when there may not be time enough for careful thought. Thus, reference to the plan keeps actions directed toward organizational objectives. Incidentally, focusing on analyses also helps define what is unknown and allows steps to be taken between planning periods to find or gather the missing information.

Finally, the plan can become a standard for comparison. It is necessary to inspect performance, and the plan can be used to see if actual performance reached the expected. Analysis of overachievement may indicate better, more efficient procedures that can be adopted by all. Analysis of underachievement may indicate potential barriers to success, which can then be eliminated in other parts of the operation. Remember, plans need not be slavishly followed because situations change, making deviation necessary.

FOREST MANAGEMENT PLANS IN THE UNITED STATES

Forest management planning may be conveniently examined by forest ownership class; federal, other public, industrial, and nonindustrial private landowners (Table 18.1). The USDA Forest Service is the largest single commercial forest land manager in the United States, managing 18.2 percent of the land. By practice and by law the Forest Service writes rather complete and exacting management plans. These include not only the timber management portion but also plans for management of the other multiple-use products that can be harvested from the forest. Over half of the other federal ownership is managed by the USDI Bureau of Land Management. This agency also writes precise and detailed management plans. Thus, the great majority of federally managed forest land is covered by detailed plans.

The other public ownerships include state, county, and municipal forests. Most state forests have sound management plans, although county and municipal

TABLE 18.1 Commercial Forest Land Ownership
in the United States

Landowner	Percent commercial forest land
Total federal	20.4
Forest Service	18.2
Other federal	2.2
Other public	7.6
Industrial forest	13.9
Nonindustrial private landowners	58.0
Total	100.0

Source: Forest Statistics of the U.S., USDA Forest Service, Review Draft, 1978.

plans are much more variable. The amount of resources devoted to forest management often depends on how wealthy a state is, measured, say, by gross state product or per capita income, and how large a proportion of the state's industrial activity is in wood-based industries. Obviously, the wealthier the state and the more that wealth is dependent on forests, the better the management planning tends to be.

Most industrial owners have thorough forest management plans. These plans emphasize timber, logically, because that is usually the reason forests are owned. However, more emphasis has been placed on multiple-use activities in the recent past. Forest planning is emphasized because in many cases a large amount of the corporation's assets are committed to timber. This and the effects of timber management on cash flow previously mentioned, make the corporate timber lands very important. Furthermore, industry is objective-oriented, and plans help to attain these objectives.

The nonindustrial private landowners control the largest single category of forest land. Their reasons for land ownership and the objectives of management are many and diverse. These owners include farmers, other rural residents, second home owners who live in urban areas, and professional persons who have invested in land. Relatively few formal forest management plans are found among these owners because of the diversity of ownership; because timber production is often not the primary reason for land ownership; and/or because owners do not have the necessary technical knowledge. Indeed, professional foresters have been long concerned that timber supply will be significantly decreased because of this situation. Recently, both state extension foresters and industrial foresters have been making progress with this group. Foresters will, on request, inspect a tract of land and write a plan for its management, which the owner is then free to follow.

Consulting foresters also perform the same service. Thus, some nonindustrial land has been well managed for a number of years.

PLANNING STEPS

Planning is essentially a decision-making process. It involves deciding beforehand the actions that will be taken in the future. The essence of the plan is to detail the course of action that is desired in the future.

There is not just one unique sequence of steps taken in planning. Different organizations will use different steps. Nor can the steps be unequivically identified in a particular sequence. In some cases it will be more efficient to take one step before another, in other cases the steps may be reversed, and in yet other cases they may be performed simultaneously. However, presenting the steps in an ordered, sequential manner will provide a framework that may be useful to those beginning the planning process.

The decision-making model discussed in Chapter 1 (Figure 1.1) can be used to define the planning steps. Recall that those steps were to define organizational objectives, identify alternative ways to reach those objectives, identify any constraints in reaching the objectives, and, finally, to choose one of the alternatives. Two more steps can be added to this sequence when discussing the planning process—establishing the planning data base and forming the subordinate plans.

Defining the organizational objectives is necessary to ensure that all members of the organization know the point toward which their activities should be directed. Objective definition provides a unity of purpose to organizational activities. This unity of purpose should be established prior to planning to make certain the plans are all directed toward the same end. Obviously, plans made to attain different, sometimes divergent objectives will be self-defeating and result in inefficiencies and dilution of effort rather than more efficient operations. Recall that there are many levels of objectives that form a hierarchy of organizational goals. Objective formulation is beyond the scope of this discussion. It is simply assumed that objectives are formulated for the level at which planning is occurring.

Establishing the planning data base requires the accumulation, publication, dissemination, and agreement on the data that will be used in making the plans. The term data base is used in the broadest sense. It can include specific data about the forest—for example, such items as forest cover type maps, compartment maps, and timber cruise and/or continuous forest inventory data. Also included in the data base might be information about external factors.

There are many external factors that might be included and, again, there is no unique set. Economic forecasts are usually one kind of external factor that is included. These might be simple forecasts for the demand for the various forest products, whether they be timber or visitor days of camping, or they might be complex forecasts including population trends, GNP, housing starts, and the like.

The external factors set the framework within which the forest must be managed and that is usually beyond the control of the forest manager.

Another set of external factors is the legal framework within which the forest must be managed. There may be extensive legislation directing specific management practices, as in the case of the public forests. Privately owned forests are influenced by many types of laws also. The most obvious are the tax laws that pervade many forest management decisions. Others include forestry incentive laws that foster reforestation and trespass and liability laws that affect plans for recreation, hunting, and fishing use.

Another set of external factors might include forecasts about the availability of labor, machines, materials, and other items necessary for forest management. Harvesting labor availability can change the mix of labor and capital used in harvesting systems, which in turn could affect the most desirable tree size. Restrictions on the use of herbicides or pesticides may alter the choice of management regime. The relative availability of fertilizer, reflected by its price, can also determine how much will be used.

The internal organization policies should also be included in the data base. These can have as much influence on plans as external factors. They can include such things as product definition, land acquisition policies, proportion of mill wood supply targeted from company land, equipment purchase policies, and so on.

The publication, dissemination, and agreement on the data base are all required to maintain the unity of purpose in planning. Publication and dissemination are sometimes difficult to accomplish. Some of the data bases are well known and the actual publication of a written document may not be necessary. In these instances, the discussion and/or verbal agreement between planners may be sufficient. In other situations, it may be desirable to document the data base for future review and revision at the next planning cycle.

Agreement on the data base is also important. Planners may disagree over what precisely should be considered "the facts." Each party could decide to follow what it believes is correct, even though it is different from what the others perceive. This, again, results in a divergency in planning and dissipates implementation efforts. Differences in opinion should be resolved before planning begins so that each planner starts from the same base. Obviously, agreement and coordination become easier the smaller the group of planners and the closer they are in geographical proximity. Large divergences can occur when there are several levels of planners geographically dispersed, as is the case with forest-level, division-level, and central staff planners.

Choosing the alternative courses of action is a very important step. As previously stated, there is almost always an alternative, even if it is to sell the forest land and invest the funds elsewhere. A thorough search with due care and thought about alternatives can add to the successful attainment of organizational objectives. This is the step during which innovation can first be brought into the organization and institutionalized. Creative alternative identification can accomplish much for an organization.

Identifying the constraints and the choice between the alternative courses of action are all part of an evaluation process. Different alternatives may have different constraints. One alternative may be capital intensive but the particular organization may be short on capital. Thus, the alternative is less desirable than one that uses less capital. Some alternatives may contribute more toward the organizational goals than others, but they may also cost more. Identifying these constraints and quantifying them may require a new data base or may be answerable from the data base established in the second step above.

Choosing between courses of action is what a large part of this book has been about. Discounting, compounding, and the decision guidelines all provide methods of evaluation and choosing between different alternatives. The harvest scheduling models help evaluate different courses of harvesting actions. Thus, these techniques and procedures are all a useful part of the planning process.

The final step in the planning process is formulating subsidiary plans. Most plans are hierarchial and making the plan at one level requires making a plan at the next level down. For example, plans may be made for broad geographic regions, and these in turn must be subdivided into plans for smaller areas. Plans may first be made for a forest region or division, then another set of plans is made for individual forests within the region, and finally plans are made for districts or working circles within the forests. The temporal sequence of planning discussed in the beginning of the chapter is another example of formulating subsidiary plans. The longer-term plans may be made first, and then the progressively shorter-term plans, which are subsidiary to them, are made.

Formulating subsidiary plans can require reexecuting the planning steps at the new level. After regional plans are made, it may again be necessary to identify forest objectives, establish a forest planning data base, and so on, until the forest plans are written. The sequence may then iterate until district level plans are also written. Working from the bottom up, sometimes called "grassroots" planning, is a variation. Here, planning occurs at the bottom level, or grassroots, first and plans are then aggregated upward to each level. One danger of this type of planning is that formulating organization-wide objectives can be difficult. Organizational suboptimization can occur if the organization plan is simply the sum of the subsidiary level plans.

MANAGEMENT PLAN COMPONENTS

It is impossible to describe a uniquely correct management plan format just as it is impossible to describe a unique set of planning steps. However, it is possible to identify components found in many management plans (Table 18.2).

TABLE 18.2   Management Plan Components

Management objectives and policies

Forest description
  Forest organization and subdivision
  Forest inventory data
  Growth and yield functions
  Maps
    Subdivisions and compartments
    Roads
    Cover types
  Narrative description
    Physiography
    Soils
    Cover types

Economic expectations
  Demand
    Timber products
    Recreation
    Hunting and fishing
    Water
    Other
  Supply
    Labor
    Capital
    Materials

Other external factors
  Legal restrictions
  Public policy

Analysis and synthesis
  Silvicultural analysis
  Regulation analysis
    Cutting budget
  Multiple-use analysis and plans

Protection
  Fire
  Insect
  Disease

Management plans covering large areas may have many or most of these components. Plans covering smaller areas may have only a few.

The first major component is a statement of management objectives and policies. These set the organizational context of the management plan. The objectives define the endpoint that is desired and the policies state at least some of the constraints within which the objectives must be attained. The statement might detail the products that are desired, proportions of company and/or open market wood, and some of the internal constraints on the management plan.

The forest description presents the physical context within which the management plan is written. It usually details the forest organization so the reader can identify areas in the field that are discussed in the plan. Furthermore, inventory data describing cover types, species, and timber volumes are also included. Formulas or tables used to predict growth and yield may be included here, as well as the predictions themselves. Descriptions of other forest aspects may also be included. These may be unique natural or historic areas, wildlife inventories, and sites with recreation potential.

The forest description can be in graphic and/or narrative form. Maps are often included to provide a visual impression of the spatial distribution. However, it is difficult to include sufficient detail on maps without their becoming cluttered and difficult to use; thus, narrative descriptions are usually found. Highly detailed descriptive material is often presented in tables and in appendices to avoid interrupting the continuity of the plan.

The management plan's social context is presented in those sections detailing the economic expectations and the other external factors. These sections describe those factors that are often beyond the forest manager's control but that must be considered when making the forest management plan. They can include forecasts of what is expected in future years as well as descriptions of the current status.

Projecting demand for timber and other forest products is very important. There is no reason for the forester to invest the resources necessary for production if demand is not likely to exist when production is completed. This is usually not a produce–don't produce decision but rather one of determining the quantity to produce. It is also important to define which product—for example, pulpwood or sawtimber—or which mix to produce.

Assessing the availability and cost of the resources needed for production is also important. These assessments can help one make cogent decisions about an alternative production process. For example, a severe scarcity of capital may indicate that seeding rather than planting would be preferable for a certain time period. Or, a projected labor shortage might indicate that a shift to a more capital-intensive process is desirable.

Remaining items in the social context are detailed in the other external factors. These need not be limited to the legal restrictions but may also include public policies with which the landowner may want to comply. These may be described and recorded here. The value of recording and describing them, as well as the other items describing the internal, physical, and social context of the plan, is that they can then be referred to in the future. This allows changing the plan when one of the basic premises changes and also facilitates updating of the plan at this next revision.

The analysis and synthesis section is where all the planning components are drawn together. It is hoped that all the descriptive material will be examined and, where possible, the interactions explored. Silvicultural analysis is essential because the forest cover must be manipulated to obtain management objectives. The silvics and silviculture of the various cover types are often presented to provide the rationale for the recommended silvicultural systems.

The regulation analysis may address two parts. First, the desired forest structure when regulation is achieved may be defined. This is the forest configuration that might be perpetuated once obtained. Second, the actions that will be taken to achieve the regulated state may also be presented. This is often called the "path" to regulation. The regulated state defines the objective of timber management; the path to regulation defines how that objective will be reached. Thus, the path identifies the cutting that will be implemented in the more immediate future.

Regulation analysis often involves using the harvest scheduling models discussed earlier. These models can be used to calculate the path to the regulated state. Recall that the regulated state is seldom reached because of constantly changing internal and external factors. However, many forest managers believe periodic recalculation will at least keep timber harvest near an optimal path if not on it. The cutting budget is usually the end product of the regulation analysis. The cutting budget specifies which stands or areas to cut and the time period, sometimes specified only to the nearest 5 or 10 years, in which the cutting will occur.

Plans for the nontimber forest products may also be formulated here. The amount and detail of these plans will vary with the management objectives. Indeed, some nontimber products may be so important as to have their own separate plans. Public forests may have recreation or game management plans that are larger than the timber management plans.

Protection plans either may be included in the general management plan or they may be separate documents. Fire, insect, and disease are the three most common areas covered but other aspects of protection may also be included. For example, timber trespass can be a problem, and sometimes protecting personal property and other policing actions can assume major proportions in recreation management.

PLANNING LIMITATIONS

Planning, as all other management techniques, has its limitations. The first is caused by change. As has been said, the one constant in the world is change. Plans must change as the internal, external, and physical contexts on which they were based change. Thus, depending on the rate of change, plans become outdated and must be recast to maintain their usefulness.

A second limitation is the accuracy with which the data base can be developed and projected. Sometimes variables are simply unmeasurable, as in the case of some nonmarket values, and sometimes time or funds do not allow precise measurement. In these cases, plans may be based on faulty data and hence be faulty themselves.

Another limitation is that the organization for which the plan is made may be inflexible. Organizations are made of people; people often resist change of any type and new plans often bring change. Thus, new plans may not be implemented. People's resistance may stem from an unwillingness to learn something new or fear that they will not learn it. It may also be based on an honest belief that the new course of action is wrong. In any event, the new plans may be resisted in both direct and subtle ways and therefore not be completely implemented.

Other organizational inflexibilities can include policies and financial limitations. Existing policies are hard to change once they have been implemented and any plan requiring such a change may take a long time to implement. Further, existing policies may be contradicted by a new plan, despite the need to consider them during plan formulation.

External inflexibilities also exist. These include a myriad of factors such as the political climate, labor availability, rate of technological change, and unforeseen market conditions. Each of these may, in its own way, prevent the successful execution of plan, even if the plan was perfectly formulated.

Finally, planning often requires a great deal of skilled labor, time, and money. Many organizations do not have these resources and hence cannot perform planning, despite its desirability. Other organizations can only do partial planning for these same reasons. Thus, planning cannot be viewed as the solution to all problems.

REFERENCES

Adams D. M. and A. R. Ek. 1974. Optimizing the management of uneven-aged forest stands. *Can. J. For. Res.*, 4(3):274–287.

_____. 1975. Derivation of optimal management guides for individual stands. In J. Meadows, B. B. Bare, C. Row, and K. Ware, Eds., *Systems Analysis and Forest Resource Management*, Bethesda, Md.: Society of American Foresters.

Bare, B. B. 1971. Applications of operations research in forest management: A survey. Quantitative Science Paper No. 26. Seattle: University of Washington.

Bartlett, E. T., K. E. Bottoms, and R. P. Pope. 1976. Goal; multiple objective programming. Range Science Series No. 21. Fort Collins: Colorado State University.

Bell, E. F. 1976. Goal programming for land use planning. General Tech. Rep. PNW-53. Portland, Ore.: Pacific Northwest Forest and Range Experiment Station.

Bentley, W. R., and R. D. Fight. 1966. A zero rent comparison of forest rent and soil rent. *For. Sci.* 12:460.

Bentley, W. R., and H. F. Kaiser. 1967. Sequential decisions in timber management—A Christmas tree case study. *J. For.* 65(10):714–719.

Bentley, W. R., and D. E. Teaguarden. 1965. Financial maturity: A theoretical review. *For. Sci.* 11:76–87.

Betters, D. K. 1978. Analytical aids in land management planning. In D. Navon, Compiler, *Operational Forest Management Planning Methods:*

Proceedings, Meetings of Steering Systems Project Group, IUFRO.
General Tech. Rep. PSW-32. Berkeley, Calif.: Pacific Southwest Forest
and Range Experiment Station.

Bueter, J. H., K. N. Johnson, and H. L. Scheurman. 1976. Timber for
Oregon's tomorrow, an analysis of reasonably possible occurrences.
Resource Bull. No. 19. Corvallis: Oregon State University.

Burkhart, H. E., R. C. Parker, and R. G. Oderwald. 1972. Yields for natural
stands of loblolly pine. FWS-2-72. Blacksburg, Va.: Division of Forestry and Wildlife Resources, Virginia Polytechnic Institute and State
University.

Charnes, A., and W. W. Cooper. 1961. *Management Models and Industrial
Applications of Linear Programming.* New York: John Wiley and Sons.

Chappelle, D. E. 1966. A computer program for scheduling allowable cut
using either area or volume regulation during sequential planning
periods. Res. Paper PNW-33. Portland, Ore.: Pacific Northwest Forest
and Range Experiment Station.

Clutter, J. L., J. C. Fortson, and L. V. Pienaar. 1978. MAX MILLION II, A
computerized forest management planning system. Athens, Ga.

Daniels, R. F., and H. E. Burkhart. 1975. Simulation of individual tree
growth and stand development in managed loblolly pine plantations.
FWS-5-75. Blacksburg, Va.: Division of Forestry and Wildlife Resources, Virginia Polytechnic Institute and State University.

Davis, K. P. 1966. *Forest Management: Regulation and Valuation*, 2nd ed.
New York: McGraw-Hill.

Duerr, W. A. 1960. *Fundamentals of Forestry Economics.* New York:
McGraw-Hill.

Duerr, W. A., J. Fedkew, and S. Guttenberg. 1956. Financial maturity: A
guide to profitable timber growing. Tech. Bull. 1146. U.S. Dept. of
Agriculture.

Dress, P. E., and R. C. Field. 1979. Multi-criterion decision methods in
forest management. In *Multiple-Use Management of Forest Resources
Symposium Proceedings*, Clemson, S.C.: Clemson University.

Field, D. B. 1973. Goal programming for forest management. *For. Sci.*
19:125–135.

_____. Various dates. Application of operations research to quantitative
decision problems in forestry and the forest products industries — a
bibliography. Orono: University of Maine (computer print-out).

Flick, W. A. 1974. Resource flows and values in the BLM's Eugene District. Guide to Land Management Rep. No. 16 (mimeograph).

_____. 1976. A note on inflation and forest investments. *For. Sci.* 22(1): 30–32.

Gregersen, H. M. 1975. Effect of inflation on evaluation of forestry investments. *J. For.* 73:570–572.

Gourley, J., P. L. Tedder, and J. S. Schmidt. 1980. TREES: Volume IV, computer analyst's guide. Res. Bull. No. 31d. Corvallis: Oregon State University Forest Res. Lab.

Gregory, G. R. 1955. An economic approach to multiple use. *For. Sci.* 1:6–13.

_____. 1972. *Forest Resource Economics*. New York: The Ronald Press.

Hanke, S. H., P. H. Carver, and P. Bugg. 1975. Project evaluation during inflation. *Water Resources Res.* 11:511–514.

Hann, D. W., and B. B. Bare. 1979. Uneven-aged forest management: State of the art (or science?). General Tech. Rep. INT-50. Ogden, Utah: Intermountain Forest and Range Experiment Station.

Hillier, F. S. 1963. The derivation of probabilisitic information for the evaluation of risky investments. *Management Sci.* 9:443–457.

Howe, C. W. 1971. Benefit-cost analysis for water system planning. Water Resources Monograph No. 2. Washington, D.C.: American Geophysical Union.

Johnson, K. N., and H. L. Scheurman. 1977. Techniques for prescribing optimal timber harvest and investment under different objectives — discussion and synthesis. *For. Sci. Monograph* 18.

Kidd, W. E., E. F. Thompson, and P. H. Hoepner. 1966. Forest regulation by linear programming: a case study. *J. For.* 64:611–613.

Klemperer, W. D. 1979. Inflation and present value of timber income after taxes. *J. For.* 77:94–96.

Leuschner, W. A., J. R. Porter, M. R. Reynolds, and H. E. Burkhart. 1975. A linear programming model for multiple-use planning. *Can. J. For. Res.* 5:485–491.

Lundgren, A. L. 1971. Tables of compound-discount interest rate multipliers for evaluating forestry investments. For. Res. Paper NC-51. St. Paul, Minn.: North Central Forest Experiment Station.

Martin, A. J., and P. E. Sendak. 1973. Operations research in forestry: A bibliography. General Tech. Rep. NE-8. Upper Darby, Pa.: Northeast Forest Experiment Station.

McArdle, R. E., W. H. Meyer, and D. Bruce. 1961. The yield of Douglas-fir in the Pacific Northwest. Tech. Bull. 201. Washington, D.C.: U.S. Dept. of Agriculture.

Meyer, H. A. 1943. Management without rotation. *J. For.* 41:126–132.

_____. 1952. Structure, growth, and drain in balanced uneven-aged forest. *J. For.* 50:85–92.

_____. 1953. *Forest Mensuration.* State College, Pa.: Penns Valley Publishers.

Navon, D. I. 1971. Timber RAM, a long-range planning method for commercial timber lands under multiple-use management. Res. Paper PSW-70. Berkeley, Calif.: Pacific Southwest Forest and Range Experiment Station.

Nelson, C. R. 1976. Inflation and capital budgeting. *J. Finance* XXXI: 923–931.

Office of Management and Budget. 1972. Discount rates to be used in evaluating time distributed costs and benefits. Circular No. A-94 (revised). Washington, D.C.: Office of Management and Budget.

Olson, S. C., H. L. Haney, and W. C. Siegel. 1981. State death tax implications for private nonindustrial forestry. *For. Products J.* 31(7):28–38.

Sassaman, R. W., W. E. Holt, and K. Bergsvick. 1972. User's manual for a computer program for simulating intensively managed allowable cut. General Tech. Rep. PNW-1. Portland, Ore.: Pacific Northwest Forest and Range Experiment Station.

Schmidt, J. S., and P. L. Tedder. 1980. TREES: Volume II, mathematical analysis and policy guide. Res. Bull. 31. Corvallis: Oregon State University Forest Research Lab.

Schuler, A. T., and J. C. Meadows. 1975. Planning resource use on national forests to achieve multiple objectives. *J. Environmental Managemen* 3:351–366.

Schumacher, F. X. 1939. A new growth curve and its application to timber yields. *J. For.* 37:819–820.

Society of American Foresters. 1958. *Forest Terminology*, 3rd ed. Washington, D.C.

Steuer, R. E. and A. T. Schuler. 1981. Interactive multiple objective linear programming applied to multiple use forestry planning. In M. C. Vodak, W. A. Leuschner, and D. I. Navon, Eds., *Proceedings of the IUFRO Symposium on Forest Management Planning: Present Practice and Future Decisions.* Publication FWS-1-81. Blacksburg, Va.: School of Forestry and Wildlife Resources, Virginia Polytechnic Institute and State University.

Talerico, R. L., C. M. Newton, and H. T. Valentine. 1978. Pest-control decisions by decision-tree analysis. *J. For.* 76:16–19.

Tedder, P. L., J. S. Schmidt, and J. Gourley. 1980a. TREES: Volume I, a user's manual for forest management and harvest scheduling. Res. Bull. 31a. Corvallis: Oregon State University Forest Research Lab.

_____. 1980b. TREES: Volume III, example problem guide. Res. Bull. 31c. Corvallis: Oregon State University Forest Research Lab.

USDA Forest Service. 1982. A guide to federal income tax for timber owners. Agriculture Handbook No. 596. Washington, D.C.

Van Horne, J. C. 1977. *Financial Management and Policy*, 4th ed. Englewood Cliffs, N.J.: Prentice–Hall.

Walker, J. L. 1971. An economic model for optimizing the rate of timber harvesting. Ph.D. thesis. Seattle: University of Washington.

_____. 1975. ECHO: Solution technique for a nonlinear economic harvest optimization model. In J. C. Meadows, B. B. Bare, K. Ware, and C. Row, Eds., *Systems Analysis and Forest Resource Management.* Bethesda, Md.: Society of American Foresters, pp. 172–188.

Ware, G. O., and J. L. Clutter. 1971. A mathematical programming system for management of industrial forests. *For. Sci.* 17:428–445.

Water Resources Council. 1973. Standards for planning water and related land resources. In the Federal Register, September 30, 1973, Washington, D.C.: The Archives of the United States.

Weston, J. F., and E. F. Brigham. 1978. *Managerial Finance*, 6th ed. Hinsdale, Ill.: Dryden Press.

APPENDIX

TABLE A.1 Future Value of a Single Payment Multiplier. The Value of a One-Dollar Payment Compounded for *n* Years.

YEARS	RATE OF INTEREST .005	.010	.015	.020
1	1.00500	1.01000	1.01500	1.02000
2	1.01002	1.02010	1.03022	1.04040
3	1.01508	1.03030	1.04568	1.06121
4	1.02015	1.04060	1.06136	1.08243
5	1.02525	1.05101	1.07728	1.10408
6	1.03038	1.06152	1.09344	1.12616
7	1.03553	1.07214	1.10984	1.14869
8	1.04071	1.08286	1.12649	1.17166
9	1.04591	1.09369	1.14339	1.19509
10	1.05114	1.10462	1.16054	1.21899
11	1.05640	1.11567	1.17795	1.24337
12	1.06168	1.12683	1.19562	1.26824
13	1.06699	1.13809	1.21355	1.29361
14	1.07232	1.14947	1.23176	1.31948
15	1.07768	1.16097	1.25023	1.34587
16	1.08307	1.17258	1.26899	1.37279
17	1.08849	1.18430	1.28802	1.40024
18	1.09393	1.19615	1.30734	1.42825
19	1.09940	1.20811	1.32695	1.45681
20	1.10490	1.22019	1.34686	1.48595
21	1.11042	1.23239	1.36706	1.51567
22	1.11597	1.24472	1.38756	1.54598
23	1.12155	1.25716	1.40838	1.57690
24	1.12716	1.26973	1.42950	1.60844
25	1.13280	1.28243	1.45095	1.64061
26	1.13846	1.29526	1.47271	1.67342
27	1.14415	1.30821	1.49480	1.70689
28	1.14987	1.32129	1.51722	1.74102
29	1.15562	1.33450	1.53998	1.77584
30	1.16140	1.34785	1.56308	1.81136
31	1.16721	1.36133	1.58653	1.84759
32	1.17304	1.37494	1.61032	1.88454
33	1.17891	1.38869	1.63448	1.92223
34	1.18480	1.40258	1.65900	1.96068
35	1.19073	1.41660	1.68388	1.99989
36	1.19668	1.43077	1.70914	2.03989
37	1.20266	1.44508	1.73478	2.08069
38	1.20868	1.45953	1.76080	2.12230
39	1.21472	1.47412	1.78721	2.16474
40	1.22079	1.48886	1.81402	2.20804

TABLE A.1 Continued

YEARS	.025	RATE OF INTEREST .030	.035	.040
1	1.02500	1.03000	1.03500	1.04000
2	1.05062	1.06090	1.07122	1.08160
3	1.07689	1.09273	1.10872	1.12486
4	1.10381	1.12551	1.14752	1.16986
5	1.13141	1.15927	1.18769	1.21665
6	1.15969	1.19405	1.22926	1.26532
7	1.18869	1.22987	1.27228	1.31593
8	1.21840	1.26677	1.31681	1.36857
9	1.24886	1.30477	1.36290	1.42331
10	1.28008	1.34392	1.41060	1.48024
11	1.31209	1.38423	1.45997	1.53945
12	1.34489	1.42576	1.51107	1.60103
13	1.37851	1.46853	1.56396	1.66507
14	1.41297	1.51259	1.61869	1.73168
15	1.44830	1.55797	1.67535	1.80094
16	1.48451	1.60471	1.73399	1.87298
17	1.52162	1.65285	1.79468	1.94790
18	1.55966	1.70243	1.85749	2.02582
19	1.59865	1.75351	1.92250	2.10685
20	1.63862	1.80611	1.98979	2.19112
21	1.67958	1.86029	2.05943	2.27877
22	1.72157	1.91610	2.13151	2.36992
23	1.76461	1.97359	2.20611	2.46472
24	1.80873	2.03279	2.28333	2.56330
25	1.85394	2.09378	2.36324	2.66584
26	1.90029	2.15659	2.44596	2.77247
27	1.94780	2.22129	2.53157	2.88337
28	1.99650	2.28793	2.62017	2.99870
29	2.04641	2.35657	2.71188	3.11865
30	2.09757	2.42726	2.80679	3.24340
31	2.15001	2.50008	2.90503	3.37313
32	2.20376	2.57508	3.00671	3.50806
33	2.25885	2.65234	3.11194	3.64838
34	2.31532	2.73191	3.22086	3.79432
35	2.37321	2.81386	3.33359	3.94609
36	2.43254	2.89828	3.45027	4.10393
37	2.49335	2.98523	3.57103	4.26809
38	2.55568	3.07478	3.69601	4.43881
39	2.61957	3.16703	3.82537	4.61637
40	2.68506	3.26204	3.95926	4.80102

		RATE OF INTEREST		
YEARS	.045	.050	.055	.060
1	1.04500	1.05000	1.05500	1.06000
2	1.09202	1.10250	1.11303	1.12360
3	1.14117	1.15762	1.17424	1.19102
4	1.19252	1.21551	1.23882	1.26248
5	1.24618	1.27628	1.30696	1.33823
6	1.30226	1.34010	1.37884	1.41852
7	1.36086	1.40710	1.45468	1.50363
8	1.42210	1.47746	1.53469	1.59385
9	1.48610	1.55133	1.61909	1.68948
10	1.55297	1.62889	1.70814	1.79085
11	1.62285	1.71034	1.80209	1.89830
12	1.69588	1.79586	1.90121	2.01220
13	1.77220	1.88565	2.00577	2.13293
14	1.85194	1.97993	2.11609	2.26090
15	1.93528	2.07893	2.23248	2.39656
16	2.02237	2.18287	2.35526	2.54035
17	2.11338	2.29202	2.48480	2.69277
18	2.20848	2.40662	2.62147	2.85434
19	2.30786	2.52695	2.76565	3.02560
20	2.41171	2.65330	2.91776	3.20714
21	2.52024	2.78596	3.07823	3.39956
22	2.63365	2.92526	3.24754	3.60354
23	2.75217	3.07152	3.42615	3.81975
24	2.87601	3.22510	3.61459	4.04893
25	3.00543	3.38635	3.81339	4.29187
26	3.14068	3.55567	4.02313	4.54938
27	3.28201	3.73346	4.24440	4.82235
28	3.42970	3.92013	4.47784	5.11169
29	3.58404	4.11614	4.72412	5.41839
30	3.74532	4.32194	4.98395	5.74349
31	3.91386	4.53804	5.25807	6.08810
32	4.08998	4.76494	5.54726	6.45339
33	4.27403	5.00319	5.85236	6.84059
34	4.46636	5.25335	6.17424	7.25103
35	4.66735	5.51602	6.51383	7.68609
36	4.87738	5.79182	6.87209	8.14725
37	5.09686	6.08141	7.25005	8.63609
38	5.32622	6.38548	7.64880	9.15425
39	5.56590	6.70475	8.06949	9.70351
40	5.81636	7.03999	8.51331	10.28572

TABLE A.1 Continued

| YEARS | RATE OF INTEREST | | | |
	.070	.080	.090	.100
1	1.07000	1.08000	1.09000	1.10000
2	1.14490	1.16640	1.18810	1.21000
3	1.22504	1.25971	1.29503	1.33100
4	1.31080	1.36049	1.41158	1.46410
5	1.40255	1.46933	1.53862	1.61051
6	1.50073	1.58687	1.67710	1.77156
7	1.60578	1.71382	1.82804	1.94872
8	1.71819	1.85093	1.99256	2.14359
9	1.83846	1.99900	2.17189	2.35795
10	1.96715	2.15892	2.36736	2.59374
11	2.10485	2.33164	2.58043	2.85312
12	2.25219	2.51817	2.81266	3.13843
13	2.40985	2.71962	3.06580	3.45227
14	2.57853	2.93719	3.34173	3.79750
15	2.75903	3.17217	3.64248	4.17725
16	2.95216	3.42594	3.97031	4.59497
17	3.15882	3.70002	4.32763	5.05447
18	3.37993	3.99602	4.71712	5.55992
19	3.61653	4.31570	5.14166	6.11591
20	3.86968	4.66096	5.60441	6.72750
21	4.14056	5.03383	6.10881	7.40025
22	4.43040	5.43654	6.65860	8.14027
23	4.74053	5.87146	7.25787	8.95430
24	5.07237	6.34118	7.91108	9.84973
25	5.42743	6.84848	8.62308	10.83471
26	5.80735	7.39635	9.39916	11.91818
27	6.21387	7.98806	10.24508	13.10999
28	6.64884	8.62711	11.16714	14.42099
29	7.11426	9.31727	12.17218	15.86309
30	7.61226	10.06266	13.26768	17.44940
31	8.14511	10.86767	14.46177	19.19434
32	8.71527	11.73708	15.76333	21.11378
33	9.32534	12.67605	17.18203	23.22515
34	9.97811	13.69013	18.72841	25.54767
35	10.67658	14.78534	20.41397	28.10244
36	11.42394	15.96817	22.25123	30.91268
37	12.22362	17.24563	24.25384	34.00395
38	13.07927	18.62528	26.43668	37.40434
39	13.99482	20.11530	28.81598	41.14478
40	14.97446	21.72452	31.40942	45.25926

TABLE A.1 Continued

YEARS	RATE OF INTEREST			
	.110	.120	.130	.140
1	1.11000	1.12000	1.13000	1.14000
2	1.23210	1.25440	1.27690	1.29960
3	1.36763	1.40493	1.44290	1.48154
4	1.51807	1.57352	1.63047	1.68896
5	1.68506	1.76234	1.84244	1.92541
6	1.87041	1.97382	2.08195	2.19497
7	2.07616	2.21068	2.35261	2.50227
8	2.30454	2.47596	2.65844	2.85259
9	2.55804	2.77308	3.00404	3.25195
10	2.83942	3.10585	3.39457	3.70722
11	3.15176	3.47855	3.83586	4.22623
12	3.49845	3.89598	4.33452	4.81790
13	3.88328	4.36349	4.89801	5.49241
14	4.31044	4.88711	5.53475	6.26135
15	4.78459	5.47357	6.25427	7.13794
16	5.31089	6.13039	7.06733	8.13725
17	5.89509	6.86604	7.98608	9.27646
18	6.54355	7.68997	9.02427	10.57517
19	7.26334	8.61276	10.19742	12.05569
20	8.06231	9.64629	11.52309	13.74349
21	8.94917	10.80385	13.02109	15.66758
22	9.93357	12.10031	14.71383	17.86104
23	11.02627	13.55235	16.62663	20.36158
24	12.23916	15.17863	18.78809	23.21221
25	13.58546	17.00006	21.23054	26.46192
26	15.07986	19.04007	23.99051	30.16658
27	16.73865	21.32488	27.10928	34.38991
28	18.57990	23.88387	30.63349	39.20449
29	20.62369	26.74993	34.61584	44.69312
30	22.89230	29.95992	39.11590	50.95016
31	25.41045	33.55511	44.20096	58.08318
32	28.20560	37.58173	49.94709	66.21483
33	31.30821	42.09153	56.44021	75.48490
34	34.75212	47.14252	63.77744	86.05279
35	38.57485	52.79962	72.06851	98.10018
36	42.81808	59.13557	81.43741	111.83420
37	47.52807	66.23184	92.02428	127.49099
38	52.75616	74.17966	103.98743	145.33973
39	58.55934	83.08122	117.50580	165.68729
40	65.00087	93.05097	132.78155	188.88351

	RATE OF INTEREST			
YEARS	.150	.200	.250	.300
1	1.15000	1.20000	1.25000	1.30000
2	1.32250	1.44000	1.56250	1.69000
3	1.52087	1.72800	1.95313	2.19700
4	1.74901	2.07360	2.44141	2.85610
5	2.01136	2.48832	3.05176	3.71293
6	2.31306	2.98598	3.81470	4.82681
7	2.66002	3.58318	4.76837	6.27485
8	3.05902	4.29982	5.96046	8.15731
9	3.51788	5.15978	7.45058	10.60450
10	4.04556	6.19174	9.31323	13.78585
11	4.65239	7.43008	11.64153	17.92160
12	5.35025	8.91610	14.55192	23.29809
13	6.15279	10.69932	18.18989	30.28751
14	7.07571	12.83918	22.73737	39.37376
15	8.13706	15.40702	28.42171	51.18589
16	9.35762	18.48843	35.52714	66.54166
17	10.76126	22.18611	44.40892	86.50416
18	12.37545	26.62333	55.51115	112.45541
19	14.23177	31.94800	69.38894	146.19203
20	16.36654	38.33760	86.73617	190.04964
21	18.82152	46.00512	108.42022	247.06453
22	21.64475	55.20614	135.52527	321.18389
23	24.89146	66.24737	169.40659	417.53905
24	28.62518	79.49685	211.75824	542.80077
25	32.91895	95.39622	264.69780	705.64100
26	37.85680	114.47546	330.87225	917.33330
27	43.53531	137.37055	413.59031	1192.53329
28	50.06561	164.84466	516.98788	1550.29328
29	57.57545	197.81359	646.23485	2015.38126
30	66.21177	237.37631	807.79357	2619.99564
31	76.14354	284.85158	1009.74196	3405.99434
32	87.56507	341.82189	1262.17745	4427.79264
33	100.69983	410.18627	1577.72181	5756.13043
34	115.80480	492.22352	1972.15226	7482.96956
35	133.17552	590.66823	2465.19033	9727.86043
36	153.15185	708.80187	3081.48791	12646.21855
37	176.12463	850.56225	3851.85989	16440.08412
38	202.54332	1020.67470	4814.82486	21372.10935
39	232.92482	1224.80964	6018.53108	27783.74216
40	267.86355	1469.77157	7523.16385	36118.86481

(*Source*: Lundgren 1971.)

TABLE A.2

Future Value of a Terminating Annual Annuity Multiplier. The Compounded Value of a One-Dollar Payment Made Every Year for *n* Years.

YEARS	.005	RATE OF INTEREST .010	.015	.020
1	1.00000	1.00000	1.00000	1.00000
2	2.00500	2.01000	2.01500	2.02000
3	3.01502	3.03010	3.04522	3.06040
4	4.03010	4.06040	4.09090	4.12161
5	5.05025	5.10101	5.15227	5.20404
6	6.07550	6.15202	6.22955	6.30812
7	7.10588	7.21354	7.32299	7.43428
8	8.14141	8.28567	8.43284	8.58297
9	9.18212	9.36853	9.55933	9.75463
10	10.22803	10.46221	10.70272	10.94972
11	11.27917	11.56683	11.86326	12.16872
12	12.33556	12.68250	13.04121	13.41209
13	13.39724	13.80933	14.23683	14.68033
14	14.46423	14.94742	15.45038	15.97394
15	15.53655	16.09690	16.68214	17.29342
16	16.61423	17.25786	17.93237	18.63929
17	17.69730	18.43044	19.20136	20.01207
18	18.78579	19.61475	20.48938	21.41231
19	19.87972	20.81090	21.79672	22.84056
20	20.97912	22.01900	23.12367	24.29737
21	22.08401	23.23919	24.47052	25.78332
22	23.19443	24.47159	25.83758	27.29898
23	24.31040	25.71630	27.22514	28.84496
24	25.43196	26.97346	28.63352	30.42186
25	26.55912	28.24320	30.06302	32.03030
26	27.69191	29.52563	31.51397	33.67091
27	28.83037	30.82089	32.98668	35.34432
28	29.97452	32.12910	34.48148	37.05121
29	31.12439	33.45039	35.99870	38.79223
30	32.28002	34.78489	37.53868	40.56808
31	33.44142	36.13274	39.10176	42.37944
32	34.60862	37.49407	40.68829	44.22703
33	35.78167	38.86901	42.29861	46.11157
34	36.96058	40.25770	43.93309	48.03380
35	38.14538	41.66028	45.59209	49.99448
36	39.33610	43.07688	47.27597	51.99437
37	40.53279	44.50765	48.98511	54.03425
38	41.73545	45.95272	50.71989	56.11494
39	42.94413	47.41225	52.48068	58.23724
40	44.15885	48.88637	54.26789	60.40198

	RATE OF INTEREST			
YEARS	.025	.030	.035	.040
1	1.00000	1.00000	1.00000	1.00000
2	2.02500	2.03000	2.03500	2.04000
3	3.07562	3.09090	3.10622	3.12160
4	4.15252	4.18363	4.21494	4.24646
5	5.25633	5.30914	5.36247	5.41632
6	6.38774	6.46841	6.55015	6.63298
7	7.54743	7.66246	7.77941	7.89829
8	8.73612	8.89234	9.05169	9.21423
9	9.95452	10.15911	10.36850	10.58280
10	11.20338	11.46388	11.73139	12.00611
11	12.48347	12.80780	13.14199	13.48635
12	13.79555	14.19203	14.60196	15.02581
13	15.14044	15.61779	16.11303	16.62684
14	16.51895	17.08632	17.67699	18.29191
15	17.93193	18.59891	19.29568	20.02359
16	19.38022	20.15688	20.97103	21.82453
17	20.86473	21.76159	22.70502	23.69751
18	22.38635	23.41444	24.49969	25.64541
19	23.94601	25.11687	26.35718	27.67123
20	25.54466	26.87037	28.27968	29.77808
21	27.18327	28.67649	30.26947	31.96920
22	28.86286	30.53678	32.32890	34.24797
23	30.58443	32.45288	34.46041	36.61789
24	32.34904	34.42647	36.66653	39.08260
25	34.15776	36.45926	38.94986	41.64591
26	36.01171	38.55304	41.31310	44.31174
27	37.91200	40.70963	43.75906	47.08421
28	39.85980	42.93092	46.29063	49.96758
29	41.85630	45.21885	48.91080	52.96629
30	43.90270	47.57542	51.62268	56.08494
31	46.00027	50.00268	54.42947	59.32834
32	48.15028	52.50276	57.33450	62.70147
33	50.35403	55.07784	60.34121	66.20953
34	52.61289	57.73018	63.45315	69.85791
35	54.92821	60.46208	66.67401	73.65222
36	57.30141	63.27594	70.00760	77.59831
37	59.73395	66.17422	73.45787	81.70225
38	62.22730	69.15945	77.02889	85.97034
39	64.78298	72.23423	80.72491	90.40915
40	67.40255	75.40126	84.55028	95.02552

RATE OF INTEREST

YEARS	.045	.050	.055	.060
1	1.00000	1.00000	1.00000	1.00000
2	2.04500	2.05000	2.05500	2.06000
3	3.13702	3.15250	3.16803	3.18360
4	4.27819	4.31012	4.34227	4.37462
5	5.47071	5.52563	5.58109	5.63709
6	6.71689	6.80191	6.88805	6.97532
7	8.01915	8.14201	8.26689	8.39384
8	9.38001	9.54911	9.72157	9.89747
9	10.80211	11.02656	11.25626	11.49132
10	12.28821	12.57789	12.87535	13.18079
11	13.84118	14.20679	14.58350	14.97164
12	15.46403	15.91713	16.38559	16.86994
13	17.15991	17.71298	18.28680	18.88214
14	18.93211	19.59863	20.29257	21.01507
15	20.78405	21.57856	22.40866	23.27597
16	22.71934	23.65749	24.64114	25.67253
17	24.74171	25.84037	26.99640	28.21288
18	26.85508	28.13238	29.48120	30.90565
19	29.06356	30.53900	32.10267	33.75999
20	31.37142	33.06595	34.86832	36.78559
21	33.78314	35.71925	37.78608	39.99273
22	36.30338	38.50521	40.86431	43.39229
23	38.93703	41.43048	44.11185	46.99583
24	41.68920	44.50200	47.53800	50.81558
25	44.56521	47.72710	51.15259	54.86451
26	47.57064	51.11345	54.96598	59.15638
27	50.71132	54.66913	58.98911	63.70577
28	53.99333	58.40258	63.23351	68.52811
29	57.42303	62.32271	67.71135	73.63980
30	61.00707	66.43885	72.43548	79.05819
31	64.75239	70.76079	77.41943	84.80168
32	68.66625	75.29883	82.67750	90.88978
33	72.75623	80.06377	88.22476	97.34316
34	77.03026	85.06696	94.07712	104.18375
35	81.49662	90.32031	100.25136	111.43478
36	86.16397	95.83632	106.76519	119.12087
37	91.04134	101.62814	113.63727	127.26812
38	96.13820	107.70955	120.88732	135.90421
39	101.46442	114.09502	128.53613	145.05846
40	107.03032	120.79977	136.60561	154.76197

TABLE A.2   Continued

YEARS	RATE OF INTEREST			
	.070	.080	.090	.100
1	1.00000	1.00000	1.00000	1.00000
2	2.07000	2.08000	2.09000	2.10000
3	3.21490	3.24640	3.27810	3.31000
4	4.43994	4.50611	4.57313	4.64100
5	5.75074	5.86660	5.98471	6.10510
6	7.15329	7.33593	7.52333	7.71561
7	8.65402	8.92280	9.20043	9.48717
8	10.25980	10.63663	11.02847	11.43589
9	11.97799	12.48756	13.02104	13.57948
10	13.81645	14.48656	15.19293	15.93742
11	15.78360	16.64549	17.56029	18.53117
12	17.88845	18.97713	20.14072	21.38428
13	20.14064	21.49530	22.95338	24.52271
14	22.55049	24.21492	26.01919	27.97498
15	25.12902	27.15211	29.36092	31.77248
16	27.88805	30.32428	33.00340	35.94973
17	30.84022	33.75023	36.97370	40.54470
18	33.99903	37.45024	41.30134	45.59917
19	37.37896	41.44626	46.01846	51.15909
20	40.99549	45.76196	51.16012	57.27500
21	44.86518	50.42292	56.76453	64.00250
22	49.00574	55.45676	62.87334	71.40275
23	53.43614	60.89330	69.53194	79.54302
24	58.17667	66.76476	76.78981	88.49733
25	63.24904	73.10594	84.70090	98.34706
26	68.67647	79.95442	93.32398	109.18177
27	74.48382	87.35077	102.72313	121.09994
28	80.69769	95.33883	112.96822	134.20994
29	87.34653	103.96594	124.13536	148.63093
30	94.46079	113.28321	136.30754	164.49402
31	102.07304	123.34587	149.57522	181.94342
32	110.21815	134.21354	164.03699	201.13777
33	118.93343	145.95062	179.80032	222.25154
34	128.25876	158.62667	196.98234	245.47670
35	138.23688	172.31680	215.71075	271.02437
36	148.91346	187.10215	236.12472	299.12681
37	160.33740	203.07032	258.37595	330.03949
38	172.56102	220.31595	282.62978	364.04343
39	185.64029	238.94122	309.06646	401.44778
40	199.63511	259.05652	337.88245	442.59256

TABLE A.2. Continued

YEARS	.110	.120	.130	.140
1	1.00000	1.00000	1.00000	1.00000
2	2.11000	2.12000	2.13000	2.14000
3	3.34210	3.37440	3.40690	3.43960
4	4.70973	4.77933	4.84980	4.92114
5	6.22780	6.35285	6.48027	6.61010
6	7.91286	8.11519	8.32271	8.53552
7	9.78327	10.08901	10.40466	10.73049
8	11.85943	12.29969	12.75726	13.23276
9	14.16397	14.77566	15.41571	16.08535
10	16.72201	17.54874	18.41975	19.33730
11	19.56143	20.65458	21.81432	23.04452
12	22.71319	24.13313	25.65018	27.27075
13	26.21164	28.02911	29.98470	32.08865
14	30.09492	32.39260	34.88271	37.58107
15	34.40536	37.27971	40.41746	43.84241
16	39.18995	42.75328	46.67173	50.98035
17	44.50084	48.88367	53.73906	59.11760
18	50.39594	55.74971	61.72514	68.39407
19	56.93949	63.43968	70.74941	78.96923
20	64.20283	72.05244	80.94683	91.02493
21	72.26514	81.69874	92.46992	104.76842
22	81.21431	92.50258	105.49101	120.43600
23	91.14788	104.60289	120.20484	138.29704
24	102.17415	118.15524	136.83147	158.65862
25	114.41331	133.33387	155.61956	181.87083
26	127.99877	150.33393	176.85010	208.33274
27	143.07864	169.37401	200.84061	238.49933
28	159.81729	190.69889	227.94989	272.88923
29	178.39719	214.58275	258.58338	312.09373
30	199.02088	241.33268	293.19922	356.78685
31	221.91317	271.29261	332.31511	407.73701
32	247.32362	304.84772	376.51608	465.82019
33	275.52922	342.42945	426.46317	532.03501
34	306.83744	384.52098	482.90338	607.51991
35	341.58955	431.66350	546.68082	693.57270
36	380.16441	484.46312	618.74933	791.67288
37	422.98249	543.59869	700.18674	903.50708
38	470.51056	609.83053	792.21101	1030.99808
39	523.26673	684.01020	896.19845	1176.33781
40	581.82607	767.09142	1013.70424	1342.02510

TABLE A.2   Continued

YEARS	RATE OF INTEREST			
	.150	.200	.250	.300
1	1.00000	1.00000	1.00000	1.00000
2	2.15000	2.20000	2.25000	2.30000
3	3.47250	3.64000	3.81250	3.99000
4	4.99337	5.36800	5.76563	6.18700
5	6.74238	7.44160	8.20703	9.04310
6	8.75374	9.92992	11.25879	12.75603
7	11.06680	12.91590	15.07349	17.58284
8	13.72682	16.49908	19.84186	23.85769
9	16.78584	20.79890	25.80232	32.01500
10	20.30372	25.95868	33.25290	42.61950
11	24.34928	32.15042	42.56613	56.40535
12	29.00167	39.58050	54.20766	74.32695
13	34.35192	48.49660	68.75958	97.62504
14	40.50471	59.19592	86.94947	127.91255
15	47.58041	72.03511	109.68684	167.28631
16	55.71747	87.44213	138.10855	218.47220
17	65.07509	105.93056	173.63568	285.01386
18	75.83636	128.11667	218.04460	371.51802
19	88.21181	154.74000	273.55576	483.97343
20	102.44358	186.68800	342.94470	630.16546
21	118.81012	225.02560	429.68087	820.21510
22	137.63164	271.03072	538.10109	1067.27963
23	159.27638	326.23686	673.62636	1388.46351
24	184.16784	392.48424	843.03295	1806.00257
25	212.79302	471.98108	1054.79118	2348.80334
26	245.71197	567.37730	1319.48898	3054.44434
27	283.56877	681.85276	1650.36123	3971.77764
28	327.10408	819.22331	2063.95153	5164.31093
29	377.16969	984.06797	2580.93941	6714.60421
30	434.74515	1181.88157	3227.17427	8729.98548
31	500.95692	1419.25788	4034.96783	11349.98112
32	577.10046	1704.10946	5044.70979	14755.97546
33	664.66552	2045.93135	6306.88724	19183.76810
34	765.36535	2456.11762	7884.60905	24939.89853
35	881.17016	2948.34115	9856.76132	32422.86808
36	1014.34568	3539.00937	12321.95164	42150.72851
37	1167.49753	4247.81125	15403.43956	54796.94706
38	1343.62216	5098.37350	19255.29944	71237.03118
39	1546.16549	6119.04820	24070.12430	92609.14053
40	1779.09031	7343.85784	30088.65538	120392.88269

(*Source*: Lundgren 1971.)

TABLE A.3 Present Value of a Terminating Annual Annuity Multiplier. The Discounted Value of a One-Dollar Payment Made Every Year for *n* Years.

YEARS	RATE OF INTEREST .005	.010	.015	.020
1	.99502	.99010	.98522	.98039
2	1.98510	1.97040	1.95588	1.94156
3	2.97025	2.94099	2.91220	2.88388
4	3.95050	3.90197	3.85438	3.80773
5	4.92587	4.85343	4.78264	4.71346
6	5.89638	5.79548	5.69719	5.60143
7	6.86207	6.72819	6.59821	6.47199
8	7.82296	7.65168	7.48593	7.32548
9	8.77906	8.56602	8.36052	8.16224
10	9.73041	9.47130	9.22218	8.98259
11	10.67703	10.36763	10.07112	9.78685
12	11.61893	11.25508	10.90751	10.57534
13	12.55615	12.13374	11.73153	11.34837
14	13.48871	13.00370	12.54338	12.10625
15	14.41662	13.86505	13.34323	12.84926
16	15.33993	14.71787	14.13126	13.57771
17	16.25863	15.56225	14.90765	14.29187
18	17.17277	16.39827	15.67256	14.99203
19	18.08236	17.22601	16.42617	15.67846
20	18.98742	18.04555	17.16864	16.35143
21	19.88798	18.85698	17.90014	17.01121
22	20.78406	19.66038	18.62082	17.65805
23	21.67568	20.45582	19.33086	18.29220
24	22.56287	21.24339	20.03041	18.91393
25	23.44564	22.02316	20.71961	19.52346
26	24.32402	22.79520	21.39863	20.12104
27	25.19803	23.55961	22.06762	20.70690
28	26.06769	24.31644	22.72672	21.28127
29	26.93302	25.06579	23.37608	21.84438
30	27.79405	25.80771	24.01584	22.39646
31	28.65080	26.54229	24.64615	22.93770
32	29.50328	27.26959	25.26714	23.46833
33	30.35153	27.98969	25.87895	23.98856
34	31.19555	28.70267	26.48173	24.49859
35	32.03537	29.40858	27.07559	24.99862
36	32.87102	30.10751	27.66068	25.48884
37	33.70250	30.79951	28.23713	25.96945
38	34.52985	31.48466	28.80505	26.44064
39	35.35309	32.16303	29.36458	26.90259
40	36.17223	32.83469	29.91585	27.35548

TABLE A.3, Continued

YEARS	.025	RATE OF INTEREST .030	.035	.040
1	.97561	.97087	.96618	.96154
2	1.92742	1.91347	1.89969	1.88609
3	2.85602	2.82861	2.80164	2.77509
4	3.76197	3.71710	3.67308	3.62990
5	4.64583	4.57971	4.51505	4.45182
6	5.50813	5.41719	5.32855	5.24214
7	6.34939	6.23028	6.11454	6.00205
8	7.17014	7.01969	6.87396	6.73274
9	7.97087	7.78611	7.60769	7.43533
10	8.75206	8.53020	8.31661	8.11090
11	9.51421	9.25262	9.00155	8.76048
12	10.25776	9.95400	9.66333	9.38507
13	10.98318	10.63496	10.30274	9.98565
14	11.69091	11.29607	10.92052	10.56312
15	12.38138	11.93794	11.51741	11.11839
16	13.05500	12.56110	12.09412	11.65230
17	13.71220	13.16612	12.65132	12.16567
18	14.35336	13.75351	13.18968	12.65930
19	14.97889	14.32380	13.70984	13.13394
20	15.58916	14.87747	14.21240	13.59033
21	16.18455	15.41502	14.69797	14.02916
22	16.76541	15.93692	15.16712	14.45112
23	17.33211	16.44361	15.62041	14.85684
24	17.88499	16.93554	16.05837	15.24696
25	18.42438	17.41315	16.48151	15.62208
26	18.95061	17.87684	16.89035	15.98277
27	19.46401	18.32703	17.28536	16.32959
28	19.96489	18.76411	17.66702	16.66306
29	20.45355	19.18845	18.03577	16.98371
30	20.93029	19.60044	18.39205	17.29203
31	21.39541	20.00043	18.73628	17.58849
32	21.84918	20.38877	19.06887	17.87355
33	22.29188	20.76579	19.39021	18.14765
34	22.72379	21.13184	19.70068	18.41120
35	23.14516	21.48722	20.00066	18.66461
36	23.55625	21.83225	20.29049	18.90828
37	23.95732	22.16724	20.57053	19.14258
38	24.34860	22.49246	20.84109	19.36786
39	24.73034	22.80822	21.10250	19.58448
40	25.10278	23.11477	21.35507	19.79277

TABLE A.3 Continued

YEARS	RATE OF INTEREST			
	.045	.050	.055	.060
1	.95694	.95238	.94787	.94340
2	1.87267	1.85941	1.84632	1.83339
3	2.74896	2.72325	2.69793	2.67301
4	3.58753	3.54595	3.50515	3.46511
5	4.38998	4.32948	4.27028	4.21236
6	5.15787	5.07569	4.99553	4.91732
7	5.89270	5.78637	5.68297	5.58238
8	6.59589	6.46321	6.33457	6.20979
9	7.26879	7.10782	6.95220	6.80169
10	7.91272	7.72173	7.53763	7.36009
11	8.52892	8.30641	8.09254	7.88687
12	9.11858	8.86325	8.61852	8.38384
13	9.68285	9.39357	9.11708	8.85268
14	10.22283	9.89864	9.58965	9.29498
15	10.73955	10.37966	10.03758	9.71225
16	11.23402	10.83777	10.46216	10.10590
17	11.70719	11.27407	10.86461	10.47726
18	12.15999	11.68959	11.24607	10.82760
19	12.59329	12.08532	11.60765	11.15812
20	13.00794	12.46221	11.95038	11.46992
21	13.40472	12.82115	12.27524	11.76408
22	13.78442	13.16300	12.58317	12.04158
23	14.14777	13.48857	12.87504	12.30338
24	14.49548	13.79864	13.15170	12.55036
25	14.82821	14.09394	13.41393	12.78336
26	15.14661	14.37519	13.66250	13.00317
27	15.45130	14.64303	13.89810	13.21053
28	15.74287	14.89813	14.12142	13.40616
29	16.02189	15.14107	14.33310	13.59072
30	16.28889	15.37245	14.53375	13.76483
31	16.54439	15.59281	14.72393	13.92909
32	16.78889	15.80268	14.90420	14.08404
33	17.02286	16.00255	15.07507	14.23023
34	17.24676	16.19290	15.23703	14.36814
35	17.46101	16.37419	15.39055	14.49825
36	17.66604	16.54685	15.53607	14.62099
37	17.86224	16.71129	15.67400	14.73678
38	18.04999	16.86789	15.80474	14.84602
39	18.22966	17.01704	15.92866	14.94907
40	18.40158	17.15909	16.04612	15.04630

TABLE A.3 Continued

YEARS	.070	RATE OF INTEREST .080	.090	.100
1	.93458	.92593	.91743	.90909
2	1.80802	1.78326	1.75911	1.73554
3	2.62432	2.57710	2.53129	2.48685
4	3.38721	3.31213	3.23972	3.16987
5	4.10020	3.99271	3.88965	3.79079
6	4.76654	4.62288	4.48592	4.35526
7	5.38929	5.20637	5.03295	4.86842
8	5.97130	5.74664	5.53482	5.33493
9	6.51523	6.24689	5.99525	5.75902
10	7.02358	6.71008	6.41766	6.14457
11	7.49867	7.13896	6.80519	6.49506
12	7.94269	7.53608	7.16073	6.81369
13	8.35765	7.90378	7.48690	7.10336
14	8.74547	8.24424	7.78615	7.36669
15	9.10791	8.55948	8.06069	7.60608
16	9.44665	8.85137	8.31256	7.82371
17	9.76322	9.12164	8.54363	8.02155
18	10.05909	9.37189	8.75563	8.20141
19	10.33560	9.60360	8.95011	8.36492
20	10.59401	9.81815	9.12855	8.51356
21	10.83553	10.01680	9.29224	8.64869
22	11.06124	10.20074	9.44243	8.77154
23	11.27219	10.37106	9.58021	8.88322
24	11.46933	10.52876	9.70661	8.98474
25	11.65358	10.67478	9.82258	9.07704
26	11.82578	10.80998	9.92897	9.16095
27	11.98671	10.93516	10.02658	9.23722
28	12.13711	11.05108	10.11613	9.30657
29	12.27767	11.15841	10.19828	9.36961
30	12.40904	11.25778	10.27365	9.42691
31	12.53181	11.34980	10.34280	9.47901
32	12.64656	11.43500	10.40624	9.52638
33	12.75379	11.51389	10.46444	9.56943
34	12.85401	11.58693	10.51784	9.60857
35	12.94767	11.65457	10.56682	9.64416
36	13.03521	11.71719	10.61176	9.67651
37	13.11702	11.77518	10.65299	9.70592
38	13.19347	11.82887	10.69082	9.73265
39	13.26493	11.87858	10.72552	9.75696
40	13.33171	11.92461	10.75736	9.77905

TABLE A.3 Continued

| YEARS | RATE OF INTEREST | | | |
	.110	.120	.130	.140
1	.90090	.89286	.88496	.87719
2	1.71252	1.69005	1.66810	1.64666
3	2.44371	2.40183	2.36115	2.32163
4	3.10245	3.03735	2.97447	2.91371
5	3.69590	3.60478	3.51723	3.43308
6	4.23054	4.11141	3.99755	3.88867
7	4.71220	4.56376	4.42261	4.28830
8	5.14612	4.96764	4.79877	4.63886
9	5.53705	5.32825	5.13166	4.94637
10	5.88923	5.65022	5.42624	5.21612
11	6.20652	5.93770	5.68694	5.45273
12	6.49236	6.19437	5.91765	5.66029
13	6.74987	6.42355	6.12181	5.84236
14	6.98187	6.62817	6.30249	6.00207
15	7.19087	6.81086	6.46238	6.14217
16	7.37916	6.97399	6.60388	6.26506
17	7.54879	7.11963	6.72909	6.37286
18	7.70162	7.24967	6.83991	6.46742
19	7.83929	7.36578	6.93797	6.55037
20	7.96333	7.46944	7.02475	6.62313
21	8.07507	7.56200	7.10155	6.68696
22	8.17574	7.64465	7.16951	6.74294
23	8.26643	7.71843	7.22966	6.79206
24	8.34814	7.78432	7.28288	6.83514
25	8.42174	7.84314	7.32998	6.87293
26	8.48806	7.89566	7.37167	6.90608
27	8.54780	7.94255	7.40856	6.93515
28	8.60162	7.98442	7.44120	6.96066
29	8.65011	8.02181	7.47009	6.98304
30	8.69379	8.05518	7.49565	7.00266
31	8.73315	8.08499	7.51828	7.01988
32	8.76860	8.11159	7.53830	7.03498
33	8.80054	8.13535	7.55602	7.04823
34	8.82932	8.15656	7.57170	7.05985
35	8.85524	8.17550	7.58557	7.07005
36	8.87859	8.19241	7.59785	7.07899
37	8.89963	8.20751	7.60872	7.08683
38	8.91859	8.22099	7.61833	7.09371
39	8.93567	8.23303	7.62684	7.09975
40	8.95105	8.24378	7.63438	7.10504

TABLE A.3 Continued

| YEARS | RATE OF INTEREST | | | |
	.150	.200	.250	.300
1	.86957	.83333	.80000	.76923
2	1.62571	1.52778	1.44000	1.36095
3	2.28323	2.10648	1.95200	1.81611
4	2.85498	2.58873	2.36160	2.16624
5	3.35216	2.99061	2.68928	2.43557
6	3.78448	3.32551	2.95142	2.64275
7	4.16042	3.60459	3.16114	2.80211
8	4.48732	3.83716	3.32891	2.92470
9	4.77158	4.03097	3.46313	3.01900
10	5.01877	4.19247	3.57050	3.09154
11	5.23371	4.32706	3.65640	3.14734
12	5.42062	4.43922	3.72512	3.19026
13	5.58315	4.53268	3.78010	3.22328
14	5.72448	4.61057	3.82408	3.24867
15	5.84737	4.67547	3.85926	3.26821
16	5.95423	4.72956	3.88741	3.28324
17	6.04716	4.77463	3.90993	3.29480
18	6.12797	4.81219	3.92794	3.30369
19	6.19823	4.84350	3.94235	3.31053
20	6.25933	4.86958	3.95388	3.31579
21	6.31246	4.89132	3.96311	3.31984
22	6.35866	4.90943	3.97049	3.32296
23	6.39884	4.92453	3.97639	3.32535
24	6.43377	4.93710	3.98111	3.32719
25	6.46415	4.94759	3.98489	3.32861
26	6.49056	4.95632	3.98791	3.32970
27	6.51353	4.96360	3.99033	3.33054
28	6.53351	4.96967	3.99226	3.33118
29	6.55088	4.97472	3.99381	3.33168
30	6.56598	4.97894	3.99505	3.33206
31	6.57911	4.98245	3.99604	3.33235
32	6.59053	4.98537	3.99683	3.33258
33	6.60046	4.98781	3.99746	3.33275
34	6.60910	4.98984	3.99797	3.33289
35	6.61661	4.99154	3.99838	3.33299
36	6.62314	4.99295	3.99870	3.33307
37	6.62881	4.99412	3.99896	3.33313
38	6.63375	4.99510	3.99917	3.33318
39	6.63805	4.99592	3.99934	3.33321
40	6.64178	4.99660	3.99947	3.33324

(*Source*: Lundgren 1971.)

TABLE A.4 Present Value of a Periodic Perpetual Annuity Multiplier. The Discounted Value of a One-Dollar Payment Made *n* Years in the Future and Every *n* Years Thereafter.

	RATE OF INTEREST			
YEARS	.005	.010	.015	.020
1	200.00000	100.00000	66.66667	50.00000
2	99.75062	49.75124	33.08519	24.75248
3	66.33444	33.00221	21.89220	16.33773
4	49.62656	24.62811	16.29632	12.13119
5	39.60199	19.60398	12.93929	9.60792
6	32.91909	16.25484	10.70168	7.92629
7	28.14571	13.86283	9.10374	6.72560
8	24.56577	12.06903	7.90560	5.82549
9	21.78147	10.67404	6.97399	5.12577
10	19.55411	9.55821	6.22895	4.56633
11	17.73181	8.64541	5.61959	4.10890
12	16.21329	7.88488	5.11200	3.72798
13	14.92845	7.24148	4.68269	3.40592
14	13.82722	6.69012	4.31489	3.13010
15	12.87287	6.21238	3.99629	2.89127
16	12.03787	5.79446	3.71767	2.68251
17	11.30116	5.42581	3.47198	2.49849
18	10.64635	5.09820	3.25372	2.33511
19	10.06051	4.80518	3.05856	2.18909
20	9.53329	4.54153	2.88305	2.05784
21	9.05633	4.30308	2.72437	1.93924
22	8.62276	4.08637	2.58022	1.83157
23	8.22693	3.88858	2.44872	1.73340
24	7.86412	3.70735	2.32827	1.64355
25	7.53037	3.54068	2.21756	1.56102
26	7.22233	3.38689	2.11546	1.48496
27	6.93713	3.24455	2.02102	1.41465
28	6.67233	3.11244	1.93341	1.34948
29	6.42583	2.98950	1.85192	1.28892
30	6.19578	2.87481	1.77595	1.23250
31	5.98061	2.76757	1.70495	1.17982
32	5.77891	2.66709	1.63847	1.13053
33	5.58945	2.57274	1.57610	1.08433
34	5.41117	2.48400	1.51746	1.04093
35	5.24310	2.40037	1.46224	1.00011
36	5.08439	2.32143	1.41016	.96164
37	4.93428	2.24680	1.36096	.92534
38	4.79209	2.17615	1.31441	.89103
39	4.65721	2.10916	1.27031	.85856
40	4.52910	2.04556	1.22847	.82779

TABLE A.4 Continued

	RATE OF INTEREST			
YEARS	.025	.030	.035	.040
1	40.00000	33.33333	28.57143	25.00000
2	19.75309	16.42036	14.04001	12.25490
3	13.00549	10.78435	9.19812	8.00871
4	9.63272	7.96757	6.77860	5.88725
5	7.60987	6.27849	5.32804	4.61568
6	6.26200	5.15325	4.36195	3.76905
7	5.29982	4.35021	3.67270	3.16524
8	4.57869	3.74855	3.15648	2.71320
9	4.01828	3.28113	2.75560	2.36232
10	3.57035	2.90768	2.43547	2.08227
11	3.20424	2.60258	2.17406	1.85373
12	2.89949	2.34874	1.95668	1.66380
13	2.64193	2.13432	1.77319	1.50359
14	2.42146	1.95088	1.61631	1.36672
15	2.23066	1.79222	1.48072	1.24853
16	2.06396	1.65369	1.36242	1.14550
17	1.91711	1.53175	1.25838	1.05496
18	1.78680	1.42362	1.16620	.97483
19	1.67042	1.32713	1.08401	.90347
20	1.56589	1.24052	1.01032	.83954
21	1.47149	1.16239	.94390	.78200
22	1.38586	1.09158	.88377	.72997
23	1.30786	1.02713	.82911	.68273
24	1.23651	.96825	.77922	.63967
25	1.17104	.91426	.73354	.60030
26	1.11075	.86461	.69158	.56418
27	1.05507	.81881	.65293	.53096
28	1.00352	.77644	.61722	.50032
29	.95565	.73716	.58415	.47200
30	.91111	.70064	.55347	.44575
31	.86956	.66663	.52493	.42138
32	.83073	.63489	.49833	.39871
33	.79438	.60520	.47350	.37759
34	.76027	.57740	.45028	.35787
35	.72822	.55131	.42852	.33943
36	.69806	.52679	.40812	.32217
37	.66964	.50372	.38895	.30599
38	.64280	.48198	.37092	.29080
39	.61745	.46146	.35394	.27652
40	.59345	.44208	.33792	.26309

TABLE A.4 Continued

YEARS	.045	.050	.055	.060
		RATE OF INTEREST		
1	22.22222	20.00000	18.18182	16.66667
2	10.86661	9.75610	8.84760	8.09061
3	7.08385	6.34417	5.73916	5.23516
4	5.19430	4.64024	4.18717	3.80986
5	4.06204	3.61950	3.25775	2.95661
6	3.30841	2.94035	2.63962	2.38938
7	2.77114	2.45640	2.19935	1.98558
8	2.36910	2.09444	1.87025	1.68393
9	2.05721	1.81380	1.61526	1.45037
10	1.80842	1.59009	1.41214	1.26447
11	1.60552	1.40778	1.24674	1.11322
12	1.43703	1.25651	1.10962	.98795
13	1.29501	1.12912	.99426	.88267
14	1.17378	1.02048	.89598	.79308
15	1.06920	.92685	.81137	.71605
16	.97812	.84540	.73786	.64920
17	.89817	.77398	.67349	.59075
18	.82749	.71092	.61673	.53928
19	.76461	.65490	.56636	.49368
20	.70836	.60485	.52144	.45308
21	.65779	.55992	.48118	.41674
22	.61213	.51941	.44493	.38409
23	.57072	.48274	.41218	.35464
24	.53305	.44942	.38247	.32798
25	.49865	.41905	.35544	.30378
26	.46714	.39129	.33078	.28174
27	.43821	.36584	.30822	.26162
28	.41157	.34245	.28753	.24321
29	.38699	.32091	.26852	.22633
30	.36426	.30103	.25101	.21082
31	.34319	.28264	.23485	.19654
32	.32363	.26561	.21991	.18337
33	.30543	.24980	.20609	.17122
34	.28849	.23511	.19327	.15997
35	.27268	.22143	.18136	.14956
36	.25791	.20869	.17030	.13991
37	.24409	.19680	.16000	.13096
38	.23115	.18568	.15040	.12264
39	.21901	.17529	.14145	.11490
40	.20763	.16556	.13310	.10769

TABLE A.4 Continued

		RATE OF	INTEREST	
YEARS	.070	.080	.090	.100
1	14.28571	12.50000	11.11111	10.00000
2	6.90131	6.00962	5.31632	4.76190
3	4.44360	3.85042	3.38950	3.02115
4	3.21754	2.77401	2.42965	2.15471
5	2.48415	2.13071	1.85658	1.63797
6	1.99708	1.70394	1.47689	1.29607
7	1.65076	1.40091	1.20767	1.05405
8	1.39240	1.17518	1.00749	.87444
9	1.19266	1.00100	.85332	.73641
10	1.03396	.86287	.73133	.62745
11	.90510	.75095	.63274	.53963
12	.79860	.65869	.55167	.46763
13	.70930	.58152	.48407	.40779
14	.63350	.51621	.42704	.35746
15	.56849	.46037	.37843	.31474
16	.51225	.41221	.33667	.27817
17	.46322	.37037	.30051	.24664
18	.42018	.33378	.26903	.21930
19	.38219	.30160	.24145	.19547
20	.34847	.27315	.21718	.17460
21	.31841	.24790	.19574	.15624
22	.29151	.22540	.17672	.14005
23	.26734	.20528	.15980	.12572
24	.24556	.18722	.14470	.11300
25	.22586	.17098	.13118	.10168
26	.20801	.15634	.11906	.09159
27	.19180	.14310	.10817	.08258
28	.17703	.13111	.09836	.07451
29	.16355	.12023	.08951	.06728
30	.15123	.11034	.08152	.06079
31	.13996	.10134	.07428	.05496
32	.12961	.09314	.06774	.04972
33	.12012	.08565	.06180	.04499
34	.11138	.07880	.05641	.04074
35	.10334	.07254	.05151	.03690
36	.09593	.06681	.04706	.03343
37	.08910	.06156	.04300	.03030
38	.08279	.05674	.03931	.02747
39	.07695	.05231	.03595	.02491
40	.07156	.04825	.03288	.02259

YEARS	RATE OF INTEREST			
	.110	.120	.130	.140
1	9.09091	8.33333	7.69231	7.14286
2	4.30849	3.93082	3.61141	3.33778
3	2.72012	2.46957	2.25786	2.07665
4	1.93024	1.74362	1.58611	1.45146
5	1.45973	1.31175	1.18703	1.08060
6	1.14888	1.02688	.92426	.83684
7	.92923	.82598	.73931	.66566
8	.76656	.67752	.60297	.53979
9	.64183	.56399	.49899	.44406
10	.54365	.47487	.41761	.36938
11	.46474	.40346	.35263	.30996
12	.40025	.34531	.29989	.26192
13	.34683	.29731	.25654	.22260
14	.30207	.25726	.22052	.19007
15	.26423	.22354	.19032	.16292
16	.23197	.19492	.16482	.14011
17	.20429	.17047	.14314	.12082
18	.18039	.14948	.12462	.10444
19	.15966	.13136	.10873	.09045
20	.14160	.11566	.09503	.07847
21	.12580	.10200	.08319	.06818
22	.11194	.09009	.07292	.05931
23	.09974	.07967	.06399	.05165
24	.08897	.07053	.05622	.04502
25	.07946	.06250	.04943	.03927
26	.07102	.05543	.04350	.03429
27	.06354	.04920	.03830	.02995
28	.05688	.04370	.03375	.02617
29	.05096	.03884	.02975	.02289
30	.04568	.03453	.02624	.02002
31	.04097	.03072	.02315	.01752
32	.03676	.02734	.02043	.01533
33	.03299	.02434	.01804	.01343
34	.02963	.02167	.01593	.01176
35	.02661	.01931	.01407	.01030
36	.02391	.01720	.01243	.00902
37	.02149	.01533	.01099	.00791
38	.01932	.01366	.00971	.00693
39	.01737	.01218	.00858	.00607
40	.01562	.01086	.00759	.00532

TABLE A.4 Continued

| YEARS | RATE OF INTEREST | | | |
	.150	.200	.250	.300
1	6.66667	5.00000	4.00000	3.33333
2	3.10078	2.27273	1.77778	1.44928
3	1.91985	1.37363	1.04918	.83542
4	1.33510	.93145	.69377	.53876
5	.98877	.67190	.48739	.36861
6	.76158	.50353	.35528	.26131
7	.60240	.38712	.26537	.18958
8	.48567	.30305	.20159	.13972
9	.39716	.24040	.15502	.10412
10	.32835	.19261	.12029	.07821
11	.27379	.15552	.09397	.05910
12	.22987	.12632	.07379	.04485
13	.19407	.10310	.05817	.03414
14	.16459	.08447	.04600	.02606
15	.14011	.06941	.03647	.01993
16	.11965	.05718	.02896	.01526
17	.10245	.04720	.02304	.01170
18	.08791	.03903	.01834	.00897
19	.07558	.03231	.01462	.00689
20	.06508	.02678	.01166	.00529
21	.05611	.02222	.00931	.00406
22	.04844	.01845	.00743	.00312
23	.04186	.01533	.00594	.00240
24	.03620	.01274	.00474	.00185
25	.03133	.01059	.00379	.00142
26	.02713	.00881	.00303	.00109
27	.02351	.00733	.00242	.00084
28	.02038	.00610	.00194	.00065
29	.01768	.00508	.00155	.00050
30	.01533	.00423	.00124	.00038
31	.01331	.00352	.00099	.00029
32	.01155	.00293	.00079	.00023
33	.01003	.00244	.00063	.00017
34	.00871	.00204	.00051	.00013
35	.00757	.00170	.00041	.00010
36	.00657	.00141	.00032	.00008
37	.00571	.00118	.00026	.00006
38	.00496	.00098	.00021	.00005
39	.00431	.00082	.00017	.00004
40	.00375	.00068	.00013	.00003

(*Source*: Lundgren 1971.)

INDEX